THE HAZARDOUS WORLD OF VICTORIAN ENTERTAINMENT

Jeopardy within the Victorian Theatre

Alan & Brenda Stockwell

VESPER HAWK

ISBN 978-0-9565013-9-4

Cover Picture:
Free Performance (Loge closest to the stage) by Hippolyte Bellangé (1800–1866)
Lithograph by Godefroy Engelmann (1788–1839) Date: 1830–40

The Elisha Whittelsey Collection, The Elisha Whittelsey Fund, 1963
The Metropolitan Museum of Art, New York, USA

Published by VESPER HAWK PUBLISHING
WWW.VESPERHAWK.COM

INTRODUCTION TO THE HAZARDOUS WORLD OF VICTORIAN ENTERTAINMENT

In the 21st century we do not consider a night at the theatre to be a hazardous occupation. The only fear we are likely to have is the possibility we might not catch the last bus or train home, or that the leading actor may be indisposed and we are fobbed off with an understudy. We do not expect somebody to fall from the balcony and land on top of us, neither do we expect the actors to maim or kill each other, and the likelihood of the entire audience rioting or panicking is such a remote possibility we do not even think of it.

However, prior to the 20th century, theatre-going was not only hazardous but downright dangerous, and the experiences given above were by no means rare. It astonishes how many people suffered injuries during a night at the theatre, how often disputes arose, and how commonplace seems to have been falling down stairs and getting trampled on. Theatre buildings themselves were particularly susceptible to fire, and partial collapse seemed to happen unexpectedly at any time. During Queen Victoria's lifetime some theatres had to be rebuilt several times.

There were some compensations in dealing with the disasters of those days. Today, when policemen no longer patrol beats at night, rarely investigate burglaries, and ignore shop lifting, it is salutary to see how often policemen were on the spot in the 19th century. While patrolling their beat in the night time they were often the first to see a fire, and they were present nightly inside theatres to quell trouble makers. They were there to prevent crime, and catch miscreants. If a constable was in trouble in the street, the sound of his whistle or rattle would bring companions running to his rescue, and most honest citizens would assist. They were supported by magistrates who took a very dim view of a person interfering with a policeman carrying out his duties. To strike a policeman or resist arrest was particularly heinous.

Magistrates were active daily, most arrests were dealt with the following day resulting in immediate fines or prison sentences. More serious offences were carried forward to the next assizes. I have often been surprised and sometimes perturbed at the variance in sentences meted out to malefactors – men sent to jail for selling a fake free pass, and a performer who discharged a cannon in a music hall killing a boy in the gallery not receiving any punishment at all!

In the matter of fatal accidents, inquests were also customarily held the following day after death, certainly within the week. A far cry from today when an inquest is often years after the tragic event. Again it is disturbing how rarely blame is attributed or compensation sought, juries concluding the affair was "a simple accident".

Another great difference between the Victorian era and today is that there always seemed to be a doctor and a chemist to hand in an emergency. Of course, there was no free health service, but if somebody was injured in the audience or on the stage, there was often a doctor in the very audience watching the show. So much so, one suspects they may have been there not for pleasure, but for the chance of possible business. Should no medical man be present, there was always one round the corner who appeared on request at the drop of a hat, and chemists seemed to be open at all hours.

This book is two-fold: Part One devoted to backstage accidents which are mainly to stage crew but also offstage performers, and Part Two accidents within the auditorium, the unfortunates included herein are mainly innocent members of the public though on some occasions accidents are propelled by individuals. A few entries – including a murder – are outside the strict definitions.

The individual entries are mainly taken from contemporary newspaper reports, in most cases amplified by research from elsewhere. Words in ". . ." commas are quotations from news items and a small number of entries are entirely brief verbatim paragraphs. The date of each entry is the actual date of the accident or incident and is as accurate as I have been able to ascertain. Where I cannot be positive, the date is followed by a small 'c' for circa.

I have used the term 'onstage' but in Victorian times that included in the circus ring, music hall and concert platforms, pleasure gardens and open-air galas, even swimming pools – in fact anywhere that performances took place. Fatalities are highlighted with the date in **BOLD.**

There is one major digression from the consecutive sequence. In my research I found many examples of accidents to performers away from their normal places of work, mainly while travelling. So while this book is devoted to audience and backstage workers there is an extra section at the end embracing accidents to performers in the world at large.

So turn the pages to find the Victorian theatres that harbour a *pot-pourri* of disaster, destruction and death . . . .

Jeopardy within the Victorian Theatre

MONEY - HISTORICAL NOTE

The currency in use during the period was based on pounds, shillings and pence (£ s d).
£1 = 20 shillings   1 shilling = 12 pence   1 penny divided into ½d (ha'penny) and ¼d (farthing)

These denominations were rendered variously as, for example,

£209 or 209*l*	(Two hundred and nine pounds)
£37.10s	(Thirty seven pounds and ten shillings)
£203.14.6	(Two hundred and three pounds, fourteen shillings and sixpence)
7/- or 7s	(7 shillings)
4/6 or 4/6d	(four shillings and sixpence – colloquially called "four and six")
6½d	Sixpence-ha'penny
1¼d	Penny-farthing

PART ONE
THE VULNERABLE BACKSTAGE OF THE VICTORIAN THEATRE

This book is a miscellany of accidents in the Victorian theatre. A companion volume *Perils of the Victorian Stage* covers onstage accidents. This one being devoted to the backstage area, and the auditorium when an audience is present at a show. The division is not rigid as if a fire starts backstage it is very likely to affect the audience — they usually flee! As you will soon realise from the chronological entries, a fire during one's evening at the theatre is no rare thing and can have a devastating effect. Thus fires are mainly in Part Two, though smaller confined fires and explosions that invariably emanate from within the stage house are recorded in Part One.

Fire was by far the greatest danger that plagued the theatre business throughout the 19th century. A theatre usually burned down through some flaw of its lighting system. However, back in Elizabethan days the theatres were open to the skies with performances taking place in the afternoon daylight, yet Shakespeare's own Globe theatre, burned down in 1613 through the wadding from cannon fire alighting on the thatched roof. Fortunately there were no deaths, the only story coming down to us being the rather whimsical anecdote of a man with his breeches on fire, extinguished by a resourceful chap throwing his pint of ale over them. Thus not all fires are necessarily caused by naked flames, but 90% of them were.

When theatres moved indoors during the 17th century some means of lighting was necessary. There was not much option of method in those days. We are talking candles in chandeliers and sconces. From that moment the quest was on to find ways to develop stronger more powerful lighting. The first candles were of tallow or beeswax, followed in the mid-eighteenth century by spermaceti wax. The five act form of play arose through the necessity of trimming candle wicks at regular periods. Whale oil was also used in simple lamps to supplement the candles, these being expensive when used in the quantity required to light a full evening's entertainment at the theatre. In 1780, a major improvement came with the patent Argand lamp, an oil lamp with a tubular wick enabling air to rise in the centre of the flame as well as outside. The flame was surrounded by a glass chimney.

A rough idea of the expense of lighting may be gained by a statement that in 1810 at Covent Garden – the largest auditorium in the country – each performance used 270 candles in the audience chandeliers, 300 Argand lamps onstage, and a similar number for front of house corridors, stairs, etc. That adds up to a lot of naked flames.

The hazards of candles and oil lamps were infinite, and much interest was given by the scientific mind to alternative forms of lighting. At the beginning of the nineteenth century the breakthrough came with the discovery of coal gas, and theatres were not slow to seize on this new form of light. In September 1815, Covent Garden announced that "The Exterior, with the Grand Hall and Staircase will be illuminated by Gas." In October, the Olympic theatre announced "The Exterior, the Saloon, and part of the Interior, will be lighted with Gas." However, it does not appear that, as yet, managements had seen the advantage of using gas for stage lighting.

In August 1817, the Lyceum opened its season proclaiming "The Gas Lights will this Evening be introduced over the whole stage." Drury Lane followed in September. Every London theatre except the Haymarket went over to gas, in some cases totally, in others with a combination of the former oil and candle set-up. Although gas in itself was more expensive, a comparison of the time shows that the value in obtaining the same amount of light worked out as 1/- for candles, 6½d for oil in an Argand lamp but only 2¾d for gas.

An alternative form of gas was oil gas, and many large buildings had a special gas room where stored oil was heated to condense into a gas form, then transferred to a gasometer. But whether gas was manufactured on the spot or piped in from outside it still meant that the created light was by a naked flame, the brightest arrangement being two jets that impinged on one another so that they splayed out into what became known as a 'fishtail'. A single jet with a glass surround formed a modified kind of Argand. That these various experiments with gas were successful in boosting light levels in theatres cannot be in doubt as complaints arose that the light was too bright! As gas flames rise naturally upwards, it is obvious that, hoisted above the level of the boxes, a large chandelier with many jets was going to cast more light on to the balcony and ceiling than downwards. Thus spectators on upper levels were dazzled, and the chandelier had to be shrouded, or a hoisting arrangement installed to lift it higher up to the very ceiling. In many cases theatres reverted to oil lamps and candles for front of house, retaining coal gas for stage lighting.

Although electricity became available, firstly using generators and batteries, then in the 1880s via mains, the first theatre to be fully electric did not arrive until December 1881. It was some years before it became the norm, throughout the Victorian period gas was king.

Over the stage – known as 'the flies' – of the Victorian theatre there was a grid system where scenic backcloths were hung. There were also battens bearing gas jets in a row. These were there to light the top part of the scenery when it was in the onstage position. To mask the lights were cloth borders. There could also be borders of gauze material to soften the light for particular effects. It takes no imagination to realise that an unexpected draught could easily waft a corner of a border into the path of a gas jet. This was a common likelihood and flymen whose job was to haul backcloths up and down always had a long pole at the ready in case a border needed easing away from danger.

Footlights were a row of naked gas jets at the front of the stage, and in the wings were 'ladders' that carried further gas jets to provide side lighting. The widespread use of coal gas for lighting purposes had to be handled carefully and any leaks dealt with immediately, otherwise a build up of gas in a confined space was very volatile should a naked flame appear.

Coinciding with the new monarchy, a novel form of stage lighting was introduced in 1837 utilising a mixture of oxygen and hydrogen. The method required each of the gases to be contained in a separate leather or rubber bag which had to be completely sealed as contact with air made the mixture volatile. To avoid explosions from mixing the gases prematurely a pipe from each bag joined in parallel immediately in front of the burner igniting a piece of quicklime (calcium oxide) the size and shape of a cotton reel. The two gases mingling in a controlled fashion produced the brightest light by far – 37 times the brightness of an Argand lamp. This new principle, called 'limelight', became exceedingly popular for special effects on the stage. A whole industry developed to service theatres. The turning and boring process of quicklime was centred on Nottingham where the quality of the chemical compound was thought to be superior.

The gases were manufactured in London and it was a common sight to see men carrying large inflated wedge-shaped bags on their shoulders in the fashion of sandwich boards. These wedge-shaped bags compressed in the manner of bellows so that they could be placed between weighted wooden boards at the theatre. As the gases were gradually exhausted the weighted boards forced the lowering gas out in a continuous steady flow. The main use of the limelight was as a floodlight, and was usually stationed in the fly gallery built on a side wall where all the ropes controlling the backcloths were anchored on a row of cleats. Space was at a premium there, so some theatres built a lower gallery underneath, especially for the use of the limelight men.

The two limelight gases encased in deflatable bags were an ongoing hazard and prone to causing explosions. Fortunately, most explosions are sudden and compact. That is they do not usually develop into widespread fires though on occasion some do and several examples follow.

1. *The point where the two gases mix*

2. *The gas bags set for use*

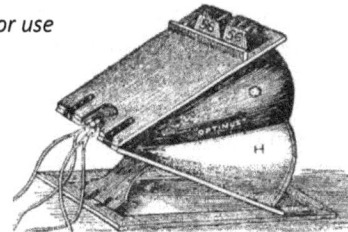

9

Backstage accidents mainly happen to those hard-working chaps the stage crew. On the Victorian stage the backstage crew was numerous because everything was done by manual labour. The scenic effects that the designers devised relied on a team of men who had to work in synchronicity. Perhaps the most important were the flymen. They had a railed gallery set high in the wings. A simple backcloth of a picture painted on canvas that had to be at least the size of the proscenium opening had a wooden batten along top and bottom. Three ropes were attached to the top batten, at each end and in the centre. These were named long, middle and short and each ran over its pulley above, then to the side fly gallery where the three ropes came together and were wound round a massive cleat. The gallery had a row of cleats so when all the backcloths in the show were hoisted up to the grid above the stage the fly gallery was swamped with coils of rope. Muscle power was the means of raising and lowering backcloths.

There were three main ways of raising a backcloth: a) if there was a fly tower the backcloth suspended on its three ropes could be hauled up out of sight completely flat. b) if there was insufficient height the backcloth could be slowly lowered while a row of men standing on the stage rolled it round the bottom batten. When fully wound, the men tied cords around the rolled up canvas together with the two bars. This was then pulled up out of view. c) The backcloth was rolled up and down like a domestic blind by means of a rope round pulleys.

1840_01_11 LONDON (Drury Lane).   ACCIDENT TO THEATRE FIREMAN

William Mills, one of the firemen at Drury Lane Theatre, was going on his rounds when he slipped on some orange peel in the pit passage and fell, breaking his leg so severely that the bone was protruding from the flesh. Not being discovered for a full hour, as soon as he was found he was rushed to hospital where he languished in a precarious state. To add to the man's woes, his wife was bedridden and his daughter suffered from dropsy, both confined to their rooms.

1840_12_23 DUBLIN (Abbey Street).   WORKER FALLS TO THE STAGE

The property man, falling from above on to the stage, caught on a protruding nail on his descent tearing off a portion of flesh near his jawbone. The man was taken to hospital where he was reported to be doing well.

1841_10_04 LONDON (Victoria).   BORDER FIRE

[The three theatres south of the river were known as the transpontine houses. Astley's was the first purpose built circus in the world and several versions entertained Londoners over a hundred years, the Surrey was created as a rival to Astley's but soon converted to a traditional theatre, and the Victoria had been built as the Royal Coburg and is still in existence as the Old Vic.]

A border that conceals the gas lights in the flies seems to have caught fire during the play at the Victoria. The audience, seeing the flames, immediately started making for the exit, but Mr Osbaldiston the manager stepped forward and begged them not to be alarmed. His staff had torn down the burning scenery and already extinguished it. The local fire engine had arrived very promptly but would not be required. Urging everybody to resume their seats, Mr Osbaldiston declared the programme would then continue.

1841_12_06 LONDON (Surrey).   BURNING FLAKES DESCEND FROM CEILING

Around 10pm, during a performance of *The Two Locksmiths* the people in the gallery noticed burning flakes floating down from above, and immediately the cry of 'Fire!' arose, causing a stampede to the exits. The panic became general throughout the house, and passages, stairs and doorways soon became blocked. Some people jumped from the boxes into the pit, others slid down pillars. "In an almost incredibly short space of time the theatre was nearly empty." With most of the audience now out in the surrounding streets, the rumour spread that the whole interior was in flames. Fire engines and police officers appeared but were not required. The fire was confined to the painting room which, like most theatres of the time, occupied the area between the ceiling and roof, the location of the fire being a small well used for collecting shavings, canvas off-cuts and other rubbish. Several painters were in the room, occupied in painting pantomime scenery but were unaware of the fire until alerted by the falling flakes and shouting. The fire was soon

3. *Surrey Theatre*

doused even though flames had gained several feet in height, as Mr Bell and other workers in the paint-shop had several buckets of water to hand. No damage was done to any part of the building, the fire being entirely confined to burning rubbish. The show resumed, but the remaining audience was very small as of those who had fled, few were disposed to trust themselves back inside.

1842_05_02 LONDON (Opera House).   SCENERY ACCIDENT AT THEATRE

Some scenery fell over on to two stage hands, Charles Honett and Daniel Brown. The latter was between 60 and 70 years of age and had worked in the theatre for over 30 years. Both men were rushed to Charing Cross Hospital with no hopes of recovery. I have not been able to find anything further about this.

1842_06_16 LONDON (Strand).   PERSON INJURED UNDER STAGE

Mr Cowell, the theatre's respectable money-taker, was walking under the stage in the late morning when it was unlit. In the dark, he stumbled into a "hole" several feet deep. His cries brought immediate attention and he was conveyed in a cab to Charing Cross Hospital. Cowell was found to have a broken leg and internal injuries.

1842_09_29 LONDON (Sadler's Wells).   PROPERTY ROOM FIRE

The theatre was crowded for a benefit night when billows of dense smoke issuing forth from the stage brought a halt to the show. The fire had begun in the property room when Mr Harvey, giving a boy a torch to hold, passed too near the blue and red fire-making materials stored with other fireworks in the room. Any audience, fearing the entire building to be on fire with themselves in it, could be forgiven for panicking, but on this occasion calmness prevailed. All the actors, supers and staff buckled to with buckets of water and the fire was extinguished within half-an-hour. It seems the audience waited patiently during all this because the performance then carried on.

4. *Sadler's Wells Theatre*

1842_12_03 LONDON (Haymarket).   THEATRE WORKER FALLS FROM ON HIGH

[A small theatre was founded in the Haymarket in 1720 in the days when theatres presenting plays needed a patent from the king. In 1754, Samuel Foote was the manager and in a royal hunting party he was allotted a particularly frisky horse as a prank. He was thrown, his leg smashed and amputated. In remorse Foote was granted a third London patent but limited to the summer months when the regular two closed so it is officially the Theatre Royal Haymarket. It was rebuilt in 1820.]

Just after midnight, George Byng was going round putting out the lights in the theatre. Having got to the second tier of boxes, he overbalanced and fell head first into the pit. The noise was heard round the theatre so other staff members were able to come to the scene immediately. They found an unconscious man with a large wound on his forehead. He was taken to Charing Cross Hospital where the wound was dressed, a sprained wrist attended to, after which Byng made his own way home.

1844_05_06 LIVERPOOL (Theatre Royal). SCENERY FIRE

During the farce of *The Man in the Moon*, flames seen among the upper scenery were initially taken as part of the production, until the stage crew ran on tearing the scenery down and throwing buckets of water about. Alarmed that the theatre was on fire, the audience rising as one speedily made for the exits. Alarm subsided briskly when Madame Celeste, the lessee and Mr Perkins the stage manager strode on to the stage and assured the audience that all was safe. It was explained that some scenery only had caught fire, this being speedily extinguished by backstage crew with some buckets of water.

5. *Theatre Royal, Liverpool*

1844_07_05 LONDON (Marylebone). FATAL INJURY TO BOY AT THEATRE

This is one of the most distressing reports I have recorded, yet I can find no more about it than a paragraph of half-a-dozen lines that was carried in a mere handful of papers. It grieves me to be unable to add any more – it seems there was no inquest.

At the Marylebone Theatre the production was a 'water piece' called *The Water Fiend* in which there was a large fall of water. A boy named Lund "was engaged in attending" – in what way I cannot elaborate – but he was carried over the fall and "in descending received such injuries as caused his death the following night."

1844_12_10 LONDON (Royal Standard). FATAL ACCIDENT TO WORKMAN

[New theatres were going up all over the country, not just to replace old or burnt out theatres but to serve the increasing population in principal towns. I decided to omit building accidents from my remit, as a fall from a scaffold is much the same whether building a theatre or a church. So this rare example must stand for many others I have ignored.]

The Theatre at Shoreditch was a new theatre nearing completion. Henry Miller (21) was an apprentice of Mr Gibson a mast and block maker. Having set up a block and tackle to raise some spars of wood 30ft in the air, Miller, to test the ropes slid down the rope, caught his fingers in the tackle, hung on for two minutes then let go, falling to strike a stove with his hip, and finishing on the ground in a pile of mortar. He was picked up insensible, taken to St Bartholomew's Hospital where it was found his leg was so shattered it was necessary to amputate immediately. Unfortunately, the young man never rallied and died on the evening of Christmas Day.

1845_02_12 LONDON (Astley's). ACCIDENT TO ERRAND BOY

Edward Woods (12) sent on an errand by one of the actors, was crossing over the stage when a platform used by some of the horses in one of the spectacles fell with a crash, trapping the lad by the leg. He was taken to Westminster Hospital where the house surgeon Mr Beaumont was able to set the fractured bone. No blame was attached to anybody at the theatre.

1845_06_09 BIRMINGHAM (Theatre Royal). FATAL ACCIDENT TO STAGEHAND

John Hickman (28) a married man with two children, by trade a pencil case maker, was also a part-time stage hand at the theatre. During a scene change, a roller that was being hauled aloft suddenly fell as the rope hauling it broke. Joshua Bolcot who was winding the scene up called 'stand clear!' but Hickman was struck on the head as the roller descended.

Doctor Wright and Mr Taylor the surgeon were both in the theatre and attended immediately ordering a swift move to the hospital. Hickman died from a fractured skull. The manager "has intimated his intention to pay all the expenses of the funeral, and provide mourning for the family of the deceased, as well as afford the widow some pecuniary assistance." A subscription appeal was set up by the theatre workers to assist the "widow and two children left totally unprovided for, to lament the loss of a protector and friend, and struggle against the vicissitudes and ills of life."

1845_06_25 LONDON (Drury Lane). ACCIDENT TO STAGE CREW

Just as the final curtain had fallen at the conclusion of *The Enchantress*, "a quantity of heavy machinery fell with a crash". Two stage hands Kirby and Hathaway were knocked down, picked up bleeding profusely and in a seemingly lifeless state. A doctor who was in the house promptly came backstage and immediately ordered the pair to be sent to hospital. Hathaway's injuries were small compared with those of Kirby, of whom there was little hope of recovery. "Not the slightest blame attaches to anyone in the theatre."

13

1845_09_08 MANCHESTER (Amphitheatre). COLLAPSE OF PART OF AMPHITHEATRE

Mr Cooke, the premier circus proprietor in the land at this time, had let out his venue to the Manchester Philharmonic Society who had hired the auditorium for two important occasions.

At this first event, in the interval, there was a mighty crash behind the scenes as the floor in the room occupied by the chorus gave way. Sixty choristers were plunged down a distance of some 12ft fortunately escaping with nothing worse than cuts and bruises.

However, passing underneath as the whole thing dropped was Edward Sudlow, first violin in the orchestra. His left leg a little above the ankle was seriously fractured and he was taken to the infirmary, where the limb was set. Mr Sudlow (59) was "advanced in age" and there were fears that the shock to his system may have proved too much. However, it was reported that he was recovering very favourably at his home, but alas, Mr Sudlow died a few days later.

The cause of the floor collapsing was simple. The building had started out as a circus with circle seating which originally continued right round the circumference of the building. At some time in the past, a stage had been erected and hence that portion of the circle would be backstage and no longer part of the auditorium. So in place of the seating some backstage rooms had been created for props, costumes etc. These were in constant use but as more space was required for some past equestrian spectacle, the beams supporting that section of the former circle were cut through and removed! Some rooms were left without sufficient support. For some time, these rooms had been used constantly for wardrobes etc, and sustained a weight of 12 tons. Mr Shorland the town surveyor inspected the site and expressed surprise that the rooms should have been allowed to remain after the supports had been removed.

1845_09_30 MANCHESTER (Theatre Royal). FATAL ACCIDENT AT NEW THEATRE

It was the opening night of the new theatre and the various workmen were tidying away all the last minute things prior to the opening of the doors for the first time. A large plank – used as part of a scaffold – had been left in the pit. Carruthers and Gill were ordered to remove it and put it under the stage. Taking an end each they took it up on to the stage. Carruthers, at the front walking backwards, stumbled into an open trapdoor and fell through to the understage cellar – a distance of 13ft – on to a brick floor. Death was almost instantaneous.

1845_11_27 LONDON (Adelphi). SMOKE ISSUING FROM UNDERSTAGE

During a performance of *The Green Bushes* a quantity of smoke was seen to emerge, apparently from under the stage. It was accompanied by a strong smell of gunpowder. Loud shouts of fire, screams from ladies and a mass rising to make for the exits followed. However, the sole occupant of the stage at the time was Madame Celeste the manager who came forward and said "There is no danger – pray keep your seats." Others of the company then entered assuring the audience there was no cause for alarm, but some time elapsed before order was restored enabling resumption of the play. "The cause of the smoke did not transpire".

6. *Adelphi Theatre*

1847_06_05 LONDON (Covent Garden). FLYMAN FALLS FROM FLIES

George Hill, one of the stage crew, fell on to the stage from a height of more than 22ft. It was feared the man was killed on the spot, but he was taken to King's College Hospital and put under the care of the house surgeon who tended to his wounds, although his condition remained distressing. However, a later bulletin said he was much improved and would shortly be back at work.

1847_09_03c LONDON (Her Majesty's). FATAL ACCIDENT TO FLYMAN

[The side 'flats' are wooden frames covered with canvas painted appropriately in keeping with the scene on the backcloth. The bottom of the flat rests on the stage floor, with a weighted brace supporting it. Formerly, the top was held in a groove. A wooden batten contained three or four of these so that a series of flats could be held closely in a stack one before another. This batten was known as 'the grooves'.]

John Chapman (47) a backstage worker in the fly gallery, while going about his normal duties stepped off the fly gallery on to the grooves. He missed his footing and fell on to the stage. He was taken bleeding to Charing Cross Hospital where he died within the hour. He was fully competent at his job having done it for several years. He was not thought to have been drinking.

1848_10_15 LONDON (Haymarket). FATAL ACCIDENT TO FLYMAN

William Winfield, slipped in the fly gallery while reefing in the lines of the stage curtain; shortly after he said that he felt ill. The following day he was unable to work and went to St Bartholomew's Hospital where house surgeon Mr Jackson said he was suffering from "erysipelas of the left side". Winfield died four days later from inflammation of the lungs, brought on by the injury.

14

1851_04_21 LONDON (Her Majesty's).   STAGE HAND FATALLY SHOT

It was the duty of Samuel Drewell (27) to fire off some guns behind the scenes. These were small cannons clamped in a frame which he held steady by placing his foot on it. However, one cannon recoiled and discharged its contents into his left leg, shattering to pieces the lower part of his leg and all the bones of the foot. Drewell was immediately moved to Charing Cross Hospital where amputation was performed on arrival. The right leg was also injured but amputation in that case was avoided.

However, Drewell died a few days later of *delirium tremens*. At the inquest the jury recommended that in future the cannons' framework should be strapped down instead of held in place by a foot. The father of the deceased promised that in future the frame would be held down with iron bands.

1852_01_09 LONDON (Colosseum).   FATAL ACCIDENT TO SCENIC ENGINEER

This venue was not an actual theatre but an auditorium for the display of panoramas, though theatre scenic devices were used. Thomas Foreman (32) who for many years had been engineer at the venue, was oiling the engine when he fell into the machinery in the presence of his fellow workmen. "Although the engines were immediately stopped, his body was taken out lifeless, horribly mutilated."

1852_03_22 LONDON (Pavilion).   HORSE BREAKS GROOM'S LEG

During a morning rehearsal of the famous hippodrama *Mazeppa* at the Pavilion Theatre in the Mile End Road starring Mrs Moreton Brooks, her groom Thomas Norton suffered a serious accident. While teaching "a fine horse, the lady's own property, to lie down on the stage" it suddenly fell on to the groom's leg snapping both bones causing one being forced upwards overlapping the other. He was taken to the London Hospital.

15

1855_03_12 LONDON (Royal Standard).   FATAL ACCIDENT TO STAGEHAND

Thomas Ray (48) was given the job of covering over a large gilt-framed mirror with a sheet of canvas. To do this he employed a ladder to raise himself some 18ft above the floor. At the top, losing his footing he fell to the floor below, blood flowing from his mouth, his body inert. Mr Roper the nearest surgeon came immediately and ministered to the limits of his meagre knowledge and had Ray sent home in a cab. As the symptoms grew worse a further surgeon was sent for, who on a brief examination stated the patient was dying and he could do nothing for him. Poor Mr Ray died at 7am the following morning from fatal injuries including a fractured skull, leaving a widow and five children in destitution.

1855_08_12 LONDON (Victoria).   EXTRAORDINARY ACCIDENT AT THEATRE

Mr Lloyd was employed as a groom. He had a ten-year-old son who was used to wandering about the building at will. On Saturday night when Lloyd was due to return home the boy was missing. On Sunday morning, cleaners found the boy lying injured on the ground with much blood on his face. A doctor was sent for and it was surmised that   the boy had fallen asleep watching the show from some backstage vantage point. He did not wake until the house was cleared and plunged into darkness. On waking, he tried to find his way out but fell through the hole on the fly floor used for the raising and lowering of the scenery counterweights, no doubt striking his head on these as he fell.

1856_03_01c NEW YORK, USA (Broadway).   HORSE AND RIDER FALL OFF THE STAGE

At the Broadway Theatre a new hippodrama called *Herne the Hunter* was being performed when Mr Sylvester reined in his horse so tightly that both horse and rider fell off the stage on to the partition dividing the orchestra from the stage. This, as in many theatres of the time, had a row of iron spikes along the top to deter invasion of the stage. Both horse and rider were severely injured by the piercing of spikes, but the orchestra played on unharmed.

1857_05_13 LONDON (Princess's).   FRONT CURTAIN CATCHES FIRE

The front curtains at this theatre were of velvet, divided in the centre. When they were down they did not fully muffle the sound on stage and a scenic cloth was dropped in behind to deaden any noise. Prior to the curtains parting the drop cloth was pulled up. So far so good. The snag was that the action of taking it out caused a draught, making the curtains belly out forwards. On this night, during which Mr and Mrs Charles Kean were staging *Richard II* with a cast of 400, the billowing curtain ignited from the footlights.

The cry of 'Fire!' and the sight of the

7. *The Princess's Theatre showing the curtains*

flames alarmed the audience to make for the exits, but while her husband and his stage crew dealt with the fire, Mrs Kean assured the audience that there was no more fire than was visible, and that they would see it very shortly extinguished. By her demeanour, calm speech and noble example she prevented a panic and the fleeing people sheepishly returned to their seats.

8. *Charles Kean*

While Mrs Kean was calming the audience, the stage crew had cut down the curtains and extinguished the blaze with water. It was estimated that no more than seven minutes had elapsed before all was well. Mr Kean came forward, taking his wife's hand and the couple received nine rousing cheers. Kean made a short speech to say there were no casualties, very little damage and performances would continue as advertised from the following night. It was reported that Kean had paid double wages to his staff who put out the fire.

9. *Ellen Tree (Mrs Kean)*

1859_02_12 LONDON (Adelphi).   ACCIDENT BY FALLING FLATS

George Hayden, a stagehand at the Adelphi Theatre, was with colleagues sorting out scenery for the evening's performance. One particular flat was required from the midst of a stack of them leaning against the wall. Hayden was holding upright the stack when they toppled over on to him. He was dragged out from the mass of scenery and taken to Charing Cross Hospital with a broken thigh.

1859_03_17c GREENOCK (Theatre).   MR LLOYD HAS HIS TONGUE CUT IN HALF

During an inspection of the new theatre at Greenock, Mr Lloyd of the Theatre Royal, Glasgow, while descending a private staircase from the boxes, slipped and fell with his face against a brick wall. He struck the surface with such violence that his tongue was cut completely in half. He was immediately attended to by Dr Macall who sewed the parts together.

1859_07_20c SPILSBY (Adelphi).   EFFICIENT DEALING WITH BORDER FIRE

The play was *Hamlet*, and new naphtha lamps had been installed to increase the brightness of the stage. Unfortunately, one of the new lights ignited a sky border. Astonishingly, there was no shout of 'Fire!' or panic stricken theatregoers fleeing for the exits. The leading man Mr Green lowered the drop scene, Mr Wigan, son of the lessee, cut down from the flies the burning material which was then extinguished. Within a few minutes the drop scene rose and the tragedy continued. "This calmness and promptitude" was given as an example to all how a scenery fire should be dealt with. The Spilsby theatre was most likely a small country venue on the lines of the extant Georgian Theatre at Richmond, Yorkshire.

1859_12_17 BIRMINGHAM (Theatre Royal).   FATAL ACCIDENT TO STAGE WORKER

In readiness for the pantomime, Thomas Field was working on some machinery in a deep well that had been dug underneath the stage. Because the newly dug well had a side of soft sandstone it was thought prudent to build a brick wall to hold back the excavation. This had been done a month previously and was shored up with timbers to allow the mortar to set firmly. Field, who had been employed at the theatre for some 25 years, was alone in the well when the wall collapsed on him and he was buried under 7ft of brick walling. It took colleagues 45 minutes to remove the "superincumbent mass" and he was clearly dead when finally revealed. He left a widow and six children entirely unprovided for, but the season, due to close at the end of March 1860, stayed open an extra day to stage a benefit for Mrs Field and her family.

1862_09_18 LIVERPOOL (Amphitheatre).   GUN ACCIDENT

A play called *The Savannah* was being performed, during which a number of guns were used. After the play Mr Jenkins the property man was clearing them away when an undischarged weapon went off in his arms. The wadding lacerated the man's face and tore his eye out. He was taken to the Royal Infirmary.

1864_02_05c PARIS, France (Châtelet).   FATAL FALL FROM FLIES

At the theatre, during the interval of *Naufrage de la Medase*, a flyman fell from the flies to the stage and was killed on the spot. He had been drinking and was considered to be quite drunk.

1865_01_02 LONDON (Covent Garden).   FATAL TRAP ACCIDENT

At the matinee performance of *Cinderella*, during the spectacular transformation scene, a stage hand called Chamont missed his footing and fell 20ft through an open trap on to the cellar floor below. The poor fellow was senseless when picked up, and on the arrival of medical aid was found to be dead from a broken neck.

1865_01_28 AGRICULTURAL HALL, LONDON.

NEW GROOM ATTACKED BY LIONS

Trainer John Crockett had recently acquired a new groom called John Reeves. At 10.30am on Thursday, piercing screams rent the air. Circus workers found that Reeves had been seized by a lion and pulled right up to the bars of the cage. His entire arm now being within the cage a second lion began eating it along with the first. The man's colleagues seized long metal poles and attacked the lions, beating them about the head and eyes as best as they were able through the bars. These measures infuriated the animals and their grip on Reeve's arm was even more tenacious. Eventually, by poking the animals in the eyes, they drove them to drop the mangled limb and Reeves was pulled free. He was taken to St Bartholomew's Hospital where his hand was amputated but his arm was saved.

image© The British Library Board

10. *Groom attacked by lion*

18

1865_02_26 LONDON (Covent Garden).   FATAL TRAP ACCIDENT

It was time for the transformation scene in the pantomime on Tuesday evening, and John Walters the crew foreman was master-minding the set change which involved opening up large traps in the stage floor to admit the hoisting up of scenery. When all was accomplished he was clearing up the stage, missed his footing and fell through an open trap into the cellar beneath, a distance of some 27ft. He was taken to Charing Cross Hospital where he expired at 3am on Wednesday morning.

1865_05_01 SHEFFIELD (Theatre Royal).   ACCIDENT TO STAGEHAND

During the performance, a stagehand named Cornelius Milner had reason to climb up to the flies at the back of the stage. Once there he lost his footing and fell to the stage below, a distance of some 35ft, where he lay a considerable time before being discovered. His injuries were serious so he was taken to the local hospital where the prognostications were said to be favourable.

1865_06_12c PARIS, France (Gaité).   SINGULAR ACCIDENT TO THEATRE MANAGER

This is an unusual one. M Arnold, manager of the theatre, worked in an office in which there was a shuttered opening for enquiries. The shutter, of heavy sheet iron, slid upwards in vertical grooves. Hearing a rap at the window, the manager slid the shutter up to deal with his visitor. By mischance, he forgot to slide the fastening bolt that held the shutter in the open position and during the conversation it fell down smashing four fingers of Arnold's right hand. The visitor had placed his hat on the ledge so this was crushed and deadened the force of the fall to some extent, but the fingers were hanging only by fragments of flesh so re-attachment was very doubtful.

1865_12_09 PARIS, France (Gaîté). FATAL FALL FROM FLIES

"A sad accident occurred at the Théâtre de la Gaîté, Paris, a few evenings back, about half an hour before the rising of the curtain. One of the scene-shifters fell from a lofty flying bridge on the stage, and so fractured his skull that he expired in a few minutes after." *Berkshire Chronicle* 1865_12_09.

1866_01_12 LONDON (Standard). EXPLOSION

During the pantomime at the Standard Theatre in Shoreditch immediately prior to the transformation scene, a large explosion took place, shaking the building, filling the auditorium with smoke and plunging the place into blackout as the gas went out. The theatre was "extremely full" and there were the inevitable shouts of 'Fire!' as the audience members blundered their way to the exits. The chaos in the dark may be imagined, but fortunately it did not last long and the lighting was restored. However, the gas pipe to the lights at the front of the circle had somehow become detached and when the gas came back, on lighting, a jet of flame shot out for several feet thus giving vent to a second panic. The blaze was immediately put out, so calming the sparse audience that now remained. Once order was restored the manager came onstage dragging what he explained was a rubber bag used for the limelight, which had exploded. No damage had been done, neither was there a report of any injuries, so the show continued to its close. The theatre was burned down on 28 October 1866.

1866_02_15 LONDON (St James's). ACCIDENT TO ASSISTANT

Mr Clare, assistant to the acting manager Mr W Emden, while moving along the flies lost his footing and fell to the stage. In his descent he struck two projections which possibly tempered his fall to immediate destruction but must have added to his wounds. Being so seriously injured he was taken to hospital without delay.

1866_02_06c CAMBRAI, France. GUN ACCIDENT TO 13-YEAR-OLD BOY

"In a piece called *La Vieillese de Brididi*, a pistol had to be fired, and, as is usual on such occasions, two had been charged with powder only for the purpose. At the end of the performance one of the scene-shifters took up the weapon which had not been used, to put it away, when a boy between 13 and 14 years of age made a snatch at it, causing it to go off in the direction of his own hand. Two of the child's fingers were broken by the wadding, which had been rammed down very tight, and his hand was otherwise so much injured that amputation, the medical men thought, would very probably be necessary." *Sussex Advertiser* 1866_02_06.

1866_09_22 CHICAGO, USA (McVicker's). FLAMING GAUZE IN THE FLIES

11. *McVicker's Theatre*

The theatre was using the dangerous expedient of hanging gauze in front of the gas battens over the stage to enable different lighting effects. The not unlikely happened as a waft of breeze caused the gauze to get nearer to the naked gas flame which set light to it with smoking portions dropping down on to the stage. Shouts of 'Fire!' arose immediately and a rush made for the exits. "The shrieking of women and the cries of the men soon told of the dreadful crush which was taking place." Mr McVicker stood on the stage imploring his audience not to panic and assured them there was no fire in the building. They had already seen as much fire as there had been confined to the stage and now it was totally out. The panic subsided and order restored, miraculously with no accident occurring.

1867_01_16 BIRMINGHAM (Theatre Royal).   SERIOUS ACCIDENT BY FALLING IRON BAR

Charles Christie was taking part in the pantomime. During the transformation scene some of the stage machinery became entangled and Christie was trying to put it right. In the process a large iron bar fell on his head, taking away the back of his skull and crashing into his shoulders. He was thought to be dead when picked up, but there was still life in him so he was swiftly despatched to Queen's Hospital where he remained "in a precarious condition."

1867_04_20c LONDON (Drury Lane).   HANSOM CAB ONSTAGE

The new drama called *A Great City* was designed to put a modern kind of realism on the stage so a proper Hansom cab with horse was introduced. The heroine of the piece – played by Madge

12.

Robertson – summoning a cab, and the genuine article appearing, then her jumping in, brought roars of delight from the densely packed audience. This sudden noise frightened the horse which backed the cab into the footlights, bending the brass rod that protects them. Miss Robertson would probably have been thrown into the orchestra pit with the cab on top of her, followed by the horse. It was prevented by the rest of the cast shouting "Whoa!" in a natural and normal style. At this the horse remembered his job and galloped off in a "spirited manner" with an unscathed Miss Robertson.

1867_06_15 HULL (Queen's).   THEATRE GAS MAN FALLS INTO PIT

On Saturday night it was the regular custom after the audience had left to cover the front of the first tier of boxes with dustsheets. Mr Lawrence the gasman of the theatre, and other employees were doing this chore. Along the boxes serving as an armrest was a rim which was loose when, reaching over to fasten the covering, Lawrence stretched too far, the rim gave way and he was hurtled over into the pit. His injuries included a dislocated shoulder.

1867_12_24 LONDON (Cabinet).   FATAL ACCIDENT TO VISITING WORKER

This accident was another that should never have happened as it resulted in the death backstage of a man not even entitled to be there. Joseph Shepherd, a coach trimmer, was engaged to repair damaged furniture and not anything else. On this night, a stagehand called Kinsman asked Shepherd if he would give him a hand with something up in the roof. Shepherd agreed and followed Kinsman up a ladder into the roof space. When he reached the top of the ladder, instead of stepping on to the bridge, not knowing how theatre matters are arranged, he stepped on to the false roof of the set which, being simply made of canvas, gave way. The poor chap not only fell to the stage, but impaled himself on the spikes that separated the orchestra from the pit.

It appears Kinsman invited Shepherd to view how the chandelier was raised and lowered. At the inquest, Kinsman prevaricated in his evidence and was severely censured by the jury.

1867_12_24 SUNDERLAND (Lyceum).   ABSENT STAGE HANDS

In this book's companion *Perils of the Victorian Stage* that covers accidents onstage this problem is mentioned several times, and it is astonishing that it was still going on at this period. In the harlequinade, characters do a lot of acrobatic stunts, including leaping through flaps in the scenery. In these cases it is necessary to have two stage hands behind the scenery with a canvas sling to catch the flying Clown or Harlequin. To ensure their presence, it was a time-honoured custom to give them a tip. Hudspeth the Clown in this pantomime, when asked for 'catch money' refused, saying Mr Holt paid them wages to do this service for him. Hudspeth was then told that he had better watch out as he might have an accident. As a result, the manager Mr Holt positioned himself to see that the two men deputed for the job, Purse and Brown, were in place. Holt watched for a while then went elsewhere. As soon as the manager had gone, Purse and Brown likewise disappeared. Mr Holt Jr and Mr Garden stepped in to deputize.

The two miscreants were sacked and new catchers appointed, but Purse and Brown had the gall to turn up on Saturday for their wages. Holt took them to court.

1867_12_24 MIDDLESBROUGH (Royal Albert).   LIMELIGHT EXPLOSION

There was a crowded house of children to see the matinee of the pantomime *Whittington and his Cat*. As the limelight was being prepared for the transformation scene there was a mighty explosion causing the actors to flee the stage and the audience to make its way to the exits. Mr Pateman the stage manager appeared to quell the panic, explaining that there was no cause for alarm and no damage had been done. He explained that the explosion was caused by the chemical mixture being prepared for the limelight, and added that in future he would not use limelight but "the magnesium wire". Mr Best the property man, preparing the limelight, had all his clothes blown to rags and was burnt around the face and head. Theatre staff calmed everything, and the panto proceeded without the aid of limelight.

21

LIGHTING BY MAGNESIUM WIRE

The magnesium wire referred to by Mr Pateman was the latest development in theatre lighting and it is likely he was announcing this via hearsay as it was not patented until 1864 by Elijah Aldis and was a very expensive means of lighting. The principle was a thin wire made of magnesium wound on a spool. The wire was ignited and produced a dazzling bluish-white light, the spool unwinding as the flame burned it away. The flame had to be centred in a curved reflector to be efficient. The wire could be produced in different lengths and thicknesses, and was very expensive to make and buy. In 1866, a German firm began producing the wire on a commercial scale. There were two main practical disadvantages apart from cost; the wire was hard to ignite so they still used oxy-hydrogen to start the flame, and burning gave off clouds of white smoke and ash which had to be constantly cleared from the apparatus.

1868_12_23 NORWICH (Mans' Circus).   GUN ACCIDENT TO SMALL CHILD

Brothers Frederic and John Allen were employees of the circus, and one of John's regular chores was to prepare and load a pistol which was fired in the ring by a trained horse pulling on a handkerchief. Having prepared the gun John placed it on a chest inside the tent, then entered the ring.

The performance had been under way for five minutes or so when he heard the report of the gun and a scream of a child. Running off he saw his five-year-old nephew Frederic Adolf Allen, screaming and bleeding from a wound in his bowels. Rushed to hospital, the little lad died six hours after admittance. The inquest verdict was 'accidental death' with the suggestion "there might be some means of putting the pistol out of the way when loaded." Which takes the biscuit for 'statement of the bleedin' obvious'!

1868_12_24 ROCHDALE (Prince of Wales). ACCIDENT TO BALLET GIRLS

The occasion was the dress rehearsal of the annual pantomime before a privileged fashionable audience. All went well up to the traditional transformation scene. This is the scene where most chorus dancers or 'ballet girls' suffer accidents. The transformation is always created for its magnificence, so the scenic effects involve the full stage crew simultaneously working different parts of the set with traps or cuts in the stage floor to allow scene pieces to rise and fall, wing pieces to slide on and off, in addition to cut cloths and gauzes being raised and lowered in the flies and so on. Integral to all this was the iron* designed so the girls in ornate fairy-type costumes could be strapped on in a tableau fashion amongst the scenery. In addition, other girls – often children – were suspended on individual wires. These poor girls were thus at the mercy of the stage engineering, the competence of the stage men, and the practical design of the thing. To add to the problems of having everything working smoothly in harmony, ambitious variations were expected of the lighting to enhance the magic of it all.

On this night, a particular platform bearing six ballet girls got stuck for several minutes, then fell suddenly through the stage to the cellars below. The rehearsal immediately stopped, and it was feared serious injury, and even death, might be found underneath the stage. But no! None of the six was markedly injured. The transformation was instantly closed down, but the rest of the panto continued.   *Not to be confused with the safety curtain also called 'the iron'.

1868_12_29 LONDON (Surrey). EXPLOSIONS

During the pantomime, two explosions were heard backstage. The first around 9pm when the stage was crowded with dancers, the second during the transformation scene around an hour later. The girls, suspended in their positions on the iron and unable to move freely, were "much alarmed" which is putting it mildly I should say. Fortunately, the two lessees and the ballet master, together at the back of the stage, were able to assure the girls all was well; the audience taking the explosions as part of the effects of the panto. They were caused by the overfilling of the two gas bags that provide the limelight.

One of the lessees immediately wrote a letter to *The Era* saying that the explosion at the Surrey was caused by "the gross carelessness of the man working that light, the said man being instantly discharged from my service." No appeals of unfair dismissal in those days.

1869_05_18 NEWCASTLE (Tyne). FATAL FALL OF DRUNKEN CHECKTAKER

Thomas Pringle (28) a joiner, had for the past week been engaged as the checktaker in the gallery. A colleague said he was tipsy every night he came. On Friday night, he was so drunk that he repeatedly fell down several of the gallery steps. On his last stumble he banged his head on the wall, and sat stupefied, leaning against it. At the end of the show he was taken to the Falstaff Inn and put in a bed. Apart from a nose-bleed – and drunk as a skunk, of course – he seemed all right. At 8am next morning a servant girl, going into the room, found him dead.

1869_05_20 LONDON (Astley's).

image© The British Library Board

HORSE ACCIDENT AT ASTLEY'S TRASHES BAND

The drama was an equestrian version of *The Battle of Waterloo*, with Napoleon and his entourage. Unfortunately, when his mount went astray one rider was at a loss what to do. The horse went backwards on to the footlights, demolished the metal bar that ran along the front and crashed into the orchestra pit, smashing instruments in all directions as it thrashed about with the rider underneath. Most of the musicians escaped without injury except the clarinettist who had his collar bone broken. The horse's front legs and head were still upon the stage, so some experienced equestrians managed to haul it back upright into position, and after two minutes all was well and the play proceeded.

1870_01_26 CORK (Theatre).   FALL OF FLYMAN DURING SHOW

The audience was enjoying a burlesque when a loud crash was heard behind the scenes. A stage hand had been perched sitting on the fly gallery rail and, losing his balance, toppled off dropping 20ft on to the stage. His fall was broken by landing on an actor. Two doctors were summoned and they agreed no bones had been broken and the dazed man was taken home. He was lucky, many flymen met death in this manner. Should the faller land on another person it is often that human cushion that suffers rather than the unwanted projectile that descends without warning. This is particularly so in audiences when somebody is liable to fall from the gallery to land in the stalls on top of some innocent person.

1870_04_28 LONDON (Covent Garden).   FATAL TRAP ACCIDENT

On Thursday evening, carpenter George Alfred Reid (38) was seen crossing the stage with some wooden steps. He moved the door that was covering a trap, and then fell down through the hole to the floor of the cellar beneath, a distance of 25ft. He broke his left thigh and the bone was protruding. He was taken to Charing Cross Hospital where he died on Saturday morning. A post mortem revealed his fractured skull to be the cause of death.

1870_09_29 LONDON (Surrey).   FATAL FALL OF PROPERTY MAN

During the day on Thursday, Dick Harvey the well-respected property man was conducting his boss E T Smith and Mr Dunn from the Lord Chamberlain's office around the theatre. They were at the top of the gallery stairs pausing while Harvey lit a gas light when he fell backwards down the steps to the landing below. He was whisked off to Guy's Hospital but the fall proved fatal as Dick died from brain injury on Saturday night.

1870_10_13 LIVERPOOL (Malakoff).   FATAL ACCIDENT TO MUSIC HALL CHILD

John Eltringham Lowrey (3) son of music hall owner Dan Lowrey Jr accidentally fell into a pail of boiling water and was so scalded no medical aid could save him, and he died the following day. Poor little lad.

23

1871_04_16 BALTIMORE, USA (Holiday St).   FATAL FALL OF FLYMAN

Samuel B Fowler fell from the fly gallery shortly after the end of the matinee performance. The distance was around 30ft and he struck a chair on the fall, fracturing his skull. He lingered until 2.30am the following morning then expired.

1871_12_26 LIVERPOOL (Adelphi).   FATAL GUN ACCIDENT

The property man was Henry Holland, his assistant John Plaistow (20). One of the many duties of this pair was to load and discharge any weapons used onstage, and make sure they were safe before putting away. On Tuesday morning around 10.30am, Mr Champion the stage manager asked Plaistow to get a gun from the theatre's collection and give it to Champion's son to take home. He stressed that Plaistow should make sure the gun was not loaded. It is not clear why Champion wanted his son to have a gun, or what his age was, but he put his finger on the nipple while Plaistow blew down the barrel. Not feeling air come through the nipple, Champion said he thought it was loaded with a charge of powder. Plaistow put the barrel to his mouth and placed the nipple in a gas light. The charge exploded, injuring Plaistow's mouth and head so severely that he subsequently died in the Royal Infirmary on Thursday morning. What an odd way to test if a gun was loaded!

1872_01_01 LIVERPOOL (Royal Amphitheatre).   FATAL FALL OF 'SUPER' FROM FLIES

14. John West falling

image© The British Library Board

At 6.15pm, three stage hands were standing on the stage prior to the performance. Hearing a noise above, and looking up, they saw a body lying on one of the rolled up scenes. As they watched, the body slipped and fell to the stage a distance of around 40ft. Dr Cross was sent for, but on arrival all he could do was pronounce the man dead. The man's head was so crushed he could only be identified by his clothes. He was John West (60) a supernumerary (the equivalent of an 'extra' in the film world) of 19 years standing at the theatre, who was known to be short-sighted. It is thought that after checking in at the stage door he had gone up to the dressing rooms, but turned in the wrong direction, walking about 10ft before falling into the hanging scenery, and thence the stage. It seems odd that a man who had worked at the place for 19 years should have lost his way, but there you are.

1872_01_06 MANCHESTER (Queen's).   FATAL ACCIDENT TO MESSENGER BOY

The pantomime was in full swing and Thomas Foxcroft (13) was employed as a messenger boy. On his way from the stage to the property room he had to cross a yard where there was a heavy hydraulic pump leaning against a wall. For some reason the lad put his foot against this pump which fell on him, crushing his foot. He was taken home, but died at 11am the following morning, his death

24

being put down to "shock to the nervous system". At the inquest the jury made a recommendation that the pump should be moved elsewhere, or if remaining in the same place should be secured. Mr Bailey the lessee promised to follow the advice.

1872_04_20 GLASGOW.   FATAL FALL OF FLYMAN

Moses Irvine (35) was lowering the front curtain with a colleague prior to the performance when he fell from the fly gallery to the stage, a distance of 23ft and fractured his skull. He died on the way to hospital. It was stated that "he was the worse for drink".

1872_11_07 LONDON (Bedford).   STAGE FIRE STARTED BY GIANT FISH TANK

[Charles Weightman (1846–1887) performed as a 'human fish' under the name of Natator. He took his act to USA and the Antipodes and wrote a book *The Art of Swimming*.] He was the attraction at this hall in Camden Town giving an underwater display in a huge glass tank. To warm this water gas battens were lit underneath the stage around 5pm. Half-an-hour later that portion of the stage was aflame, and before it could be extinguished the blaze had spread to scenery. The fire was promptly dealt with by breaking the tank and flooding the place with water. One side of the stage was badly damaged but the show went on as usual – except, of course, without Natator. I wonder how soon he got a replacement tank, and who paid for it?

25

1872_11_09 BOSTON, USA (Theatre).   THE GREAT FIRE OF BOSTON

This was Boston's largest ever fire, the blaze beginning at 7.20pm in the basement of a commercial warehouse and spreading to 776 buildings. The flames prevented the actresses from getting out of their theatre and they fled to the upper reaches where they became trapped. One resourceful actress, realizing there was a telephone pole outside the window, resorted to standing on the sill and leaping across the five feet gap. Others followed suit, they must have been limber.

1873_02_24 BLACKBURN (Theatre.)   EXPLOSION

During the play *The Jewess*, a loud explosion from the stage was heard and all the lights in the theatre went out. Instant panic ensued with people making for the exits. However, Chief Constable Potts happened to be present in the boxes and, believing the danger to be over, calmed the boxes, then went to those in the pit and then into the gallery. In the latter place the ticket taker and a policeman were manning the door, not allowing anybody through. This was a wise precaution as the exit door led to a flight of narrow stairs, and a mass of people fleeing in the dark would have brought inevitable serious accidents, as happened on several similar occasions.

The explosion was caused by one of the limelight bags, apparently in the fly gallery under the charge of a youth named Whittaker. An escape of gas from the bag ignited with a bang when it came into contact with a gaslight. The result was that part of the fly gallery some 5ft wide and 10ft long was blown down, Whittaker falling with it on to the stage 18ft below. The light restored, medical aid was summoned and Whittaker was found with wounds on scalp and neck which were dressed and he was taken home. The performance continued after the delay.

1873_02_28 EDINBURGH (Theatre Royal). FATAL ACCIDENT TO STAGEHAND'S SON

On this Friday night, a little boy called William Raeburn, the son of a stagehand at the theatre, accompanied his dad when he went to work. He fell on to the stage, a distance of around 20ft, and was taken to the Royal Infirmary with a fractured skull and thigh. He died on Monday morning.

1873_05_25 MALTA (Theatre Royal). RAZED TO THE GROUND BY A SCENIC FIRE

16. *The aftermath of the fire*

This beautiful theatre was built to the designs of Edward Barry the designer of the Covent Garden Theatre. On Sunday evening, the company was holding its dress rehearsal for a new opera due to open the following evening. About 10.30pm one of the side scenes caught fire and in a moment the place was a mass of flames. Being a rehearsal, there were very few people attending who were not directly concerned in the production, so all persons were able to make their escape.

All the interior was gutted, only the outer walls remaining standing though, as these were cracked in several places from the great heat, it was thought they would have to be demolished and a new theatre started from scratch.

26

1873_12_24 LIVERPOOL (Amphitheatre). EXPLOSION

During the opening night of the pantomime everything was progressing normally until the scene called *The Palace of Playing Cards* when there was a loud bang backstage followed by smoke and dust. The audience rose to flee, but the principal players Rachel Sanger, Mr Scanlan and Mr Flockton dashed on to the stage and urged the audience not to panic but keep their seats. They succeeded in preventing a mass exodus after explaining the minor explosion was caused by the bursting of a limelight bag brought about by "one of the gasmen incautiously treading on one of the pipes."

1873 AN AMERICAN FIRE SAFETY IDEA

The wooden buildings of America were particularly prone to fire and the latest idea for a new hotel was to have a long safety gallery on the top floor fed by stairs from all parts. From this gallery an iron fireproof bridge 10ft wide crossed the road to a building also owned by the hotel. People fleeing across the bridge would find themselves on a large area at the top of the building surrounded by a balustrade on all sides. Internal stairs from this platform led down into the building. An impressive idea, but probably unfeasible in crowded London, until one learns that there already existed such a link between the Gaiety Theatre and some refreshment rooms opposite. However, this was closed by an Act of Parliament thus compelling theatregoers to descend by stairs to the street, cross over and ascend another set of stairs to gain the refreshment rooms. Well done, Parliament!

1874_02_18c PARIS, France (Gaîté).   FALL FROM FLIES MID-PERFORMANCE

The play was *Orphée*, which was a version of the work the English know as *Orpheus and Eurydice*. Théâtre de la Gaîté, the fourth incarnation of a theatre that first opened in 1759 was known for its melodramas. It is not clear whether this was a play or an opera, but during the scene with the duel between Eurydice and the King of Boetia a body fell from the flies on to the stage, to lie a "crushed and inert mass" alongside the actors. As soon as the audience realised they were probably looking at a corpse many ladies and some men fainted. The curtain was dropped and the play put on hold while the man was attended to. He had broken one arm in several places and his skull was fractured.

1874_03_07 LONDON (Covent Garden).   FATAL TRAP ACCIDENT

A stagehand called Henry Parr fell through an open trap a distance of 16ft to the cellar below. He was taken up insensible and carried to Charing Cross Hospital where he died from his injuries.

1874_05_23 DETROIT, USA (Theatre).   ACCIDENT TO VETERAN ACTRESS

The Holman English Opera Troupe was appearing in a repertoire of light operas. Halfway through the week, Mrs C Hill (73), going along a passage under the auditorium to the stage entrance, fell down a flight of steps, hitting her head and injuring her spinal column. She was immediately taken to her hotel and every attention given by her friends and colleagues. Because of her advanced age it was thought that the accident may well prove fatal.

1874_10_03 COBHAM (Holt's Puppet Theatre).   DESTITUTION BY FIRE

This accident is not just backstage but auditorium, stage and home. It is both a family and professional tragedy on a small scale by the dimensions of theatres razed to the ground but totally shattering for the little family involved. Holt's Royal Collection and Theatre of Marionettes was temporarily situated on a piece of waste ground in the Kent village. Around 4am a gale sprang up with such force that the canvas booth which provided the auditorium of the theatre was blown down. As it fell on to a portable stove kept burning in the tent overnight, the booth immediately burst into a mass of flames. Alongside the booth was a four-wheeled wagon which served as the stage for the theatre and the dwelling of the Holt family in which Mr and Mrs Holt were asleep with their two children. Mr Holt, fortunately roused by the fire, desperately tried to get his family out of the wagon. He managed to save his wife and baby, but the flames fanned by the strong winds, meant the older child of four years could not be reached and thus "miserably perished".

The fire burned itself out within an hour leaving only the ironwork of the former wooden wagon, and the charred remains of the child among the debris – a colossal tragedy for this little family. Not only had they lost a child, but their home and livelihood had also vanished, leaving them at 5am penniless in the middle of a piece of waste ground with only the clothes they slept in.

The following week after the report in *The Era,* the paper received two guineas from the London Stereoscopic Co. and 10/- from Miss Lydia Howard the "fairy actress". Mr Holt was asked to urgently get in touch, but had he got 5d to buy the paper? As a professional puppeteer for forty years I was especially interested in this case but so far, in spite of all my research, the trail has remained cold.

27

1874_12_26c LONDON (Alhambra).   FATAL FALL BY HEAD SUPER

William Edgcombe, described as "master of the supers", fell down some stone steps leading from the stage to the canteen. He was found at the bottom crying out that his legs were broken, and was promptly taken to hospital where he expired. It was acknowledged that the steps were well lighted, and had been used without incident for two and a half years. After the accident, the management had installed a handrail. The jury returned a verdict of 'accidental death' and expressed the opinion that the rail should have been installed before.

1874_12_29 STOCKTON-ON-TEES (Theatre).   SCENIC ARTIST FALLS FROM FLIES

The pantomime *Robin Hood* was in full swing, and Furnival Hughes the chief scenic artist was engaged in duties in the flies. Around 9pm, he lost his balance and fell to the stage a distance of 30ft and was picked up insensible "and now lies in a very precarious state." A later bulletin expressed more optimistic auguries.

1875_01_12 NORWICH (Theatre Royal).   EXPLOSION

The pantomime wittily titled *Ali Baba and the Thirty-nine Thieves* was underway when, following an explosion under the stage, all the lights in the theatre went out. As this particular performance was a treat especially for the juveniles, the audience was unusually large. The people in the boxes tried to fumble their way to the exit, while the pittites made a stampede of getting out which could have developed into a dangerous melee if the manager and stage manager had not been on the ball and got the lights working in double quick time. It did not help that in the darkness the dancers and children onstage started screaming and rushed outside in their flimsy costumes, to be taken in by a neighbouring house. Hurst, the manager made a conciliatory speech assuring the audience that there was no danger, the damage was but a trifle and the performance would continue.

So what was the cause of the explosion? Well, by now the reader will probably have twigged that it was the old punctured limelight bag accident. It seems that the theatre did not normally have limelight, but had installed one or more for special lighting effects in the pantomime. Regrettably, the apparatus had been put in the care of an inexperienced youth called Austin who had allowed a heavy weight to fall on one of the bags thus puncturing it. The explosion forced up a section of stage and the footlights, and brought down a shower of debris from the flies.

While the manager was placating the audience and the cast returning, a frantic woman dashed on stage shouting that her son had had his brains blown out. This was Mrs Austin, of course, so she had to be bundled off to prevent her blabbing to the audience. The damage to her son, actually lacerations to one side of his head, needed immediate attention at hospital. And the show went on.

The next morning, Hurst conducted an examination into the cause of the accident. Lee, the machinist of the theatre, removing the bag used for the limelight, held it up to the gaslight when it promptly exploded again. Clearly it still contained an amount of oxygen. Lee's reward for his clumsy incautiousness was a broken arm and a broken finger.

1875_11_13 LONDON (Albion).   GUN ACCIDENT TO PROPERTY MASTER

John Hicks was the Property Master at the theatre in Poplar. He was loading a pistol prior to the play when it burst, completely shattering his hand. He was swiftly moved to the Poplar Hospital

28

where three fingers of his right hand were amputated. He was still in hospital while further possibilities of removing his entire hand were mooted. The stage manager of the Albion sent a heart-rending letter to *The Era* begging for funds to support the man who "in the prime of life and manhood" was suddenly reduced to "abject pauperism." The subscription list went on to 15 January when it closed, Hicks still being in the Poplar Hospital "in a precarious state".

However, in *The Era* of 1876_03_26, a letter from Hicks revealed he had had his entire hand successfully amputated and, itemising them all, thanked the fund subscribers for their support, which had raised a grand total of £70. 03.10d (£6661 in today's money).

1875_11_18 SHEFFIELD (Alexanda). STAGE CREW INJURED BY COLLAPSE OF STAGE

It was a Thursday afternoon and five men were arranging scene-shifting tackle when a bridge over the front portion of the stage gave way and all the men were thrown violently on to the stage. All were injured, one rather seriously.

1876_04_25 ROUEN, France (Des Arts). BACKSTAGE FIRE

On this night, the actors were dressing ready for a performance of the opera *Hamlet*. There were many people backstage when a stage curtain caught fire, and they all made a rush to get out of the place as flames rapidly spread to the stage and scenery.

Having been built in 1774, the theatre was over 100 years old and, as such, lacked modern facilities, passages being narrow and winding, exits few and small. When the artistes rushed to the exit

from the dressing rooms they found the fire had penetrated under the staircase, thereby cutting off their only means of escape. The poor chorus singers' only recourse was by leaping out of the windows. By this time people from neighbouring houses were outside, stacking up mattresses etc to cushion the dropping bodies. All the principal singers bar one got out safely as their rooms were on the first floor. The exception was Madame Preys who, learning her husband was on an upper floor, went searching in defiance of the colleagues who showed how they could save themselves, and thus perished herself. The most unfortunate were the 40 chorus singers and 35 supers (soldiers of the 24th Regiment) who were on the third and fourth floors.

17. *Théâtre des Artes*

M Guillemot, who was to sing Hamlet, saved many of the female singers, guiding them through his dressing room, along smoke filled corridors to the stage door, until he himself could make his escape only by climbing from a window. Madame Dallier, a poor dresser to the chorus, was prominent in urging the performers to jump from the window on to the mattresses below, until all were out. A rope was thrown to her from an adjacent building and, tying it round her waist, she too made the leap but alas, the rope broke, and she was dashed on to a stone abutment and killed.

The attending fire engines were virtually useless, and the flames had total control through the night. When it was possible to search the wreckage there were additions to add to the known fatalities, the final count being 13 dead. M Goutchalde, the manager of the theatre was arrested on the double charge of embezzlement and arson.

Goutchalde, real name Adolphe Godefroy, came to trial in August. The accusation was that, being on the verge of bankruptcy, he was relying on the insurance money to save him. There was some evidence against him but, with the balance of the testimony decidedly in his favour, he was acquitted. However, he was then charged with fraud. He had made deductions from the salaries of the performers on the pretext of giving New Year presents to the working staff, whereas only a small proportion went to that purpose. He was convicted and sentenced to one month's imprisonment.

1876_08_21 YORK (Theatre Royal). EXPLOSION

Just prior to the show, a loud explosion was heard emanating from backstage. The audience was naturally alarmed but, when reassured that the theatre was in no danger, relaxed to enjoy the show. Backstage was a very different matter. The reader will have surmised by now, the ubiquitous limelight bags were to blame. William Pinder (50), a jack-of-all trades at the theatre, was deputising for the regular gasman, a job he had often done before. The explosive force rammed him against the wall, damaging his right side and breaking his leg. Sent to hospital, on Tuesday it was deemed necessary to amputate Pinder's right leg. The unfortunate man succumbed to the operation, and died on Wednesday. He had been employed at the theatre for 20 years. The limelight apparatus had been installed for 12 years and Pinder had operated it "a thousand times without incident."

1876_09_06 LONDON (Queen's). HORRIFIC FATAL INJURY TO VISITING LABOURER

This is a truly horrid thing to picture. It was a Wednesday morning when labourer Henry Emeric (34) was working under the stage with other men clearing things from around a spring trap. Not accustomed to working in theatres, he would not have been aware of the principle of a powerful spring trap which was used to propel pantomime gymnasts through a star trap high into the air. A star trap opens with flaps like the wedge shape slices of a round cake. Essential in trap work is the necessity of first sliding sideways the portion of stage above the trap apparatus. The spring trap was held down in its low position by a timber strut. It was conjectured that Emeric was actually standing on the trap when he removed the strut, the released spring thus propelling him upwards with a mighty force, smashing his head on the underside of the stage and resulting in a fractured skull from which he died.

There is an interesting short video on YouTube showing all the wooden apparatus under the stage of the Gaiety Theatre, Isle of Man including a demonstration of the only remaining Corsican trap in the world. https://www.youtube.com/watch?v=-TyNJKbB88g

1876_09_23 HAMBURG, Germany (Central Halle). ONSTAGE FIRE

This venue – a theatre and pleasure garden combined – was crowded on a Sunday when the fire broke out. Panic sent the crowds rushing wildly about with "women fainting, and children crying piteously". The fire – caused by the familiar curtain blowing into a gas light – rapidly spread. Some of the actors and ballet girls received burns before they got out, and a dozen members of the public had limbs broken in the fleeing melee.

1876_11_20 LIVERPOOL (Sefton).   GUN ACCIDENT

The companion book *Perils of the Victorian Stage* about onstage accidents details no fewer than 56 incidents. This is an additional offstage one. It is astonishing, considering how all these had been reported in the press, that more care was still not being given to firearms. This accident – actually in the wings – was caused by hesitation alone. The actress was Mrs Creamer, the wife of the lessee, who was playing a role in *The Dead Hand*. In the course of the play a pistol had to be fired in the wings, and Mrs Creamer was deputed to do this. At the very last minute when the cue came she thrust the weapon to a male colleague, asking him to do it. Then, suddenly changing her mind, and deciding she would fire the gun after all, reached out to take it back at the moment the man pulled the trigger almost blowing her fingers off.

1877_01_06 LONDON (Alhambra).   FATAL ACCIDENT TO STAGEHAND

During the interval before the last act of an opera all was bustle onstage as the scenery was changed. Among the crew was Frederick Thomas (40) an employee of many years standing, and well acquainted with the work. As there had been a delay in lowering a backcloth, Thomas tied a stage weight to the rope to make it easier to lower at future performances. Having done that, the backcloth was raised up into the flies. When the weight was about 16ft up, the knot came undone, and the weight (26lb) fell on to Thomas's head fracturing his skull. He was dead on arrival at Charing Cross Hospital.

31

1877_01_17 MANCHESTER (Theatre Royal).   SCENIC ARTIST FALLS THROUGH STAGE TRAP

During the afternoon, scenic artist Charles Fox (55) was watching his son, also an artist, at work. Fox stepped sideways and instantly fell through an open trap to the cellar 25ft below. Colliding with various beams and fittings as he fell, he was "considerably stunned" when found. He was taken to the Royal Infirmary by the manager Mr Sidney, where it was discovered that apart from a shock to the system he had suffered no injuries, and was able to resume his duties within a few days. Remarkable!

1877_11_06 HULL (Theatre Royal).   EXPLOSION

The play was *Nell, or the Old Curiosity Shop*, one of the many dramatic versions of Dickens's novels brought out while he was still writing them. A gas bag readied for lime light effects exploded blowing a piece of wood from the scenery which hit John Marshall, a stagehand, on the head. Fearing fire, many rushed from the building but the damage was not great and the danger now non-existent. The manager strolled on and told the audience that there was no cause for alarm and the play would continue as soon as the fleers returned to their seats.

1878_01_23 BALTIMORE, USA (Gilmore's).   EXPLOSION

Four men – including James Knapp – were deputed to handle the stage lighting effects for the matinee. Knapp, assuming that all had been set up ready for operation, turned on the hydrogen and applied a match. The explosion was terrific, with parts of the mangled cylinder blown completely across the auditorium, and the concussive blow breaking several windows as far as front-of-house, and extinguishing every light in the building.

Fortunately nobody was injured in the explosion except for the four men supposed to be in charge. Equally fortunate was the fact that daylight had access to the interior, though confusion reigned for some time until the Stage Manager and the Treasurer came on stage to explain that there was no further peril, the explosion had been the accident, and it was now over. The lights came on again, and the musicians who had fled the pit crept back into place. The audience who had left their seats returned, the stage cleared of debris, and the show started. Of the four men, only James Knapp was badly hurt, having among his injuries a shattered leg. This was amputated, after which he lingered some days in great agony before he died, conscious until the end.

1878_10_07 GREENWICH (Theatre).   EXPLOSION

The gas used for the limelight suddenly exploded putting out all the lights and filling the auditorium with dust and smoke. Instantly there was a mad rush for the doors, but appeals not to panic, and assurances of safety from the management were sufficient to calm the people and they returned to their seats.

1878_11_10 DUMFRIES (Theatre).   EXPLOSION

On Sunday 10 November 1878, "though the day was Sabbath", Captain Gordon's company was setting up and making preparations for opening on the next night with *Bonnie Prince Charlie*. While a supernumery was adjusting a limelight, the retort exploded and a piece of flying metal struck him on the throat, completely severing the carotid artery. "Death was almost instantaneous". Well I think that is truly terrible, but the good folk of Dumfries were more put out about something much more serious viz: "The utmost consternation is felt, as clandestine labour at the theatre on Sunday was never suspected by the community".

1879_05_15 LONDON (Covent Garden).   ACCIDENT TO FLYMEN

At the end of Act I of the play *La Prophete* the curtain came down in a fierce and startling rush injuring two flymen who were either caught up or flung aside when the over-weight curtain was released to fall. One suffered a broken leg, the other a broken arm and leg. The men were taken to Charing Cross Hospital.

1879_12_23 LIVERPOOL (Adelphi).   FATAL GUN ACCIDENT

Samuel Ackers (42), a house painter by trade, also worked as a stagehand at night. A fellow stagehand was George Snape whose job at a particular part of the play was to shake a thunder sheet with one hand and fire a gun with the other. The gun "went off sooner than anticipated" and shot the nearby Ackers in the leg. He was taken home, dying on 30 December. At the inquest, Snape was very much concerned to say that before Ackers died he had said "it was purely an accident", and that was the verdict returned.

1880_09_29 COVENTRY (Theatre Royal).   COLLAPSE OF DRESSING ROOM FLOOR

The play was *The Danites*. In the same dressing room were actors Clifford, Elmore, Fisher, Granville and Moore. Suddenly the piece of floor Mr Moore was standing on gave way and he fell through the resulting aperture, grabbing a section of the remaining floor with his hand. He was left hanging until help could arrive with means of rescue. It was found that the 4" square beam supporting the floor had snapped in two because it was rotten through and through, and could be crumbled in the fingers like a loaf of bread. The floor planking was similarly rotten, and it was a wonder the weight of all five men had not caused the lot to collapse. If Moore had entirely fallen through he would have fallen on to a flight of steps.

1880_11_13 LONDON (Her Majesty's).   EXPLOSION

Gounod's opera *Faust* was being presented and all was passing favourably until the middle of the last act when a loud explosion backstage was heard by the audience. Mdlle Widmar, in the middle of an aria as Margherita, sang on "with wonderful *sang froid*" and was emulated by Signor Runcio. But the audience was restless and a few had left, so the conductor, halting the orchestra, called out that there was no cause for alarm. The stage manager then entered and explained the explosion was caused by the limelight apparatus, and the show continued. The only difficulty caused by the explosion was the apotheosis of Margherita and the angels which took place in *chiaroscuro* instead of celestial limelight.

1881_04_23 PORTSMOUTH (Theatre Royal).   EXPLOSION

The gasman put a quantity of hydrogen into an oxygen bag which exploded with a loud report. The stage and front rows were enveloped in dust, but the players staunchly carried on acting and panic was averted. The gasman must have been extraordinarily careless.

1882_07_07 DARWEN (Theatre Royal).   EXPLOSION

The show had progressed until 9pm when an explosion occurred backstage. The resulting flame set light to the immediate area with clouds of smoke rolling out on to the stage and thence into the auditorium. "The audience fled in an excited state" while manager Woodfield tried to assure them there was no danger. The theatre emptied without panic or accident and the show abandoned.

1882_08_12 OLDHAM (Theatre Royal).   EXPLOSION

The London Pride Company was presenting a new play called *May Day*. At around 8.30pm there was a backstage explosion caused by the negligence of the man working the gas pipes for the limelight. The tanks exploded, blowing up the floor of the ladies' dressing room which was immediately above. In the room were Mrs and Miss Jane Rignold, the latter found lying half-way though the broken floor, covered with debris and suffering from a broken leg. She was given medical assistance and then taken to her lodgings nearby. Manager Stringer announced the cause of the interruption, and the play continued. The company included Mr Lionel Rignold who was, presumably, the husband of Mrs R and father of Jane R. Lionel was a cousin of the more famous William Rignold and his brother George who became a major actor in Australia.

1882_09_28c OREBRO, Sweden.   SPREADING SCENERY FIRE

The theatre in this large town caught fire due to a dangling decoration first catching light. Very soon the entire stage was ablaze. The doors had not yet opened, but the players had arrived and were dressing and making up in their dressing rooms. Ladders were put up at the windows and many

33

actresses escaped that way, though the normal stairs were still available. Soon the fire burst through the roof and by the time engines arrived it was too late to save the theatre. The building was insured for 100,000 krona.

1882_10_05 BERLIN, Germany (Royal Opera House).   SAFETY CURTAIN CAUSES PANIC

The venue had a crowded glittering audience gathered to witness *Tannhäuser*. Many theatres had put modern safety measures in place and here a new iron safety curtain had been installed. As the vast majority of theatre fires emanate from the stage the logical thing was, and is, to install a massive fireproof screen that shuts off the entire proscenium opening. This had been done, and as the audience was settling in, the whole thing suddenly dropped with a "fearful crash" among the footlights. The audience at once rushed to the exits in a panic, and the house was soon entirely clear. It was found that the iron had fallen because the suspension chain had snapped.

18. *Berlin Opera House*

[Most conventional proscenium theatres of size are required by law to have a safety curtain. It is referred to as 'the iron' whatever the actual material. At one time asbestos was favoured but not any more. By the nature of the thing it is extremely heavy and has its own raising and lowering equipment. Nowadays electric motors are used and usually prove reliable. In the UK the law demands that the safety curtain should be lowered and raised each performance in the presence of the audience. This usually takes place in the interval. Older theatres used to have the slogan 'For thine especial safety' on the front of the iron which is a quote from *Hamlet*. The Barbican Theatre in London has a very intriguing one, where half comes down and half rises up meshing like a giant set of false teeth.]

Personal Note: I recall a panto season in Scotland when the safety curtain was duly lowered in the interval, then would not rise again, leaving a choice of either performing the second half on a 2ft strip before the iron, or sending everybody home. Fortunately, the clever stage crew found a way to raise it by winching by hand so we had an elongated interval watching the massive thing – taking an inordinate amount of time – inching its way skywards.

1882_11_07 ACCRINGTON (Prince's).   GUN ACCIDENT TO OFFSTAGE ACTOR

The play was *Uncle Tom's Cabin*. As the play was proceeding, the audience heard gunshots from the wings, the players stopped acting, and the curtain was lowered. Colonel Grover came onstage to announce that actor-manager Charles M Hermann, playing the role of George Harris, had met with a serious accident. While checking over the revolver he was to use in a later scene two of the chambers had exploded in his face. It was feared he would lose his sight. Another actor took over the role so that the play could finish.

1882_12_22 LONDON (Drury Lane).   FATAL ACCIDENT TO FLYMAN

Flyman Partridge, over-balancing, fell 25ft down to the stage. In his descent his head struck a bolt in some scenery, inflicting a severe wound. He was taken to King's College Hospital where he died five days later.

FIRE PREVENTION SCHEME

From time to time somebody decides that something must be done to halt all these fires that not only interrupted performances but in many cases razed theatres to the ground. Fire prevention ideas were mainly based on dealing with them rather than preventing them in the first place. The companion volume to this book has a special section on costume fires which points out methods of fireproofing material take a back seat to how to deal with young females dashing about in clothing ablaze.

Similarly, ideas came up for dealing with fires rather than methods of fire-proofing scenery. In November 1882 in Austria-Hungary, a British firm was touting an ingenious fire prevention idea. The London firm's proposal was a water sprinkler system for use in theatre fires. Basically, it comprised of forcing water through the existing gas pipe system, so turning the gas jets into water jets. Very ingenious. I assume this was the patent 858 (Feb 22) applied for by the McLennans and R Owen. There is no record of it being installed and effectively used.

1883_01_12 LEAMINGTON SPA (Theatre Royal).   SEVERE ACCIDENT TO MANAGER

Mr D'Albertson, up in the flies, was making arrangements about the scenery for the forthcoming pantomime when his jacket caught the windlass handle that controlled some heavy scenery. This released it and, whipping round with great force, it struck Mr D'A knocking him off balance. To prevent a fall of some 30ft on to the stage he grabbed at the windlass, with the result that his right hand and arm became enmeshed in the cog wheels. Fortunately, he was swiftly rescued but his hand was mangled with several broken bones. It seems that amputation was not considered necessary, but obviously it would be many weeks before the poor chap was restored to normality.

1883_01_12 LONDON (Lyceum).   ACCIDENT TO ACTOR COLLECTING HIS WAGE

The actor was the veteran Henry Howe. He had been to the usual 'Treasury Call' at 1pm on Friday, *de rigueur* at all theatres until many years later – I could never understand why one had to trail in specially, and not be given your money when arriving for work in the evening. Anyway, the poor chap fell down the steps on his way out and "broke the sinews of the leg joint". He was still on crutches in mid-February, unable to resume work. This dapper man had been inspired to take up acting by seeing Edmund Kean (1787-1833) and suffered an early accident when a gun went off in his face at rehearsal. He was honoured with a cheque for 10/- from young Queen Victoria on that occasion. After his early acting years, he really only had three contracts in his entire life. He was with Macready until the latter retired, then he spent 40 years with Ben Webster at the Haymarket, and finally became a member of Irving's company remaining until his death at the age of 84 while on tour in America.

19. *Henry Howe*

1883_01_18 MILWAUKEE, USA (Opera House). EXPLOSION

An explosion occurred during the performance as one of the tanks feeding the limelight shattered. All the lights went out, the scenery ended in fragments, one stagehand was killed and two fatally injured, with several others suffering minor injuries. A panic was avoided by an employee boldly sitting on the remaining tank. He would have known he was perfectly safe because the explosion had been caused by an illicit mixture of the two gases, and after the explosion only one was present. There were no injuries among the 600 people in the audience.

1883_02_16 PLYMOUTH (Theatre Royal). KEEPER TRAPPED BY CAMEL

The pantomime was *Robinson Crusoe* wherein a live camel was introduced. William White the keeper, finding the camel would not follow his orders, struck the beast across its legs, whereupon it promptly knelt on him. Not willing to budge, it took another man to come on and rescue White. He was then found to have a broken thigh, and whisked off to hospital. One would think a camel keeper ought to be conversant with the spiteful behaviour of a cross camel.

1883_02_21 LINCOLN (Masonic). EXPLOSION

This explosion was a very modest one as it was merely a stage effect. The play was *Money*, in which an "infernal machine" explodes killing the villain. On this night the explosion was a bit over-egged, and the crowded house saw Charles Hermann the actor-manager severely burned on the hand and arm. Infernal machines were a staple of Victorian melodrama.

1883_03_24 PRESTON (Theatre). GUN ACCIDENT CHASING RATS

William Coward was the bar-keeper and cellarman at the theatre which was rat infested. After baiting the pit and having gone up to the gallery with a shotgun, he took potshots at the vermin as they emerged to take the bait. Pausing to change position he laid the gun on a seat. Taking it up again to start firing it went off, the charge entering the inner part of his right thigh. He collapsed to the floor crying out "Oh, I'm shot!" James Park the stage-carpenter rushed up to find him lying between the seats, bleeding profusely.

1883_03_27 ROCHDALE (Theatre Royal). SERIOUS ACCIDENT TO PROPERTY MAN

The theatre was empty of people except for Edwin Birch the property man who, for unknown reasons, was climbing up the iron ladder fixed to the wall to reach the flies. Attacked by giddiness, he fell 20ft, landing astride an open door beneath. The lower part of his body was dreadfully injured and partially disembowelled. Fortunately, hearing Birch cry as he fell, a curious passer-by poked his head into the stage door to enquire its cause. Seeing the dramatic state of affairs he rushed next door to the Theatre Hotel to summon aid. Mr Smith the landlord, with others, hastened round to rescue the poor man and take him to the Watson Infirmary. A benefit was given by the theatre whose company, orchestra and staff all gave their services to raise "a nice little sum for the man's wife and children."

1883_04_10 REVAL, Russia (Theatre). EXPLOSION

In contrast to the above (*see* 1883_02_21), the explosion at the theatre in Reval was a terrific affair. Reval is a town in the Gulf of Finland, not all that far from St Petersburg. It was reported that

2000 people were watching a performance in the town's theatre when there was a mighty explosion, all the lights went out, and the audience panicked like mad things. When the lights came on again the scene resembled the aftermath of a battle, with hundreds thrown to the ground and trampled on, others lying crushed by fallen stones and beams, and many more simply hurled bodily against the walls by the force of the blast, to lie slumped and bleeding.

Help was soon to hand, the building cleared of bodies, the wounded taken to hospitals, the dead consigned to their relatives. As to be expected, the cause of the explosion was the escape of gas from the *gutta-percha* bags employed for the limelight. The Paris papers started off this story, and it was widely disseminated throughout the UK, but further details of fatality numbers etc are impossible to locate.

1883_04_24 PARIS, France.   FATAL ACCIDENT TO STAGEHAND

The latest operatic success in Paris was *Lakmé* but on its fourth airing stagehand Lefort was moving a piece of scenery when part of it fell over on to him, breaking his skull. The unfortunate man was taken without delay to the hospital Beaujon in a hopeless state. The audience were unaware of the accident.

1883_04_25 PARIS, France (Ambigu).   EXPLOSION

The play was *L'As de Trèfle*. The audience was assembled, but a few minutes before curtain-up there was a loud explosion on the fourth floor. This was the dressing room of 20 supers and, on arriving, several said they could smell gas, so the windows were thrown open and one sensible chap said not to light any candles until they got the gasman up to examine the room. But one bright spark (Ho! Ho! Ho!) struck a match and all the guys were blown off their feet in the explosion. 14 of the men were taken to hospital, three in a particularly parlous state.

As the explosion was backstage on the fourth floor the seated audience may not have realised what it was, or how bad. They remained in ignorance because the manager M Simon walking on before the curtain, told them that the star of the show had been suddenly taken ill and could not appear. "Your money will be returned, or you may have tickets for another night." That's a clever one from M Simon; the public withdrew in an orderly manner without knowing what had actually occurred.

1883_06_24 DERVIO, Italy (Tavern).   TAVERN FIRE

Dervio is a village near Como. The venue was not a proper theatre but a large room above the local tavern that had been set up to accommodate a travelling puppet show. The audience numbered around 90 people. The play was *The Martyrdom of St Philomena* – hardly suitable children's fare, but the audience included many. During the show the puppeteer let off Bengal lights as a special effect, but unfortunately several stray sparks set light to some straw and hay behind the fit-up stage. The showman, first to realise, gave a cry of "Fire!" but his audience sat on, thinking he was simply making his effects more realistic. The puppeteer leapt out of the window, but his wife and mother perished. He, himself, was so badly injured he "expired shortly afterwards". People outside, seeing the flames, they too started shouting. The folk in the tavern, thinking it was some sort of affray happening out in the street, barricaded the door with a mighty table in case the trouble-makers should attempt to enter.

37

They realised their mistake when the flames burst upon them. When all was over and the fire extinguished, 48 persons were found burnt to death. Two more were fatally injured and several others severely injured. The village had a population of only 750, so many families were devastated, one losing five children, and one losing three.

1883_10_01 BIRMINGHAM (New).   FATAL FALL OF WORKMAN

The new theatre was nearing completion and John Evans (30) was putting in stage equipment on a scaffold some 60ft from the ground when he slipped, falling head first towards the ground. In his descent his head struck an iron girder and "his skull was completely smashed, and his brains scattered about". He died on the way to hospital leaving "a widow and four children to lament their sudden bereavement."

1883_10_03 BATH (Theatre Royal).   FATAL FALL OF BOY FROM FLIES

"After the performance, a youth named Walter Bartlett accidentally fell from the flies and was instantly killed." This terse report appeared in many newspapers but, although basically correct, the subsequent enquiry told a very different story. Walter was actually a five-year-old child, the son of Arthur Bartlett the theatre's gasman. It is thought that he fell asleep sitting on the fly floor while his dad attended to his duties after the show. Bartlett and Davis the stage door keeper were the only remaining staff, and the theatre was in darkness except for one light. The surmise is the boy awoke and in trying to find his way from the fly gallery, fell to the stage 25ft below. Davis saw him fall, and Pc Newton – who was outside the theatre – heard the commotion and hastened in. He raised the boy and carried him in his arms to the nearby Royal United Hospital, with blood streaming from Walter's head and nose. The boy had died ere the constable arrived at the hospital.

1883_12_22 NEWPORT (Victoria).   STAGEHAND FALLS FROM ON HIGH

The unfortunate man was the master carpenter James Crowley who fell some 25ft sustaining "internal injuries of a serious nature".

1883_12_26 BLACKBURN (Theatre Royal).   ACCIDENT TO PANTO MANAGER

This accident was during the opening night of the pantomime *Robinson* Crusoe, the unfortunate man was Mr Elliston manager for Mrs Duval the lessee. Pantomimes still had major scenes and harlequinades, where characters were shot up from understage, passing through star traps to make a soaring entrance; also transformations worked by machinery below stage, raising and lowering scenery pieces through sloats in the stage floor. A sloat is a long narrow trap – imagine a hinged floorboard. The understage of a Victorian theatre was a mass of wooden beams, wheels and ropes, with similarities to the mechanics of both sailing ships and windmills. Elliston was down under the stage directing all these operations. Passing from one side to the other he was struck by a trap in the process of catapulting a pantomimist on to the stage. The blow caught him just above the eye, laying bare the bone of his eyebrow. Dr Stephenson, whose surgery was near at hand, dressed the wound, enabling Elliston to return to his home at Bolton. Though an excellent house for Mrs Duval's first panto, it was not as crowded as customary for a panto first night, this being attributed to the number of men on strike against a reduction in their wages.

1884_01_08 BELFAST (Theatre Royal). FATAL ACCIDENT TO MASTER CARPENTER

Owen, the unfortunate victim, was master carpenter supervising the moving of a piece of scenery in *The Silver King*. A stage weight fell from a height on to his head, fracturing his skull. Taken to the Royal Hospital in a precarious position, he died the following morning. Several master carpenters in other theatres held collections for his widow, and around £50 was raised.

1884_02_25 LONDON (Covent Garden). EXPLOSION

The location of this explosion was the Covent Garden office of manager Ernest Gye. Signor Salvini the Italian tragedian was starring in a farewell season at the theatre, and his manager had seen a wonderful lighting effect which mimicked lightning. Salvini wanted this effect to be incorporated in one of his plays. In charge of this device was 'firework artist' Harry Cardwell assisted by his brother Andrew. Mr Gye requested a demonstration, and asked his brother to come along to witness it. The apparatus was sound and safe, but the firework artist was holding an open glass bottle of magnesium filings. While showing the procedure for creating the lightning, a stray spark ignited the powder in the bottle, which exploded. The window of the office was shattered, and both men were injured. Harry, receiving cuts on face and hands and injuries to both eyes, was taken to hospital, whereas brother Andrew had his lesser wounds dressed and was despatched home. Harry was not detained long, being soon up and about.

20. Ernest Gye

21. Signor Salvini

39

1884_06_06 LONDON (Drury Lane). EXPLOSION

[This accident happened at "a morning performance" which meant at a matinee that, as now, took place in the afternoon. I am aware that 'matinee' comes from the French for 'morning' but how ludicrous to go on calling it a morning performance when it is in the afternoon. If they want to be French, why not call it 'après midi'? Adverts would say "Morning performance at 2pm" which is ridiculous. Why did the Brits not simply call it an afternoon performance? Having gone on for 200 years, we now all know 'matinee' in English means 'afternoon' but I still think it is stupid. When it is an actual morning show, as often in the pantomime season, they have to say 'Morning matinee'!]

The explosion was under the stage where the limelight bags were operated. Oxygen escaped into the hydrogen bag so – boom! Clouds of dust which the audience mistook for smoke, permeated the auditorium, making a shout of 'Fire!' highly probable. Stagehands James Harris (36) and Benjamin Creed were injured and taken to hospital. Harris died from his injuries two days later. At the inquest it was said there was insufficient evidence as to the cause, the limelight was operated by incompetent men, and under the stage was an unfit place for it to be located. Both seem likely causes to me!

The show in progress was Haverley's Minstrels and two of them interpolated a gag which went "Did you hear my trunk fall then?" To which the response was "No, that's too heavy for your trunk." This feeble *ad lib* brought a reader's letter to the *Morning Post* praising the quick-witted pair suggesting their employers "will testify their gratitude in a substantial manner." I can find no further information on this suggestion, so doubt it was acted upon.

1884_10_19 PRAGUE, Czech Rep. (German).   FATAL ACCIDENT TO STAGEHAND

"During the performance of *Aida* at the German National Theatre here this evening, the vaulted tomb which was in readiness behind the scenes for the fourth act fell in, killing one of the workmen." *Morning Post* 1884_10_20.

1884_11_01 BRADFORD (Prince's Theatre).   ACCIDENT AT THEATRE TREASURY

Miss Beddard's *Gabrielle* company was in residence and her actors went in for their week's wage on a morning. Loyale Frere, seeking the treasury office along a dark passage, fell down a flight of stone stairs leading to the orchestra pit. She was badly cut about the chin, receiving many body bruises and a severe shock to her system. Miss Beddard immediately had the poor actress taken to Dr Evans who, after dressing the wounds, certified that Miss Frere would be obliged to relinquish her professional duties for some weeks.

1885_01_28 NEWCASTLE (Tyne).   FATAL FALL OF FLYMAN

William Blake Brewis (23), while repairing a border above the stage, attempted to reach the fly rail by swinging. He failed, falling a height of 30ft on to the stage where he suffered severe injuries including concussion of the brain. Taken to – and remaining in – Newcastle Infirmary until his death on 8 February.

40

1885_11_20 PARIS, France (Ambigu).   STAGEHAND FALLS FROM GREAT HEIGHT

The play, *The Silver King* by Henry Arthur Jones, was a huge hit for Wilson Barrett since first produced by him in 1882. The actor manager performed 300 consecutive performances at the Princes Theatre, London. This was a French version, and the stage crew was not attuned to the rapid changes of scene. In 1822, when the first English company to present Shakespeare in Paris since Elizabethan times performed *Othello*, the audience was totally confused – they thought with every scene change a new play had started. French classics observed the three unities of time, place and action, as in the ancient Greek theatre. Modern methods had become more acceptable 60 years later but scene changes were still conducted in a leisurely manner. Thus, when one scene changed in *The Silver King* on this night, one of the stagehands got caught up in the cloth flying out and dropping from it at a great height, broke his arm.

1886_01_02 GLASGOW (Theatre Royal).   TRAP ACCIDENT TO STAGEHAND

Archibald Crawford (48), spreading out canvas on the stage, fell through an open trap into the property room below. His injuries included a broken collar bone.

1886_05_09 NOTTINGHAM (Grand).   FLOOD ACCIDENT AT NEW THEATRE

This was a newly built, recently opened theatre and the architect had made good provision against fire by means of a huge water main running under the stage. On Sunday afternoon, when the theatre was locked and empty, this main burst. The fire brigade was called to pump the water out and away. Not only was the stage flooded, but a huge tank 47ft long by 42ft wide cut out of the rock was full to the brim and overflowing; 90,000 gallons was drawn off, and it was rumoured that the foundations had been affected, the stage sinking some inches. Not true, probably a modern folk tale.

1887_04_07 NEWCASTLE (Tyne).   FATAL ACCIDENT BACKSTAGE DURING OPERA

[The Carl Rosa Opera Company, formed in 1873, was the major opera company touring the provinces for the following 85 years. The company presented 150 different operas during its lifetime, and many eminent singers and conductors performed with the company. Rosa himself died in 1889. *Personal Note: My own introduction to opera was the company's 'Cav and Pag' at Bradford Alhambra in the 1950s.*]

The second act of the opera *Nordisa* featured a thunder storm. Storm effects nowadays are recorded, but formerly done live by shaking large panels of tin called 'thundersheets'. Prior to that, since time out of mind, thunder was created by a 'thunder run', sometimes called 'race', which comprised sloping wooden gutters down which cannon balls were rolled, rumbling down before falling off at the bottom into a metal container with a crash. These were permanent fixtures in the theatres of the time.

On this night, one of the balls, jumping out of the gutter, fell on the head of stagehand Robert Crowther who was standing in the wings. He was taken to the Infirmary, but died the next day leaving a widow and four children. He was 30 years of age and a millwright by trade. Two of the leading singers with the Carl Rosa company, donating ten guineas, started a fund for his dependents.

I believe there are only three UK theatres still with thunder runs – Her Majesty's and the Playhouse in London, and Bristol Old Vic.

1888_02_03 LOWRY'S MUSIC HALL, DUBLIN.   PHOTO CALL FOR LION QUEEN

22. *A Lion Queen*

There were several female lion tamers working in Victorian times which gave an extra frisson to the entertainment. Mdlle Senide, a popular 'Lion Queen' had been appearing at Dan Lowry's for some weeks and this was her benefit night. She performed her usual act, receiving the usual acclaim, and all had gone well. However, after the show she had a photo call and had to go through her act for different pictures to be taken. Several satisfactory photographs had captured various groupings, then Mdlle Senide requested one of her with her head in a lion's mouth. This being a feature item in her act, she wanted it for publicity purposes as it was a trick that not every lion tamer did. If you have ever been in a photo session at a wedding you will know how much fiddling about the photographer does and how slow it all is.

Mdlle was there with her head in the lion's mouth for fully two minutes, perhaps even a little longer. She called out "Are you ready? Hurry up!" The reply came "Just a minute" as the man fiddled, trying to ignite the magnesium flash. Whether the voice issuing from its own throat, or the sudden flash alarmed the lion, who can say? But the result was it closed its mouth. Fortunately, Mdlle was able to get her head out, but not without receiving a rent from cheek to chin from the lion's tooth. The friendly lion also put its paw on her shoulder making an ugly scratch across her chest.

Medical attention came and stitched up her cheek and chin, during which Mdlle refused chloroform. She sent word to Dan Lowry that she was willing and able to work the next night with her lions, tigers and bears, but Lowry declined to let her do so as she had not fully recovered. Her main concern was being left with disfiguring facial marks but was reassured by the medics that it would not be so.

1888_11_17 LONDON (Shaftesbury). OPENING NIGHT CANCELLED BY FAULTY IRON

[The first iron safety curtain installed in London was 1794 at Drury Lane, together with a great water tank that could open to flood the stage. When the theatre burnt down in 1809, the iron was no longer there, it had been removed several months before because it was so rusted up as to be useless. One was installed in the Grand Theatre of St Petersburg in 1837, and the continent in general was keener on the idea than the UK. However, the New Alexandra Theatre at Liverpool built in 1865 incorporated one, and the Edinburgh Theatre Royal of the same year also included one, although in the fire ten years later it was reported that the iron was "crumpled like wallpaper". Many leading theatres throughout Europe had installed iron safety curtains by 1878, and after the Ring fire of 1881 they were compulsory in all Vienna Theatres, and in all Paris Theatres.

This theatre was very new, opening on 20 October with *As You Like It* starring Miss Wallis the wife of the owner. It boasted of being the safest house in London as it was completely isolated from other buildings, having streets on all four sides, with 18 exits directly into these. Also the stage could be completely isolated from the rest of the building at a minute's notice by an iron safety curtain, painted a dark blue colour to match the coverings of the seats.]

On this night the audience was eagerly awaiting a revival of the popular play *Lady of Lyons* but, at the appointed time, the curtain did not rise. Neither did it rise within the next hour, the reason being the iron curtain mechanism would not function, and the defensive barrier twixt stage and auditorium would not move. A large team of men was desperately trying to get the thing to slide up in its grooves, but some part of the machinery had got bent and essential tools to correct it were not in the theatre. When 9pm arrived it was necessary to cancel the show and refund money. This event did not encourage other managers to lash out a lot of money for such an unreliable gadget.

23. *Shaftesbury Theatre*

1889_01_12 GLASGOW (Grand). FATAL FALL OF FLYMAN DURING SHOW

The pantomime *Babes in the Wood* was in progress and at the moment of the accident Ada Bemister was the only artiste on stage. Mid-song a body fell from the flies on to the side of the stage, fortunately not in the view of most of the audience. Miss Bemister, with great presence of mind, carried on singing while moving to the front of the stage taking the spotlight away from the body and thus "prevented any excitement among the audience". The few people who actually witnessed the fall

thought it was a dummy body such as was often used in the harlequinade. In fact, it was Robert Potts (37) principal flyman who, while leaning over the fly rail reaching for a rope, over-balanced to fall 22ft to the stage. Although a doctor was in the audience and hastened to assist, Potts died of a fractured skull within minutes. He left a widow and five young children.

1889_02_08 ALDERSHOT (Theatre Royal).   ONSTAGE FIRE PRIOR TO CURTAIN UP

The pantomime was *Sinbad*, very popular at this period. There was no agreement about how to spell the hero's name – sometimes as above, other times with a D as Sindbad. In this book it varies as I spell it as it was at the venue in question.

A quarter hour before the show started a fire broke out onstage; an actor going before the curtain, asked the audience to file out and not panic because there was no danger. An understandable white lie, but within 15 minutes the whole building was ablaze. The theatre was totally destroyed within 1½ hours but nobody was injured as the bulk of the audience had not yet arrived.

1889_08_23 HARTLEPOOL (Victoria).   GUN ACCIDENT TO ACTOR

George Slow, an actor who worked at the Victoria Theatre – a wooden erection in the market place – was sorting and cleaning guns in readiness for that evening's performance of *Buffalo Bill*. Finding a blockage in one of the pistols, he took it to a blacksmith's shop and, presumably with an idea to expand the metal, heated the weapon in the fire. He then placed it in a vice to take out the nipple. The gun exploded and the charge, which was paper and wadding, shot him in the breast tearing through his waistcoat and shirt, entering his body.

43

1889_09_06 LONDON (Arcadia).   GUN ACCIDENT

At the Arcadia Theatre within London's Agricultural Hall, an explosion injured an actor-manager William Walton who was loading an old fashioned horse pistol when it exploded in his hands, igniting the powder used in *Jack Robinson and His Monkey*. There was little damage to the room and contents, but Walton was burnt in hands and face, as was Nat Wallace a member of his company. Their parts in the play were taken at very short notice by Mr Levite taking Walton's role as the monkey, and Mr McNulty replacing Wallace as Jack Robinson.

1889_11_25 MANCHESTER (Palace).   COLLAPSE OF NEW WALL AND FLOODING

The Rochdale Canal passed behind the back of the Palace of Varieties theatre, and actually up against the back wall of the stage was a dock used by timber merchants that extended along the entire rear of the theatre. The theatre owners drained the dock and laid down a base of thick concrete. Work then started on building up the back wall of the theatre planned to be 50ft long and 70ft high. Once the workmen had reached a certain height the dock basin was refilled. As the work continued, adding further courses of bricks, water was seen trickling through the lower courses, then a bulge appeared in the wall. The men were brought out of the building, which was fortunate, as a few hours later the whole thing gave way, water pouring from the canal into the theatre, bringing with it bricks and chunks of the concrete lining of the basin. A 100 men were employed on the scheme and had to be put on hold as the dock basin water drained away finding its destination under the stage of the theatre.

1889_12_23 STOCKTON-ON-TEES (Theatre Royal).   ELEPHANT FALLS THROUGH STAGE

The pantomime was *Blue Beard* and the performers were Professor Henry and his elephant Sheriff. The elephant had done its act though this had been curtailed by the Prof as both he and the elephant were apprehensive about the strength of the stage. The Prof had got Sheriff to the back of the stage and turned him ready to walk off when the boards gave way and the back legs and hind quarters disappeared into the hole. The curtain was lowered and the lessee Lloyd Clarence in his Blue Beard costume, coming before the curtain, asked the audience to be calm and not panic as all was under control. The elephant was soon freed unharmed, the curtain rising again to continue the panto.

No doubt the theatre owner, the lessee and Professor Henry had fun and games blaming each other as in a wrangle about who was responsible for a weak stage floor in following case 1891_08_03.

1890_08_04 NEWPORT (New).   ACCIDENT TO STAGE MANAGER

Tom Herman, the stage manager of the company presenting *The Denounced*, was injured on the head by falling scenery. The manager was "quickly on the spot with a medical gentleman" who dressed the wound. The plucky fellow then carried on for the rest of the show. The speed that medical attention was whistled up in those days must seem astonishing to modern readers.

1890_08_25 SOUTH SHIELDS (Theatre Royal).   FATAL ACCIDENT TO FLYMAN

44 The time was 1.30pm and the stage crew were setting up for that night's production. William Newman (36) went on to the grid to fix an errant rope. The next anybody knew was Newman's body hurtling down to the stage 42ft below. His mates, dashing to help, heard him utter three words only before dying. "His head lay in a pool of blood" and two of his limbs were broken.

1890_08_29 GLASGOW (Grand).   FATAL ACCIDENT TO FLYMAN

Just before curtain up, flyman Joseph Fletcher (49) fell from the flies to the stage floor, a distance of 36ft. Dr Adams advised he be moved to the Royal Infirmary where his injuries were found to be a compound fracture of the right hand middle finger, and a fractured rib. These do not sound life threatening injuries, but the poor man died in the infirmary two days later, so probably suffered undiagnosed internal injuries.

1890_12_ 24c BUDAPEST, Hungary (National).   DEATH OF ACTOR VIA MAKE-UP

Louis Benedek, a prominent member of the National Theatre slightly cut himself when shaving. Before the wound was closed he applied theatrical make-up. As a result the paint got into the wound causing inflammation followed by gangrene and death. Benedek was only 32.

1891_08_03 LONDON (Elephant & Castle).   HORSE FALLS THROUGH STAGE

This accident to a horse raised an interesting point of law. Mr Tilling was a well-known owner of horses, Mr Balmain a theatre manager of long experience, and currently the short-term lessee of this theatre. Balmain, requiring a horse to take a part in a play, hired one from Tilling at 30/- for the week. A man was to come with the horse and position it in the wings, whereupon an actor would mount it and ride to the centre of the stage during the action of the play. On this, the first night, the planks gave way and the horse, falling through to the floor underneath, around 4ft to 5ft, was injured.

Tilling took Balmain to court for damages which had been refused. In court, the judge said that as far as could be seen the floor was safe, Balmain had no reason to believe that it was insecure and that it was not used in an improper way. Balmain had prudently carried out all duty of care therefore judgment was given in his favour. Tilling appealed against the decision, the matter trailed on, coming up at the Queen's Bench in April 1892, where the learned judge upheld the decision and dismissed the case. Press comments argued that the man supplying the horse should not be expected to suffer loss, especially as there was no want of care by owner or man. It was conjectured whether a case could be made against the owner of the theatre for having an unsubstantial floor, whereupon he in turn could claim that he had not been told an extra weight was to be placed upon it, and thus had no reason to examine its bearing properties. Interesting.

1891_08_10 BOLTON (Victoria). FATAL FALL OF ATTENDANT

After the night's show, it was attendant Birch (35) who had the duty of covering the front of the balcony with a dust sheet. He overbalanced, and falling forward into the pit landed on his head "which was driven into his chest, breaking the spine and causing instant death." None of his colleagues actually saw the accident but several heard the thud of the landing body.

1891_08_08 LONDON (Pavilion). EXPLOSION

At this theatre in London's Whitechapel district, the play was called *The World* in which a "mimic ship is blown up". On this night the explosion was too realistic and stage-hands Frederick Chappel (22) and Francis Figgins (39) were "shockingly burnt about their faces and hands" by the explosion. They were taken to the London Hospital.

1891_09_06 PARIS, France (Châtelet). FATAL ACCIDENT TO STAGEHAND

During the performance of *Lakmé* at the Opéra Comique all the electric lights went out causing a minor panic. Presuming the Châtelet Theatre opposite was served by the same cabling, M Carvalho went over to where a rehearsal was in progress to see if they were similarly affected. He was soon told the gruesome reason. A stagehand in the act of greasing the machinery for the electric light, had fallen between two cranks and been instantly torn to pieces. Death was so sudden the man had not even the time to cry out. It was necessary to stop the generator to recover the man's remains, hence the loss of electric light while the macabre toil was accomplished. The man left a widow and two children.

1892_01_20 PARIS, France (de la Gaieté). REHEARSAL FLOODED OUT

For reasons that remained unexplained, during a rehearsal at this theatre a stagehand opened a hydrant and water gushing out drenched the actors and flooded the stage. The scenery suffered major damage and the fire brigade had to be called out at midnight to pump out the cellar under the stage – in five minutes it had taken in water to a depth of three feet.

1892_02_03 NEW YORK, USA (Metropolitan). THEATRE RAIDED BY POLICE

On the show was the notorious dance known as the *Can-Can*. When the dance started the police entered and stopped the performance. The girls were rounded up and led away, laughing and crying, some fainting, some begging for mercy, but all banged up in cells.

45

1892_02_22c SUNDERLAND (Avenue).   ACTOR FAILS IN DAMAGES CASE

William Goodwin, an actor in W Bourne's *A Big Fortune* company, was playing at C E Machin's theatre. Going into the theatre for a rehearsal Goodwin found that the stage door led into the porter's hall where a further door would take him to the stage. The passage was "quite dark" and after a few steps he should have turned left up a staircase but, missing these, went straight forward for some way falling down a flight of steps to the right leading to the machinery room. Injured in the fall, he sued the theatre owner for £50 damages and medical expenses.

The case came before the court in May when the judge said that Goodwin was not an employee of Machin, so there was no duty of care involved; that Goodwin was a free agent and if he chose to wander along a dark passage it was entirely at his own risk and Mr Machin was under no obligation to provide lights in that passage it being one that Goodwin, or any other person except machinists, was unlikely or permitted to go. Judgment was in favour of Machin with costs.

It has to be said that some of the judgments revealed by legal cases are surprising to the modern eye and ear though there is a clear attitude alien today that a person is responsible for his own welfare and blaming somebody else is not the first thing that springs to mind.

1892_08_27 COATBRIDGE (Theatre Royal).   SHOOTING ACCIDENT CAUSED BY HORSEPLAY

46

The property master had been cleaning pistols and other weapons assisted by a girl Agnes Rooney. Wilson a youthful programme seller passed by and Agnes, pointing a gun at him in jest, pulled the trigger. Unknown to her the pistol was loaded with a blank charge. As the lad was only a couple of yards away he was knocked to the ground and severely scorched over the left eye. How many more accidents with guns have to happen before people realise they are not toys?

1892_09_11 PARIS, France (Cluny).   EXPLOSION

It was a 2pm matinee performance with the audience settled awaiting for the curtain to rise. A sudden explosion under the stage caused by gas blew open all the stage traps through which smoke began to rise. The large hose connected to the hydrant was swiftly brought into play, rapidly flooding the entire stage and cellar underneath with water. The audience, completely ignorant of all this happening, was starting to mutter about the delayed start. The manager came before the curtain and regretted that the condition of the stage floor made it impossible to give the performance. The audience filed out, to be refunded on the way. Only when they got outside and saw a fire engine and firemen did they realise they had been in danger. The head of the stage crew, the chief gasman and two others were seriously burnt by the explosion.

1892_12_24 LONDON (Britannia).   DRASTIC ACCIDENT TO HEAD STAGEHAND

Shortly before 10pm an accident interrupted the dress rehearsal of the *Man in the Moon* pantomime. A trap in the stage had been left open, and William Smith, supervising the change for scene five, fell through into the cellar below, a drop of some 17ft. He was found unconscious with a gaping wound in his head from which part of his brain was protruding. He was taken to St Bartholomew's Hospital where the surgeons regarded survival as hopeless. But, dear reader, be not distressed; on 1 January it was revealed that Smith's injuries were slighter than as first reported. He had suffered a cut on his head after which, it having been dressed, he recovered and returned to work.

1893_02_14 NEWCASTLE (Tyne).   FATAL ACCIDENT TO HIDE-AND-SEEK CHILD

Arriving early before the show so they could play together, William Wood (12) met up with two other boys engaged for the dolls scene in the pantomime *Humpty Dumpty*. Running around on the stage playing 'tiggie' (also known as 'tag') William fell into an open trap to the cellar floor 22ft underneath. He was taken to the Infirmary with severe injuries to his head from which he died. At the inquest the jury expressed the opinion that the lad was in a part of the theatre where he had no right to be. I am surprised that discipline was so slack; child performers nowadays would certainly not be allowed to roam loose backstage, much less allowed to play chase games; confined to their dressing room until required they are then escorted to and from the stage.

1893_03_18 SHEFFIELD (Alexandra).   FATAL FALL OF FLYMAN

It was the last night of the pantomime *Sinbad the Sailor*. During a scene change, flyman William Jessop (46) overbalanced and fell to the stage 22ft below, landing on his head. He was taken to hospital but died shortly afterwards. The audience was unaware of the accident and the show carried on uninterrupted. Jessop was an experienced flyman having worked at the theatre for 26 years. Known to be a quiet and sober man, he had only been drinking to the extent that five of the stage crew had shared three pints between them. It was assumed that he had been kneeling on the fly-floor using a long clearing stick to steer a backcloth from catching as it was let up or down – a regular procedure. He may have become dizzy and fallen below the lower guard rail. Jessop left a widow and eight children. The lessee Mr Britlebank paid all the funeral expenses, and the theatre company and staff had a whip-round on behalf of the Jessops.

47

1893_08_28 CARDIFF (Theatre Royal).   ACCIDENT TO MP'S CURIOUS SON

This is a bizarre one. Wilson Barrett's Company was presenting *Claudian*, a play which had an impressive earthquake scene with a thunderous battery discharge as part of the effects. Son of an MP, John Arch a retired sergeant-major from the Welsh Fusiliers, was in the lane outside the theatre near the stage door and scene dock doors and was struck in the face by some exploding material, causing a wound to his forehead and his face blackened with powder marks. A friend took him to hospital where he was treated, and then to the police where he reported the accident, threatening to sue for damages. It transpired that the only way the injury could have occurred was via a circular hole 3" in diameter in the scene dock door about 5ft from the ground. It was assumed that Arch had contributed to his injury by peering through the hole at the time of the explosion.

1893_09_28 NEWPORT (Empire).   MAGICIAN FALLS FROM A GREAT HEIGHT

This is a rum accident with a bit of a comically odd twist. Allan McAskell, a magician who, during the day while appearing at the Empire, climbed up to the fly-floor some 30ft above the stage. There, for reasons known only to himself, he hung by his hands from a cross beam, then losing his hold fell to the floor, more or less landing on his feet but spraining both ankles. I cannot conjecture what possible purpose there could have been in these antics, and one can only wonder if the man himself realised how lucky he was not to suffer more bodily damage.

In the evening, though "suffering great pain" he was carried onstage and gave his show "kneeling across two chairs to the interest and satisfaction of the audience." All very odd.

1893_11_12 ROTTERDAM, Holland (Cirque Bonyn).   FATAL ACCIDENT AFTER THE SHOW

After the performance, one of the employees, climbing to the top of the building to take down the trapeze, fell into the ring which was boarded over. The force of the fall smashed in several boards. The poor chap, taken to hospital, died shortly after arrival. He left a widow and four young children.

1894_01_26 SWANSEA (Empire).   ACCIDENT TO PERFORMING ELEPHANT

An elephant called Nancy was exploring her stable and discovered a trapdoor in the roof. An elephant's trunk is an all purpose nose extension full of muscles and tendons used for grasping, breathing, feeding, dusting, smelling, drinking, lifting, and sensing. Asian elephants have one finger-like projection at the tip of the trunk while African elephants have two. These finger-like projections have many sensitive nerve endings and are capable of fine motor skills, such as grasping small and delicate objects.

So with all those attributes Nancy not only discovered the trapdoor but opened it. Unfortunately, she let the door fall back while her trunk was still there, damaging the end of it. This had to be amputated, which presumably caused her to lack much of her future motor skills. Ouch!

1894_01_29 DUBLIN (Gaiety).   DANCERS INJURED BY FALLING CHIMNEY POT

Minnie Mullen and Rosanna Kearns (both 17), dancers in the pantomime at this theatre, were sitting in the dressing room at 7pm when a chimney pot crashed through the roof with bricks, mortar and debris, striking both girls causing injuries to their heads. The collapse of the chimney was probably due to the strong wind blowing at the time. The girls were taken to Mercer's Hospital and though their injuries were of a painful nature neither was in any danger. It was considered fortunate that the other dancers had not yet arrived.

1894_02_19 LIVERPOOL (Shakespeare).   FATAL FALL OF FLYMAN

On Monday afternoon during a performance of *Cinderella* a flyman called Fuchie fell from the fly gallery on to the stage, receiving such injuries to his skull that he died on reaching the Northern Hospital.

1894_03_13 LONDON (Niagara).   ACCIDENT TO MR EDWIN DREW

[Niagara Hall was a circular building that housed a panorama. It opened in 1881 as the Westminster Panorama with the Battle of Waterloo, then in 1883 became the National Panorama, showing the Battle of Tel-el-Kebir, changing yet again in 1888 to become the Niagara Cyclorama and Museum, exhibiting a cycloramic painting called Niagara in London. This was so popular that the building itself came to be known as Niagara. In 1895, it became an ice rink which lasted until 1902 when the picture – measuring 400ft x 38ft – was sold for £200 and the building became a garage.]

Edwin Drew, the popular entertainer and author, after giving a performance at the Niagara Hall, was about to leave at the end of the night and, calling out a farewell to Mr Pulling the secretary, made for the exit. In the effort of trying to open the door he fell down the staircase with a cry. This brought Pulling with a light which revealed the fallen man in an inert heap at the bottom of the stairs. It was 90 minutes before a doctor could be found – perhaps they were all at the theatre? Eventually Drew was taken to Westminster Hospital where he had concussion of the brain, injury to the head, and injuries on his left side and arm. Following the accident, a rail was installed on the staircase.

On 2 June, Drew's wife organised a benefit for him, herself and their children at the St George's Hall, when many kind friends came to sing his songs, and four of them act "not very brilliantly" in a new play of his devising. The dearer seats were not very well filled – at benefits not everybody who bought tickets in support used them – in spite of wooing the presence of the Duchess of Teck, the Earl of Northbrook, the Marquis of Bute, and many theatrical and literary celebrities.

1894_08_04 BLACKPOOL (Winter Gardens). DANCER FALLS THROUGH GLASS ROOF

A story of a silly girl. Maude Dalle, a member of the Belle Quartette of speciality dancers, was so warm after her exertions that during the interval she opened the window of her dressing room which overlooked the glass roof of the promenade. She thought it would cool her down if she shed her clothing and stepped out of the window. The thought no sooner popped into her vacuous mind than the action followed. To her horror the roof immediately gave way and she fell some 15ft into the crowd of promenaders. One gallant gentleman covered her up with his coat and carried her to a private apartment. There Dr Richardson found that, apart from several bruises and a gash on her face, she had broken her right wrist. The injuries would prevent her working for several weeks. It sounds like the start of a Mills & Boon novella but I am afraid it ends here.

1894_10_20 SUNDERLAND (Avenue). FATAL ACCIDENT TO RESPECTED EMPLOYEE

Above the entrance to this theatre it was the practice at the end of Saturday night's performance to place a canvas banner advertising the following week's attraction. John Churchill (35) the gas-man, and another employee were in the act of doing this chore which necessitated climbing through the window from the dress circle bar. While they were untying the existing banner – *Morocco Bound* to replace it with *Don Juan* – a gust of wind caught the canvas, jerking Churchill to the ground 30ft below. Dr Watson, who happened to be at the theatre, ministered to the fallen man by bandaging his head. Churchill was then taken in a cab to the Infirmary by Mr Clark the Acting Manager. Dr Bain discovered that his patient's skull had been fractured by hitting the concrete pavement, and he died within minutes of his arrival. Mr Churchill had been employed at the theatre for many years. He left a widow and three children.

1894_11_13 CARDIFF (Empire). ACCIDENT TO MR FRED KARNO

[Fred Karno (1866–1941), born Frederick John Westcott, was a Music Hall impresario and head of a popular slapstick pantomime sketch troupe. Among the unknown comedians who worked for him were Charlie Chaplin and Stan Laurel. He bought an island in the River Thames and engaged the doyen of theatre architects Frank Matcham to build a music hall he called The Karsino. He was bankrupt in 1925, and in 1929 went to the USA where Chaplin and Laurel were now big stars in silent films, but a job with film studio boss Hal Roach did not work out well and he returned home. Thereafter he did little of importance before retiring to a village in Dorset.]

Between houses two members of the Karno troupe were pumping air into a siphon when it burst, sending glass flying about the room.

24. *Fred Karno*

Pieces of broken glass hit Fred Karno in the face and Dr Wallace was called in to render assistance. He dressed the injuries and the troupe was able to give its sketch as usual at second house. Karno, managing to carry on his business, swiftly recovered.

1895_02_06 LONDON (Metropole).   ACCIDENT TO CHILD PERFORMER

    The Metropole Theatre at Camberwell was a new venue and the lessee had programmed the pantomime for six weeks but, owing to demand, extended the run for a further week by buying out the company he had already engaged to follow. During this extension week one of Mdlle Marie's pupils while playing in the flies – surely not permissible, what was Mdlle thinking of? – fell from a height of 26ft, hitting a light fitting which broke away, before landing on the cellar stairs. The injury sustained by the child was described as "concussion of the spine".

1895_05_04 DEWSBURY (Theatre Royal).   STAGE GUTTED BY FIRE

    Around an hour before the theatre was due to open its doors a fire broke out at the stage end of the building, the blaze consuming all the scenery of the evening's attraction *Uncle Tom's Cabin*. The stage end was destroyed but it was not clear if that alone could be rebuilt.

1895_05_27 LONDON (Metropole).   FATAL ACCIDENT TO PLUMBER

    Plumber John Curtis Ashdown (49) had arranged to meet Mr Brough, clerk of works, backstage at the theatre. A workman called Gardner took him to a wall ladder at the side of the stage floor and told Ashdown to stop and wait on the landing at the top of the ladder, cautioning him not to move from there, while he went to get Mr Brough. Before Gardner could go off in search he heard a noise and saw Ashdown falling headfirst down the ladder he had just climbed. The man was estimated to weigh around 17 stone and the distance of the fall 25ft. He landed on a rail in the wings and broke his back. Death was instantaneous.

1895_06_15 EDINBURGH (Empire).   POISON ACCIDENT TO LOIE FULLER

25. Loie Fuller

[Loie Fuller (1862–1928), born Marie Louise Fuller, was an American actress and dancer who pioneered modern dance, and patented theatrical lighting techniques. She created the Serpentine Dance wherein her costume itself was included in the choreography with lighting effects part of the spectacle. Moving to Paris where her creations chimed with the Art Nouveau movement, her popularity enabled constant engagements at the Folies Bergère. She was a fore-runner and champion of Isadora Duncan, and assisted her career in France. Her Serpentine Dance can be seen on You Tube.]

    "An unfortunate accident occurred last Saturday to Loie Fuller after her matinee performance at the Empire, Edinburgh. By mistake she took a dose of cocaine instead of another medicine, and so serious was the case that she was taken to the infirmary, where the stomach pump was applied. Happily she was quickly brought round and able to fill her post at night, where it is needless to say she met with a tremendous ovation." *Music Hall & Theatre Review* 1895_06_21.

1895_09_02 NOTTINGHAM (Theatre Royal).   ACCIDENT ON STAIRCASE

Gladys Olga Ffolliott was a comedy burlesque actress who, playing boys' parts, singing and dancing roles, had obtained a good class of engagements for some ten years at weekly salaries of between eight and fifteen guineas a week. Appearing with the Ben Greet Company on a tour of *Buttercup and Daisies*, she was allotted a dressing room on the first floor. In the play with a costume change after Act I, she had to go upstairs. In doing so she injured her ankle and could only walk with agony. She staggered through the rest of the play because she had no understudy, but afterwards saw a doctor and was taken to London by train having to be lifted in and out of the carriage.

Having suffered five weeks in bed and a long recuperation, at a hearing on 7 March 1896 she sued the theatre owners on the grounds that the steps were worn and dangerous. The owners denied any responsibility stating hundreds had used those same steps since her accident without any mishap. They also claimed they had no duty of care; it was her own responsibility to go up and down steps safely, the same as everybody else. They also alleged she was exaggerating the result of her own carelessness. The lessee's lawyer said the company had let the venue to the company of Mr Ben Greet. The position was exactly the same as a man who let out his furnished house for a week or month, the landlord not being bound to keep his house in repair – which seems bizarre even for those days.

Miss Ffolliott (or her lawyer) was no fool. An architect had been employed to accurately measure the steps to make a model. The steps were all found to be worn away between 1½ to 2½ inches. She had also had her foot photographed using the latest medical technique – X-rays. This was very early in the use of Röntgen's discovery which only startled the world on 6 January 1896. Miss Ffolliott won her case and was awarded damages of £76.10.0.

1895_10_11 BIRMINGHAM (Prince of Wales).   FATAL ACCIDENT TO STAGEHAND

Arthur David Jones (33) attending to scenery at the back of the stage, paused to rest with head on arms against a canvas flat. Falling backwards he landed on a scene brace, the point penetrating his bladder so deeply it was only removed with much difficulty. He was taken to the General Hospital where he died in terrible agony four days later.

1895_10_15 WORKINGTON.   ACCIDENT TO ACROBAT DURING PRACTICE

Brete Fenello was practising a new stunt in preparation for a string of forthcoming engagements. This was a back somersault over four chairs. He slipped and fell, severely injuring his head and neck. This, putting him out of action for a month, lost him his run of engagements. It is worthy of note that most accidents to gymnasts of all types are either from practising new tricks or, if in public performance, more often from dodgy apparatus rather than lack of skill.

1895_11_20c NEW YORK, USA.   FATAL ACCIDENT ON IRVING'S FIRST NIGHT

After the first night of *Macbeth* in New York, Sir Henry was called before the curtain and during his speech there was a loud crash behind the curtain. Not knowing the cause, he glibly passed this off as the witches "still up to their diabolical antics". The audience thus left the theatre without knowing that two men, Harper and Daniels, who were in charge of the limelight on a platform 15ft above the stage, had been leaning against the rail to listen to Irving when it gave

26. *Sir Henry Irving*

51

way, throwing them on to the stage, along with the limelight gas bottle which landed on Harper. Both men were shaken but neither seemed hurt, Daniels walking home and Harper taking a cab. On the way home, the latter was seized with illness, and the cab diverted to hospital where it was found he had a fractured skull. Harper died the following morning, Irving cancelling rehearsals on hearing the news.

1895_12_01 LONDON (Metropolitan).   FATAL ACCIDENT TO PREACHER'S SMALL SON
[The popularity of some charismatic preachers of those times meant they attracted crowds far larger than could be encompassed in normal religious venues. It became the practice of hiring out Music Halls on Sundays to religious groups.]   On this evening, the popular preacher Mr Cooke arrived at the Metropolitan Music Hall with his small son Oswald. While his father was preaching, Oswald wandering about in the backstage area ventured into the painting room where a feature was a long fissure across the floor. This enabled a complete backcloth to be painted from one level by hauling the cloth up and down on pulleys. This was the alternative to having the painters on a gantry arrangement which had to be hauled across horizontally and vertically – like window cleaners on a tall building – to paint a backcloth hanging stationary. The meandering little chap fell down this slot in the floor and "was *in extremis*" when found by the theatre's gasman and taken to St Mary's Hospital where he died shortly after admittance.

1896_03_05 MANCHESTER (Palace).   ACCIDENT TO HARRY TATE

[Harry Tate (1872–1940), born Ronald Macdonald Hutchison, was a popular music hall comedian who made his debut in 1895 as a personable young man with an act of impressions of star performers of the time. He went on to become known for his broad comedy sketches such as Motoring and made a dozen films. He was fairly new to the business when he had this accident.]
      Harry Tate, the well-known mimic, fell down the stairs, injuring his knee so seriously that he had to have an operation thereby losing work in Cardiff they following week.

27. *Harry Tate*

1896_04_06 LONDON (Gaiety).   ACCIDENT TO THEATRE FIREMAN
      Fireman Dent, while going round the theatre at 2am doing his duty, overbalanced from the gallery falling into the pit. He was taken to Charing Cross Hospital where it was found he had broken both legs.

1896_10_07 LONDON (Alhambra).   ACCIDENT TO STAGE CREW
      The attraction was the ballet *Rip Van Winkle* in which a scene change in the last act involved hoisting a scenic piece representing a cottage weighing around 6cwt up into the flies. Whatever was supposed to hold it stored secure up there failed, and the whole thing crashed down on to three men on the stage beneath. Stage crew Joseph Bennett, Joseph Player and Robert Ritchie were all rushed to Charing Cross Hospital by Mr Ford the stage manager. As the scene change took place behind a front cloth, the audience was unaware of the accident while watching the final item of the evening taking place. Astonishingly, after treatment the three men were allowed home.

1896_10_29 LONDON (Prince of Wales). LIGHTING BOARD DESTROYED DURING SHOW

Around 10.30pm during Act II of *The White Silk Dress* it was observed that something was amiss with the electric lights. Then flames appeared from the back of the lighting switchboard. The curtain was lowered, the lights turned off and a fire hydrant brought into use to douse the flames which had set light to the woodwork and melted most of the wiring. In swift order, the gas system and such of the electric circuits that remained undamaged were brought into use allowing the play to continue. The audience – in ignorance of the reason for the hiatus – left full of entertainment and satisfaction. NB: Fires involving electricity should not be fought with water.

1896_12_11 LONDON. ACCIDENT TO TRICK CYCLISTS

The Grover siblings – Stella, the leading artiste, two younger sisters and a young brother were the personnel of a trick cycling troupe. They were practising in their back garden for their Christmas engagement in Manchester. The stunt they wished to include consisted of Stella bearing a pyramid of the other three on her shoulders while riding a unicycle. During a rehearsal on a mock stage of laid out boards the tyre burst. The three young ones, jumping down, landed safely, but big sister thrown to the ground, was carried into the house semi-conscious. It was not considered that their Manchester contract was in jeopardy.

1896_12_26 LIVERPOOL (Star). CLEANER KILLED BY SAFETY CURTAIN

As a precaution against the still all too frequent fires, many more theatres were now installing iron safety curtains which could be lowered in an emergency, cutting off the stage house from the auditorium. The Star Music Hall had been closed for some months while major alterations were carried out, and this day was the grand re-opening. Mary Edmondson a cleaner was working during the morning to make all ready for the evening's show. Working at the front of the stage, she realised too late that the safety curtain was rapidly descending. The iron struck her a tremendous blow to the side of her head fracturing her skull and killing her instantly.

1897_01_16 HULL (Theatre Royal). GUN ACCIDENT

During the pantomime *Babes in the Wood*, Miss Chadwick finding a gun in the wings that had been recently used in the duel scene, handed it to the property master. When last used it must have misfired, because in the handing over it went off, the blank wadding hitting Miss Chadwick's face injuring the area near her left eye. She had the wound dressed at the Infirmary but fortunately there was no damage to the eye itself.

1897_02_24 LIVERPOOL (Grand). PARTIAL COLLAPSE OF WALL AT REAR OF STAGE

The company was that of T Morton Powell, the play was *Greed of Gold*. A most appropriate title in view of the following. Around 6.50pm the brick wall at the back of the stage began bulging forwards forcing a few bricks out at the top and in the centre to drop on to the stage. Not anticipating any further movement, Grafton the lessee decided to carry on regardless. Meanwhile the police had arrived, deeming it necessary to send for Mr Shelmerdine the City Surveyor. He advised Grafton not to proceed with the show but dismiss the audience and close the theatre. Now heeding the advice, Grafton went before the curtain and explained to the audience while assuring them "there was not the shadow of ground for alarm." The audience members were offered their money back or a ticket for the next performance as repairs were to be instantly put in hand and the theatre guaranteed to open the following night.

1897_03_01 ROCHDALE (Royal).   ACCIDENT TO FRANK HERTIE

Frank Hertie was an actor-manager until he broke his leg in an onstage accident. As a result he was indisposed for nine months before relinquishing his status as an actor and turning to resident management. In September 1896, he became acting manager at Rochdale. On his way home on this night he slipped from a high kerb and broke his leg. Seemingly unlucky in keeping his legs intact, he may have been suffering from brittle bones due to a lack of calcium and vitamin D. This latter comes from sunlight and it may be his mode of life confined him to an excessive amount of time indoors. He was thought likely to be off for several months judging by his previous leg break, so Mr Anstead of the Halifax theatre was drafted in as a substitute. Hertie resumed duties on 24 May.

1897_05_17c WIGAN (Empire).   CHEMICAL EXPLOSION INJURES JAMES ENGLISH

James English of the English sketch company was asked by the owner of the theatre if he would attend to some coloured fires that had been prepared by a local chemist. Being an obliging sort of chap he did as requested and as soon as he lit the stuff with a fuse there was an explosion that hit him directly, injuring his hands and face. As a result he had to cancel several imminent engagements and remain in Wigan under medical treatment. It does not always pay to be helpful and obliging. A benefit was held for English on 11 June which "proved a big success."

1897_08_17 WEDNESBURY (Theatre Royal).   USA ACTRESS SAVES THEATRE FROM FIRE

28. *Miss Go-Won-Go-Mohawk*

[Go-Won-Go-Mohawk (1860–1924) was born Carolina Mohawk on the Cattaraugus Indian Reservation in Western New York, her father being chief and medicine man Dr Allen Mohawk. She was an accomplished athlete who possessed masterful horsemanship skills and appeared for a time with the western shows of Buffalo Bill Cody and Wild Bill Hickok. Go-Won-Go, one of the first Native American actresses to perform on the American stage, married Captain Charles in 1889; Charles an ex-Army officer and former actor, became her manager. They came with horses to the UK to star in "authentic American Indian" plays.]

Miss Go-Won-Go-Mohawk, outside the ladies' dressing room, smelled smoke. Peering into the room she saw that a large screen had toppled over on to the gaslight fixed to the dressing-table, and was fully ablaze. Dashing into the room she threw down the screen – some 9ft square – on to the floor, and emptying a bucket of water on to it stamped out the remaining flames. As she was clad only in her fringed Indian dress, she had put herself in jeopardy, but avoided injury except some burns to her hand and a wound to her thumb. The theatre was crowded, and the show only part way through, so the hint of even a whiff of smoke escaping into the auditorium could have started a panic. Being the only person present, Miss Mohawk very capably dealt with the problem rather than running madly about.

1897_09_03 BIRMINGHAM (Prince of Wales). CEILING FALLS ON ACTRESS

Frances Ivor of Mr Tree's Company was sitting in the dressing room ready and awaiting her call when without any warning, the entire ceiling fell in covering her with a mass of broken laths and plaster. Fortunately, she remained conscious although badly shaken and in a visual mess. When her cue call came she had to brush herself down as best she could, and after making her entrance managed to get through her part with barely a hint of what she had just suffered. On the following night she appeared as Queen Gertrude in *Hamlet* after spending the whole day in bed "in a state of prostration".

1897_09_18 LONDON (Drury Lane). PLAY CANCELLED AND AUDIENCE SENT HOME

The play was a new one called *The White Heather*, the staging too also novel. The concept of the system was basically to build up the scene below stage level and then raise it into place complete. When the curtain was due to rise it was found that the hydraulic lift which lifted the opening scene refused to function. The stage was, in effect, a huge chasm and it was impossible to start the play. J M Glover the conductor of the orchestra announced the fact, and the audience good-naturedly filed out with no trouble or panic either in front or behind the curtain and money was refunded at the box office. Engineers and carpenters worked from 6am on Sunday to 5pm on Monday building a temporary stage in the massive space left by the lack of the hydraulic lift. The performance went off satisfactorily and the box office was besieged by ticket buyers.

The cause of the failure of the £8000 system was the loss of air-tight packing on one of the joints. Scenic effects relying on mechanics are always unreliable. In very recent times West End and National Theatre shows have had to be cancelled or abandoned part-way through because of recalcitrant revolves and similar mishaps.

55

1897_10_04 LONDON (Haymarket). ACCIDENT TO JAMES BARRIE

[J M Barrie (1860-1937) born in Kirriemuir, was the ninth of ten children. He gained a reputation as a writer by submitting articles and stories to journals. Moving to London he embarked on a successful career writing novels and plays. He had several successes but is now mainly known only for *The Admirable Crichton* and the ever-enduring *Peter Pan*.]

29. *J M Barrie*

Barrie was directing rehearsals of his play *The Little Minister*. As was the custom before microphones were invented, a platform was built over the orchestra pit, with table and chairs for production personnel. Barrie was standing leaning on the rail surround when it gave way precipitating him into the orchestra pit. He was unconscious for a time but, coming to, appeared to be none the worse other than suffering a shock to his system.

1897_10_06c CHESTER (Prince of Wales). GUN ACCIDENT

During the prologue of the play *The New Magdalen*, stagehand Smith was handed a gun by a member of the company and instructed to fire it on a given signal. The pistol was proffered barrel forward and, as Smith had something else in his hand at the time, on taking it he accidentally caught the trigger shooting one of his fingers to pieces. *The New Magdalen* company "generously offered to pay Smith's wages while disabled, and also to defray the medical expenses."

1897_12_14c DOVER (Tivoli).   FATAL ACCIDENT TO FLYMAN

"A sad accident occurred at the Dover Tivoli, when an employee fell from the flies, a distance of 60ft, and was killed this week." *Music Hall & Theatre Review* 1897_12_17.

1898_02_08 LONDON (Canterbury).   ACCIDENT TO FLYMAN

Flymen were still tumbling over the safety rail of the fly gallery. This example being the fortieth recorded herein. The unnamed man, leaning over for a better view, toppled down a distance of 25ft on to his head. He was taken to St Thomas's Hospital in a "critical condition".

1898_04_19 LONDON (Palace).   PAINTER'S FATAL FALL FROM FLIES

Frederick Wooller (37) had been employed as a painter during the day, and a fly-man in the evening. At 2pm he fell from the flies to the stage suffering serious injury. He died three days later.

1898_10_17 LONDON (Tivoli).   FIRE DESTROYS CINEMATOGRAPH APPARATUS

At the end of the century it was commonplace on music hall bills for scenes to be shown on a cinema screen. On this day the projector lantern catching fire destroyed the whole cinematograph apparatus. This led to discussions on the matter at London County Council which, while deciding not to impose regulations, decreed that a letter be sent to all venues that were licensed by the LCC informing them that express permission must be obtained before any cinematograph exhibition can be given.

1899_03_04 LONDON (Hammersmith Varieties).   EXPLOSION

This explosion presaged a new form of entertainment that would eventually drive music halls out of business. The latest novelty on a variety bill was to replace one of the turns with a short film show. Here the projector was housed in a fireproof room at the back of the stage, thus the films were back-projected on to the translucent white screen. At 10pm as the films were being shown, flames shot up skywards followed by an explosion. Projectionist Andrew Wraight was badly injured and rescued by his assistant Mr Brock. The collection of film spools was entirely destroyed. The audience had no reason to panic as most of the calamity was concealed. The show continued minus the moving pictures segment.

1899_03_16 LONDON (Brixton).   HORSE FALLS ONSTAGE

[Several managements have attempted to place a real horserace onstage. The most famous was in a play called *The Whip* at the Theatre Royal, Drury Lane in 1909 which not only had a race with eight horses but a spectacular train crash. However, there were several previous attempts to put racehorses onstage by brave producers in the Victorian era (*See* 1893_12_16c)]

Brixton Theatre presented a play *In Old Kentucky* that had a race scene with real horses. At the performance on this night, Queen Bess and her rider Lilieth Leyton came rushing onstage and the mare fell, landing with its front legs hanging over the footlights, with broken glass shattering everywhere. Miss Leyton, remaining calm, neatly slid from the saddle and taking the reins coaxed the horse to its feet. The audience also rose to its feet showering applause on the "plucky little lady".

1899_05_05 COLCHESTER (Theatre Royal). FATAL ACCIDENT TO PROPERTY MASTER

The property room had a door opening to a yard outside the theatre. The floor level of the room was 9ft 8in above the ground level of the yard. The purpose of the door was to enable props and scenery to be off-loaded from wagons in the yard, directly into the backstage area where Arthur Johnson (33) and Thomas Dyer were at 9.30pm. Johnson brought in a chair from the stage to put on top of some boxes, and on placing his hand against the door to steady himself, it flew open and he fell out into the yard. Dyer hastening down found him quite conscious, sitting up with his head bleeding. He said the door was unfastened and his "head was broken". Dr Becker was summoned, and finding a 10in wound and another of 3in on Johnson's head, stitched and dressed them before sending him home in a cab. Johnson, acting and speaking normally, ascended the stairs to bed without assistance. On 12 May, after being regularly attended by Dr Becker, lockjaw set in and he died that evening.

At the inquest it was pointed out that the door fastening – a bolt – was found only partway across and as it appeared that Johnson himself was the last to fasten it, he must not have shot the bolt fully home. The jury foreman said if the door had opened inwards the accident could not have happened. He was told it was a legal requirement for theatre doors to open outwards as a fire precaution. He then suggested a platform could be erected outside the door and was told that getting stuff in and out was awkward as it was, a platform would make it even more difficult. The lessee said there had never been any accident there previously but he would do whatever was possible to make the doorway safe. The management would pay the funeral expenses to which the jury foreman said "I think that is very kind" – the jury adding "Hear, hear!"

57

1899_06_28 CROYDON (Grand). FATAL ACCIDENT TO ACTOR

Barton de Solla (66) who had been playing the role of Dr McGrath in *The Broken Melody* was leaving the theatre when he slipped on the stone steps at the entrance, falling on his head. Picked up unconscious, he was taken immediately to Croydon General Hospital but, in spite of every attention, he died at 6am the following morning.

1900_03_20 PARIS, France (Folies Bergère). BULL BREAKS LOOSE IN THEATRE

The pantomime *Flamenca* in imitation of a Spanish bullfight featured a real live bull. The animal managed to break the bars of its cage, causing many spectators to flee. However, the toreadors successfully drove the bull into a safe place so no accident occurred. The only concessions to actual bullfighting were a few passes with the cape and the placing of two banderillos in the bull, although these were not actually stabbed into the bull but stuck on with pitch. It seems the electric light frightened the animal.

1900_04_18 WOOLWICH (Barnard's). FATAL ACCIDENT TO ENGINEER'S BABY

Though electricity was being adopted by more and more theatres, many still clung to gas. Those using electricity did not always take it from the mains. James Hamilton McCullum was at work in Barnard's Theatre on the engine that generated electric light. He had his eleven-month old daughter Margaret in his arms when his coat caught in the fly-wheel of the machinery throwing them both to the ground. McCullum was severely cut about the head, the injured child died the following day. Truly awful!

1900_10_19 LEICESTER (Opera House). LIMELIGHT LENS FALLS ON HEAD OF ACTRESS

The play was *Quo Vadis?* and as Caroline Barrett was waiting to enter for her first scene, the limelight man let the glass lens from the light fall from the fly floor. It struck the unfortunate actress on the head and only by suffering much pain, did the game gal get through her part.

1900_12_19c HANLEY (Imperial). FATAL GUN ACCIDENT

The play was *Rich and Poor of London*. The manager was backstage showing a faulty gun to Joseph Glover one of the actors. The trigger was defective, failing to work after having been pulled several times to no avail. Then a blank cartridge exploded burning a hole in Glover's shirt sleeve and causing a slight wound. This did not seem serious and the man was able to carry on acting for some further evenings until Monday night. However, he died the following day from "shock caused by inflammation and gangrene." It is salutary to realise how primitive medicine was a century ago and the astonishing progress over the following hundred years.

SUICIDES

From the evidence of the above text there is no doubt the Victorian backstage was a very dangerous area and an unconscionable number of people were maimed and killed there. It also seemed to some unfortunate souls the perfect place to commit suicide. It is difficult to ascertain what drove these unhappy individuals to do away with themselves because they did not go in for leaving notes behind them. Perhaps in most cases they did it on impulse, perhaps full of alcohol? There have been suicidal people in the entertainment profession under all kinds of circumstances.

Mr George Percy (45) was the property-master and modeller at the Surrey Theatre in London. He had complained to his wife Rebecca and several colleagues about being overworked as for some time he had been employed both day and night. He told his wife he was going to leave on Saturday next. His main complaint was that his supervisor constantly demanded too much of him, abusing him to such an extent that he could take no more. Percy also suspected another person wanted to replace him upsetting him greatly. On Monday morning of 19 June 1854, he again remarked to John Clements the watchman, a colleague for the last six years, that he could no longer tolerate the abuse he was receiving at the theatre. Later in the morning Percy's assistant came down greatly agitated, shaking and unable to speak. After calming down he told his workmates to go to the property room. There they found Percy hanging. He was cut down but life was extinct. At the inquest the jury's verdict was 'Temporary Insanity'.

In June 1857, A pot-man from a pub next door to the Princess's Theatre habitually called in to take orders. At 10am one morning he went in saying he had come to collect empty pots. He then disappeared and nothing more was seen of him until two flymen, going up to the fly gallery, found the pot-man hanging by the neck with a rope attached to an overhead beam. He was speedily cut down and an alarm raised, but the man was already dead, "the vital spark had fled."

On 26 August 1899, while a performance of *A Prodigal Daughter* was taking place at the Grand Theatre, Derby, a stagehand called Heathcote Henry Hill (38), a blacksmith by trade, was seen climbing up the fire escape. When asked where he was going he replied he was "getting some fresh air." Shortly after he was found hanging by his necktie from a gas-pipe in the narrow back yard of the theatre. Colleagues said he had been acting strangely of late, often bursting into tears, and had several times remarked on taking his own life. At the inquest, Hill's brother said the deceased had been recently troubled regarding his wife's conduct. It would seem that an outside fire escape existed at this theatre.

I have evidence of more suicides but the perpetrators were all discreet enough to carry out the deed away from their place of work.

MURDERS

While, like many of us, theatre workers have sometimes felt like murdering a colleague, none of them do so. Well, that's not strictly true – in the companion volume *Perils of the Victorian Stage* there is an actual onstage murder in front of the audience! And this is an example of another cunningly planned plot by one actor to murder another. As it involves l'amour you won't be surprised that we visit Paris on 5 July 1862.

Mr and Mrs Dumongeot were actors in the minor theatres of Paris. On this night Mrs D was performing at the Island Theatre in the Bois de Boulogne, while Mr D was at the little theatre in Montparnesse. A colleague of Mr D was a young actor of 19 called Dumont. Dumongeot and Dumont were good friends. But Dumont had fallen seriously in love with Mrs D and had written several love letters to her, which she had ignored.

On this night, while Mr D was onstage, Dumont went into the dressing room and stole from Mr D's street clothes the key to his apartment and made his way there letting himself in with the key. He then partially undressed and armed with a dagger and a carving knife hid under Mrs D's bed.

Mr D arrived home at midnight, followed half an hour later by his wife. They sat and chatted while they ate supper, so it was around 2am when they went to bed – in separate beds. All the while Dumont had been lying under Mrs D's bed for about four hours. At 3am he surfaced, went to Mr D and stabbed him 15 times with his weapons. Fortunately, "none were fatal or even dangerous". Mrs D, forcibly awakened by her husband's screams and shouts, ran down in her nightdress out into the street where she soon found a police sergeant (*at 3 in the morning?*) and a neighbour who rushed back to help her. There they found the two men rolling over and over on the floor, locked in a struggle enabling the policeman to rescue Mr D and arrest Dumont. In November, Dumont was on trial for pre-meditated attempted murder.

The usual place to murder a thespian is not to hide under the bed but to lurk at the stage door. That was where a disaffected young woman launched her attack on actress Eliza Vincent in June 1849.

Eliza Vincent (1815-1856) was daughter of a newspaper vendor and first appeared on stage at the age of six. In 1826, when she was 11, she made a marked success at Drury Lane as Oberon in *The Elfin King,* and a print of her in the role was made. She then went on to have a long career becoming a star actress known as "The Heroine of Domestic Drama", and manager at the transpontine theatres.

59

Miss Vincent's somewhat turbulent private life included a long-lasting affair with Surrey Theatre manager David Webster Osbaldiston by whom she was rumoured to have had a child. The pair took over the management of the Victoria in 1841 and when Osbaldiston died in 1852 she continued as sole manager.

The "diabolical attempt to assassinate Miss Vincent of the Victoria Theatre" took place as the actress-manager was leaving the theatre after the show.

She was about to enter a carriage at the stage door when a young woman hurled herself upon her and attempted to strangle her with bare hands. Mr Johnson, an actor also leaving the theatre, rushed to Miss Vincent's assistance and, manhandling the woman who was loudly declaring that she would kill her victim, dragged her away into the theatre where he handed her to Murray the constable of the theatre. On being taken into custody the prisoner was found to have a quantity of stones and a sharp knife.

30. *Osbaldiston*

Before magistrates it was established the woman was Harriet White aka Cole who claimed to have been a ballet girl when Miss Vincent had appeared at the Haymarket theatre and had assisted her there. Having since fallen on hard times, she had sought help from Miss Vincent but having been spurned vowed to have her revenge. She had been watching the actress for several nights and seeing her alone had taken the opportunity to launch the attack. Miss Vincent declared she did not know the woman. The magistrate, realising that Cole was "not in a proper state", detained her until friends came forward to be answerable for her future conduct. The woman appeared to be friendless and was jailed for three months. At the expiration on the sentence Cole threatened "to do for" Miss Vincent and so the proposed bail was withdrawn and she remained in jail.

After Osbaldiston died, Eliza Vincent at the age of 37 married Benjamin Crowther (28), an equestrian formerly of Astley's and currently appearing at the Victoria. The courtship was short and after the wedding the happy couple went for a brief honeymoon to Brighton. They returned after four days to their home at Barkham Terrace, where the groom suffered some kind of brain fever. After this he settled into a melancholic gloom that defeated all efforts by physicians, and was placed in a private asylum at Peckham.

Well after two failed attempts at murder we close this part of the book about backstage matters with two successful notorious stage door murders.

Nathaniel Curragh, widowed manager of Crayford Waterworks, had three daughters and a son. Beatrice, the middle girl, developing a desire to become an acrobat after seeing acrobats at Sanger's Circus, answered an advert wanting girls to train with the Letine Troupe performing on bicycles, and was offered a job. She begged her father to grant consent which, to humour her, he did.

The troupe comprised George Gorin aka Mr Letine, Mrs Olga Letine, three young women – one being Beatrice – and a boy apprentice. At first Beatrice was a very apt pupil showing talent, working the music halls of the UK and Europe throughout 1887. Her older sister Gertrude also joined the troupe prior to Christmas 1887 from when until Easter 1888 they had the following daily schedule: Royal Aquarium, afternoon 3.15; evening, 8.45; Oxford Music Hall, 10.20 ; London Pavilion, 11.20. So the troupe was performing four times a day at three different venues, travelling between in its own horse-drawn minibus taking the six personnel and the bikes. Beatrice was permanently tired and often fell asleep on the journeys. At one performance when she was supposed to balance a little boy on her shoulder she dropped him. Letine picking him up, replaced him, whereupon Beatrice dropped him again. The audience hissed, Letine tried the stunt a third time, but again the boy was dropped, and the hissing renewed.

The Letine Troupe, highly regarded for its attractive and graceful females, was constantly in work, rarely playing fewer than two venues a night. In April 1888, the Letines had a twelve day contract in Cardiff and here Beatrice's condition grew markedly worse. Complaining of feeling tired and ill, and barely able to dress herself, she had to be helped to change into her performing costume. She had become so thin and frail that Mrs Letine pulled Beatrice's performing tights over her day stockings to help disguise her stick-like legs. Examined by a doctor he said the girl should rest more and get out in the fresh air. He did not say – what surely must have been obvious to all – she was in the throes of 'galloping consumption'. After the Cardiff engagement, the troupe returned to London, and the Letines took the wretched Beatrice back home. She did not want to go home, and cried. The Letines now found out the girl was weak and delicate, and that her mother had died of tuberculosis. This contagious disease had no cure and 80% of those contracting it died. In the last 50 years of Victoria's reign some four million people died from TB, it was a disease that aimed at young adults.

Her father was appalled at the change in his daughter who had left home a happy active healthy thirteen-year-old and returned within a year as a decrepit wasting invalid. Mr Curragh blamed George Letine for mistreating her and with the connivance of the recently formed NSPCC, made Letine defend himself in three court cases. The charges of mistreatment were thrown out in all three. So, with his distorted outlook, Curragh looked to other avenues than the courts of law. He wrote to eminent social activists and newspaper editors, his brain being finally turned when Beatrice died on 5 December. According to Curragh's son his father had become demented with grief, waking in the night screaming out, evil tempered, talking aloud constantly about his daughter, and perhaps most peculiarly, tying knots in pieces of string and showing them around to men at the waterworks. The story of Beatrice, only lightly fictionalised, was published as *An Acrobat's Girlhood* in the June 1889 issue of the *Sunday Magazine* which her father constantly read over and over moaning aloud. The son said his father's sister had been in and out of asylums for years, another member of the family was also insane.

And so we come to the evening of Friday 21 June around 11pm when the Letine Troupe arrived in its minibus at the Canterbury Theatre having travelled from the Paragon Music Hall. A man stepped from the shadows, a knife blade glittering in the lights from the theatre, "I have been waiting for you a long time; now I have you!" Nathaniel Curragh, for it was he, thrust his knife over and over into Letine who slumped to the pavement. Bystanders, too stricken to move, were stunned when Curragh crossed the road, produced a revolver, and placing the barrel in his mouth, pulled the trigger.

Police were soon on the spot and the two men, placed in the minibus that had arrived only five minutes before, were taken to hospital.

Mrs Letine arriving at the hospital found that her husband had died within 30 minutes of admittance.

33. *Death of Lutine*

image© The British Library Board

Curragh was saved to face the death sentence but when tried, with the evidence showing him clearly insane, he was ordered to be detained during Her Majesty's pleasure.

This final murder at the stage door on 16 December 1897 shocked the world because the actor attacked was with the possible exception of Sir Henry Irving, the most popular actor in Britain. It was the most celebrated and appalling murder in English theatre history.

William Terriss (1847–1897), born William Charles James Lewin, was known for his swashbuckling hero roles, as well as parts in Shakespeare and classic dramas. Athletic as a child, Lewin tried several professions abroad and at home but, having enjoyed amateur theatricals, he decided to try the stage, adopting the stage-name William Terriss. His first appearance on the professional stage was at the Prince of Wales Theatre, Birmingham in 1868. His London debut was in 1871 and he was soon one of Britain's leading actors, popularly known as Breezy Bill. In 1880, he joined Henry Irving's company at the Lyceum Theatre. From the mid-1880s he also played hero parts in the Adelphi melodramas, regularly returning to the Lyceum company both in London and on USA tours. By 1897, he had appeared in a play *The Harbour Lights* in which an actor called Richard Prince had a minor role. During the run of this play Terriss, having been offended by Prince, had him sacked. However, he sent small sums of money to the wretched actor and tried to find alternative work for him. On 12 December, while appearing at the Adelphi Theatre as Capt Thorne in a play called *Secret Service*, Terriss was visited by Prince and they were seen arguing in the dressing room. On this day, 16 December, Prince had gone to the Actors' Benevolent Fund office to ask for another handout only to be told that was not possible and to return another day. Prince then lurked in an alley near the Adelphi stage door and when Terriss arrived for work Prince stabbed him to death. Terriss died in the arms of his lover and leading lady Jessie Millward.

34. *William Terriss*

The nation was appalled, and Sir Henry Irving who was not only the head of the profession but also a close friend of Terriss took command. Terriss was a married man with two children but since 1885 had lived with his paramour. It was an unheard thing in those days for a man's lover to attend his funeral, in fact some people thought it not proper for any women to attend a funeral. Irving arranged through the appropriate channels that he should deliver a message of condolence to Mrs Terriss. This was an expected formality but Irving went further. On the morning of the funeral he called at Miss Millward's flat with a bunch of violets and a message of condolence from the Prince of Wales. He then asked if he might escort her to the funeral. He knew that there would be no adverse comments if she was with him.

Irving forecast that "Terriss was an actor, so his murderer will not be executed." At the trial Prince was found "Guilty but insane" and sent to Broadmoor where he remained until his death in 1937.

63

PART TWO
THE TURBULENT VICTORIAN AUDITORIUM

Many buildings used for professional entertainment in Victorian times were of some antiquity, often converted from non-theatrical premises. Others were entirely of wood, some were jerry-built and even impressive brick and stone structures housed flimsy interiors which were unable to bear the weights imposed by hundreds of tramping feet.   The very popular circuses in the early Victorian era carried on operating as they had since the first circus founded by Philip Astley in 1768. When they toured, they built wooden amphitheatres much like the theatres of the day, with a ring in place of the pit but still including a stage. The circus stayed several weeks changing the programme frequently before moving on to the next town. The building was then dismantled, or left for other entertainments. Often these temporary buildings lasted many years, being improved and converted into traditional theatres.

The circus 'big top' marquee (invented in America in 1825) did not come into common operation in the UK until later in the 1840s, and for some years circus managers continued building wooden amphitheatres in tandem with canvas big tops. Circuses operated much like the theatres of the day with melodramas, pantomimes and sensation pieces. Horses being the main distinguishing feature of circus programmes they were the foundation of dramatic pieces known as 'hippodramas' located in 'hippodromes'. The name became attached to later places of entertainment that had never seen a horse inside.

Equestrian tricks and stunts that had been around for years began to acquire a meaning via presentation and costuming. Andrew Ducrow who succeeded to Astley's devised *The Courier of St Petersburg* where the rider straddles two cantering horses while other horses, bearing the flags of countries on the route passed between his legs. As each horse went through his arched legs Ducrow picked up the reins each time until by the end of the act he was driving a dozen horses.   Even Shakespeare was grist to the mill with equestrian versions of *Macbeth* and *Richard III* being particularly popular. Perhaps the most enduring equine drama was *Mazeppa* which could be done on theatre stages.

The Victorian theatre and circus staged spectacular displays. Stage scenery comprised canvas on wooden frames known as 'flats', and canvas backcloths hanging on wooden battens and ropes. The scenery was often constructed and painted on site, with the workshop either over the auditorium between the ceiling and roof, or backstage. Glue was boiled in pots over a naked flame; paint was mixed with flammable spirits, all of which contrived to make scenery highly combustible, acting as a conduit from the smallest spark to complete destruction of a theatre. Apart from the efforts of a few individuals, there was little unified movement to find a way of fire-proofing wood and canvas.

Although today we think of theatres, music halls and circuses as being completely different forms of entertainment, in Victorian times they were much more intermingled. Although theatres continued developing from the ones of the Georgian era they were not restricted to offering only straight plays. Even London's august Theatre Royal Covent Garden (now the Royal Opera House) staged circuses as well as plays, opera, ballet, pantomimes and variety. Music hall arose from the free-and-easy song and supper rooms. Originally they were concert halls with food and drink served at tables but developed into buildings akin to conventional theatres. I have not attempted to distinguish between these places of entertainment and in this book they are all called theatres.

The outstanding danger to all places of entertainment of the period was FIRE. In researching the Victorian period for this book I located details of 283 theatre fires which resulted in 212 buildings being totally destroyed. Reader don't be alarmed, I shall not be inflicting all those upon you! The thankful fact is that the great majority of fires occurred at times when the theatres were devoid of people. These are eschewed from the book, only fires that burst out during a performance are included although this is not as rare as one might suppose.

In the latter case audiences are clearly in danger and desperate to get out. On a few notorious occasions when a fire started during the performance, people struggling to get out were trapped, injured and died. However, included are some of the most infamous cases of panics and frenzy with many injuries and fatalities stemming from a very small beginning. One voice mistakenly or deliberately crying "Fire!" can start a frenzy that sets the entire place in a desperate panic *when there is not a vestige of a flame* but can cause more human suffering than when an actual fire razes a building to the ground. In many of the following entries of panic and frenzy there was no necessity of alarm at all and are unwarranted and highly reprehensible for one reason or another.

Another surprising thing is the number of accidents caused from defects in the interior such as stairs and entire balconies collapsing through the weight of increasing numbers. Often the damage to a theatre is deliberately wrought by the audience itself rioting and wrecking the place because of some dispute with the management. The following entries include all of these plus a few amusing oddities and one or two actual murders. Two facts should remain in mind throughout:

a) Until very late in the 19th century there were no official regulations imposed by law, and all theatres were hazardous by modern day standards.

b) The average life of a theatre in the 19th century was 23 years.

1838_06_14 WINDSOR (Theatre Royal).   ACCIDENT TO SCHOOLBOY

[Because of the proximity to the school, normally the Windsor theatre was not allowed to open during the periods when the Eton College boys were resident. Thus the theatre was only open on school holidays. The only exception was during the annual race week in June. The manager then followed the practice of staging an early performance for the boys of Eton prior to the normal one that attracted the race-goers.]

As usual, the young toffs got up to their high jinks, scrambling all over the auditorium, calling out to the players, firing missiles at the band, and similar japes. The Hon Thomas Milles – son of Lord Sondes – a young gentleman of fifteen or sixteen years of age, and a pack of chums, gained admission to the gallery then let themselves down into the boxes and pit. In this instance one boy held Milles's hands in the gallery, while another stood in the boxes underneath to guide his feet to the pillar. The gallery boy let go too early and Milles crashed into the pit. He was carried into the greenroom and surgeons speedily arrived in the shape of Sir J Chapman and Mr Soley who discovered the boy had a severe fracture to the head and other injuries of a serious nature. The injured lad was taken home in a carriage and was "believed to be out of danger but still lies in a very bad state."

1838_09_03 LONDON (Surrey).   A FIGHT IN THE GALLERY

Two men who paid for their seats in the gallery quarrelled during the performance. The theatre was very crowded and the men started fighting at the back of the gallery where, during the day there were windows, but prior to the performance these were removed and wooden shutters with bars replaced them. During their fight, the men lurched against the shutters which gave way precipitating them on to the portico of the theatre which was half way up the facade. The pair were seriously injured, one being sent with broken limbs to hospital. "Both men were in liquor at the time."

67

1838_10_02 BIRMINGHAM (Theatre Royal).   RIOT

[Riots in the theatre have a dishonourable history. If our ancestors were displeased about something while watching a play or opera they did not content themselves with simply booing, or leaving the theatre. No! They rioted. Probably the best known were the Old Price Riots of 1809, a little before our period. These arose because after Covent Garden Theatre burned down, the rebuilding of a new one was an incredibly expensive £150,000. Inevitably, the management increased the admission prices. Boxes went from 6/- to 7/- and the Pit from 3/6 to 4/-. Both galleries remained at the old prices. On reopening, audiences rioted. They did not despoil or vandalise anything – they shouted and stormed throughout the performances so not a word could be heard, and they kept this up for 67 consecutive nights. Eventually, the defeated management conceded and lowered the prices to the former rates, upon which the audience unfurled a banner reading "We Are Satisfied".]

In Victorian times riots had degenerated into dissatisfied audiences wrecking the place to a greater or lesser extent. The riots throughout the book are varied in cause but the responses are typical. Harvey Leech, known as Hervio Nano, an aggressive little man with peculiarly stunted legs but a very powerful torso and arms, appeared as The Gnome Fly. He was to star in a new afterpiece *The Demon Dwarf*. During the course of the main feature he asked Simpson the resident Stage Manager for some pay he claimed he was owed. It was pointed out that Nano's agreement was with Mr Yates the manager of the touring company therefore he should address his claims to him. This threw the little man into a rage and he refused to appear. Simpson explained this to the audience so a substitute play would be given.

At this announcement, with Hervio whipping them up into a frenzy, the gallery started a riot by shouting out "Clear the pit!" pulling up the benches and throwing them into the pit below, smashing glass chandeliers on the way. Flying wooden planks hurtling down was a major threat of injury if not death, so not surprisingly, the pit emptied immediately. The riot eventually ended when police arrived, Hervio being led off in handcuffs shouting, and the theatre emptied by dousing all the lights.

Hervio was bailed and carried on with Mr Yates's tour until the next assizes when he was tried for instigating a riot but, the jury voting in his favour, the case was dismissed.

35. *Hervio Nano*

1839_05_05c MANNHEIM (Germany).   ONSTAGE FIRE

Some of the decorations at this theatre caught fire during the performance causing the audience to rush out screaming. The Dowager Grand Duchess of Baden, though urged to flee, remained seated in her box, while her niece the Princess of Hesse Darmstadt dissolved into hysterics. The flames were soon put out, but during the fire four small children dressed as fairies were left dangling on ropes in the air, "surrounded by flames, screaming with fright, while their mothers, terrified to death, rushed on to the stage to rescue them from danger."

1839_11_26 LONDON (Victoria).   MAN FALLS ASLEEP IN THEATRE

A man called Giles went to the theatre where he partook of gin and water after which he fell asleep. Presumably the play was not very gripping. Not even the finale applause woke him. Eventually awaking at 2am he found himself alone and in the dark. Realising where he was, he saw a solitary light that he assumed was the lobby of the theatre. In fact it was at the back of the stage and he was in a box in the upper circle. It seemed logical to him that he could jump into the lobby, which is what he thought he did. In fact he jumped into space and landed wedged between two seats in the pit – a drop of some 20ft. His groans were eventually heard by the night watchman who, on finding Giles, summoned medical help. "He still remains very much indisposed." Which is hardly surprising.

1841_05_21c LONDON (Victoria).   SPECTATOR OFFERS AID TO ACTRESS

Eliza Vincent, "The Heroine of Domestic Drama", playing a sobbing and distraught heroine in a piece called *Simon Lee*, was assailed with a sequence of shillings thrown on to the stage from one of the boxes. It was occupied by John Gill a sailor recently returned from the Brazils, who was celebrating with a pocket full of wages and a bottle of spirits. He stood up and declared: "Avast there; I'm damned if you shall want while Jack has a copper in the locker to give you!" and threw the series of coins on to the stage.

Gill was arrested and hauled up before a magistrate the following day, having spent the night in custody. He explained he was "a little groggy" and his feelings were overcome by the young lady reduced to such a state of destitution that he felt he must help her, and the only thing he could think of was to toss her some money from where he was sitting. He certainly had no intention to injure the young lady. The policeman explained it was in the best interests of the defendant to keep him in custody as he was in a tipsy state carrying a large amount of money in the form of his hard earned wages from a long sea voyage. He thought it would prevent him from either being robbed or squandering away the rest. Gill thanked the constable for looking after him, after which the gullible sailor was discharged.

1841_10_04 LONDON (Victoria).

BORDER CATCHES FIRE FROM LIGHTS

[The Victoria Theatre was built in 1818 as the Royal Coburg. The roof and walls remain the same today as the Old Vic though inside has had many major rebuilds.]

A border that concealed the gas lights in the flies seems to have caught fire during the play. The audience, seeing the flames, immediately started making for the exit, but Osbaldiston the manager stepped forward and begged them not to be alarmed. His staff had torn down the burning scenery and already extinguished it. The local fire engine had arrived very promptly but would not be required. Urging everybody to resume their seats, Osbaldiston declared the show would then continue.

36. *The Royal Coburg*

69

1841_10_12 LONDON (Victoria).

COLLAPSE OF STAIRS

[The three theatres south of the river – Astley's, Victoria, and Surrey were, the reader will recall, known as "the transpontine houses" – Astley's the first circus in the world; the Surrey built as a rival but soon converted to a regular theatre; the Victoria still going strong today as the Old Vic. All three were famous for 'blood and thunder' melodrama, catering for the working class population that had grown in that area. All had large, crowded galleries and frequently feature herein.]

At 5.30pm, the normal time for gallery doors to be opened for the evening show, there were some 200 people waiting on the stairs at the Victoria Theatre. The pay box was situated part way up the stairs, thus having paid the admittance fee people then rushed up the stairs to bag the best seat possible. One of the flights of steps collapsed with around 50 people on it, crashing down on the flight below. By good fortune that flight was clear of persons otherwise they would have been crushed by the falling stairs and people from above. There were some injuries but not of a serious nature. Mr Brooks a surgeon in the Waterloo Road came and attended to eight people who waited at the stage door. All were able to walk home apart from a female who required a cab.

1842_05_30 MARKET DEEPING (Theatre).   COLLAPSE OF GALLERY

The performance of *The Poor Gentleman* was being given under the auspices of the Oddfellows, and as a result the house was full to suffocation point. During the epilogue, the gallery collapsed with a fearful crash burying everybody in the boxes beneath. As a result, women were screaming and crying, blood was gushing from many wounds, and fine dresses ruined. Fortunately, considering the scale of the disaster, there were no deaths. Blame was heaped on the carpenter who built the building, but the management had just employed Mr Northhouse of Boston for new painting and decorating, so his work was also under a cloud. The theatre was repaired and back in business by 10 June.

1842_06_06 SCHLEITZ, Germany.   CEILING COLLAPSE AT CHARITY SHOW

A charity performance was being held for the benefit of people who had suffered from a fire in Hamburg. A performance of a play called *The Czar and the Carpenter* was underway when ominous creaking was heard, rapidly followed by the ceiling suddenly collapsing and crashing down into the pit covering the audience there. The gallery people and most of those in the boxes were unscathed, but the 81-year-old matriarch of the Grand Ducal Family and her ten-year-old grandson, leaning out of their box, were both knocked into the pit by flying timbers. Incredibly, neither suffered injury. All help was instantly summoned, including the soldiery who desperately strove to remove the debris. When all was cleared it was found that the horrendous toll numbered 29 dead and 87 seriously injured. Of the latter a further 32 died in hospital. The theatre was not a permanent one but the Duke's riding house converted for the occasion by an architect called Khristen who was immediately sought for arrest, but had gone into hiding "to escape the vengeance of the people".

1842_06_28 GLASGOW (Cooke's).   NEW CIRCUS DESTROYED BY FIRE

[William Cooke was a circus man with a family of performers. More than that he was a circus entrepreneur. He built wooden temporary circuses not only all over the UK but also in the USA. In February 1838, Cooke's Baltimore $120,000 building was totally destroyed by fire. From 1853 to 1860 he leased Astley's Amphitheatre.]

The new building on Glasgow Green was a substantial one believed to have cost in the region of £800. This was only the second night of an anticipated lengthy season and 300 people were already seated. The fire was spotted by a policeman who ran to where he saw the flames, there meeting up with Mr Barlow the manager. Some straw was burning and flames had already reached the hay loft above which was soon alight, and in less than five minutes the whole roof was blazing. By the time of arrival of fire engines, the building was lost. Everybody escaped promptly and safely, and all the animals were rescued except for a single donkey. Most of Cooke's lavish wardrobe was destroyed thus adding to the cost of the disaster as nothing was insured. In spite of all this, Mr Cooke, who had "been in indifferent health since the serious calamity which befell them in New York" was determined to have a new amphitheatre up and running in time for the imminent fair.

1843_07_03 DUBLIN (Theatre Royal).   ATTEMPT ON THE LIFE OF ONSTAGE ACTOR

Not an accident but attempted murder. The play was *Macbeth* and the part of Macduff was played by John Calcraft the actor-manager and lessee. Just after curtain up, a respectable young wood carver William Sillary took a seat at the extreme end of the upper gallery. When Calcraft made his entrance, Sillary threw a glass bottle at him and exclaimed 'Damn you, oh Calcraft, Calcraft, Calcraft, – villain, villain, villain!' He then produced a knife clutching it like a dagger and adopted a menacing posture while uttering more violent and incoherent oaths. Thomas McCabe the duty policeman that night, struggled with the youth to capture the knife, and in the quarrel Sillary went over the edge of the gallery landing on his feet in the middle gallery. Immediately, he leapt over the edge again to land spread-eagled in the pit. The violence of the fall rendered the youth totally insensible. He was taken on a stretcher to Mercer's Hospital where he died at midnight.

The bottle was found to be filled with gunpowder in which were mixed pieces of broken glass, buttons etc with a partially spent match fixed to its mouth. The presumption could only be that Sillary had lit this bomb before throwing it, and whilst in flight the match had blown out.

At the inquest, it came to light that the young man, who was about 21 years of age, was estranged from his family because of his violent and excitable irritability. His father was not on speaking terms as he was not a dutiful son, but he stated his son was not a drunkard, and he had never considered him deranged. Mr Calcraft said he had never seen the man before he rose to his feet in the gallery, and could offer no explanation for the man's objection to him. Very strange.

1843_12_26 LONDON (Surrey).   BOY INJURED IN GALLERY

Being Boxing Day, the gallery at the theatre was very full. Galleries in those days were simply rows of backless benches and people grabbed a place wherever they could. William Parrott and his brother were sitting together towards the back of the gallery when a powerful man called Charles Hughes attempted to force a place for himself between them. The pair resisted this and Hughes pushed Parrott forward which resulted in the lad tumbling down over the heads of the rows in front, only stopping himself by grabbing the rail at the edge of the gallery. In the fall his arm was broken, and Hughes, realising what he had done, tried to make his escape but was arrested by constable Selwood who placed him in custody, returning to take William to St Thomas's Hospital.

Next day, in the magistrate's court, Mr Traill the magistrate declared himself at a loss on how to deal with this because the maximum fine he could impose was £5, none of which would go to the complainant; or he could send the case to court before a jury, but this would be at the cost of the boy's family who were very poor. This being the position here, he gave the father of Parrott the choice of which procedure he would prefer to take. Mr Parrott pleaded poverty and so would have to accept the inadequate fine being imposed. He said his son may be maimed for life, and certainly would not be able to work for several weeks, and it was unfair that there should be no benefit from a fine.

Mr Traill imposed the maximum fine of £5, or six weeks in jail if it should not be paid. Mr Traill doubted that the fine would be paid, and advised Mr Parrott that if that should occur he could appeal to the Lords of the Treasury who had the power to divert the money to the victim. For his part, if he was permitted to give the fine immediately to Parrott he would not hesitate to do so.

1843_12_27 LONDON (Prince's).   FIRE IN THE BOXES

Wafts of smoke were seen emerging from the private anteroom behind a box. It was found that a metal gas pipe leading to the lamps had melted, and the escaping gas was on fire, setting light to the ceiling above. The fire which had burnt no more than about a square foot of ceiling was put out.

71

1844_03_29 GLASGOW (Adelphi).   MISTAKEN FRENZY

It was a benefit performance for Mr J Grey, a popular member of the company, so a very large audience had gathered. Mid-performance a call went out for any firemen sitting in the theatre. It was the custom for firemen, like doctors, to give notice of where they were sitting so they could be discreetly summoned out for an emergency elsewhere. Clearly discretion was not used in this case, and a public announcement for fire fighters made. This was because a fire had broken out in another part of town. The audience, assuming it to be within the theatre, panicked, and all fought for the exits. The noise and shrieking drowned out any attempt to explain there was no fire in the theatre. Utmost confusion occurred with many bruised and wounded, as large numbers were thrown down and trampled underfoot. Surgical assistance was sent for and doctors attended to the sufferers promptly. Much damage was done to the theatre, and the box-keeper, an elderly man named Livingstone, was knocked down by some miscreant and robbed of several pounds.

1844_10 _05 LONDON (Drury Lane).   BOY INJURED IN PIT PASSAGE

In many theatres of the period, access to the pit was along a subterranean passage that passed under the side boxes. Three boys, who one assumes should have been on their way to the pit, decided to fool about when they discovered in the passage some hefty wooden frames leaning against the wall. These were occasionally used to form scaffolding when access to the ceiling was required. The boys clambered on these, until the frames, not tethered in any way, fell over to lie flat on the ground. Two boys escaped unharmed but one, a lad of about 12 years, caught underneath, suffered a broken leg. He was taken up almost insensible and as his whole body was bruised and injured he was immediately taken to King's College Hospital "where he now lies in a hopeless condition."

1844_11_01 LONDON (Cooke's Circus).   CIRCUS BIG TOP BLOWN DOWN

Cooke was the circus impresario who built circus buildings all over the place including America. Among his various ventures, Cooke was doing one-night stands with a one pole big top. The centre pole – known as the king pole – was some 20 inches in circumference and 40ft high. This tent was pitched behind Hackney Grove. Just before 7pm when the show was due to start, a strong wind blew up shaking the tent violently, suddenly ropes snapped and the king pole crashed to the ground dragging the canvas mushroom with it. Mrs Isbiter was struck on the head by the falling pole, and near her was sitting Mrs Laws, a relative whose child was knocked out of her arms. Immediate medical attention to Mrs Isbiter proved useless as her head was "literally crushed". The two-year-old child died the following day.

At the inquest, discussion was made concerning the safety of the tent, and a constable who had examined the structure earlier in the day had found it sound. The coroner made the point that just as a bus-driver was responsible for the safety of his passengers, and must convey them in a safe vehicle, so must the equestrian be responsible for the safety of his audience in his marquee. He would, therefore, like to have evidence from experts regarding marquees. There was evidence that a main guy rope had been cut – the ropes were all new – and that the pole would not have fallen otherwise. Suspicions were aroused concerning this cut rope, with rumours of foul play, until one man spoke up saying there had been cries for ropes to be cut while the struggle to free the audience buried under canvas was going on. It was agreed this was when the rope was severed. The verdict was accidental death in both cases.

1844_12_24 WINDSOR (Theatre Royal).   AUDIENCE MEMBER FALLS FROM GALLERY

Only the gasman and the orchestra leader were present in the theatre when Mrs Sarah Hume (63) entered the gallery. She was with her daughter Laura, and her husband was following outside on the stairs. The entrance was at the very back, and Mrs Hume, with her arms folded, stepped over the rows of benches to get to the front row, this being the usual procedure in a theatre gallery. On this occasion the Humes were the first customers and when she reached the front Mrs Hume toppled over the rail and plummeted down into the pit. Laura turned and ran out to her father, meeting him on the steps. They both then hastened down into the pit. Mrs Hume was lying on her back across the benches. A plank was brought; she was laid on it, and carried up on to the stage. As yet there were no other people in the house, and Mr William Moss, a local surgeon, was sent for. He found a very weak pulse and ordered Mrs Hume to be taken home on her stretcher plank. He accompanied her but on arrival at her house she was dead. Her back was broken.

At the inquest, the theatre manager Mr Reeves explained there were four rows of seats in the gallery with a space of eighteen inches between rows. The total distance from front row to back was eight feet. The back row was raised five feet above the front row so the rows would be tiered with twelve to fifteen inch risers. The height of the railing in front of the gallery was only 2ft 8in. There was some consternation about this and the coroner expressed surprise. Mr Reeves explained if it were higher the view from the back row would be impeded.

The verdict was accidental death and the manager was instructed to increase the height of the railing which he undertook to do without delay. Remarkably, the evening's performance had proceeded as usual after this accident, though to a sparse house.

73

1845_03_05 WASHINGTON, USA (National).   THEATRE DESTROYED BY FIRE

The audience was in the middle of enjoying *Beauty and the Beast* when the manager interrupted the piece by walking on to announce with the utmost calmness that the theatre was on fire but there was no cause for alarm. He asked the audience to withdraw in good order and peaceably, and once the theatre was empty they would be able to put out the blaze. The audience obeyed notwithstanding the alarm, only one lady having to be carried home in a dreadful state of convulsions.

Once empty, the fire burst forth with terrible rapidity. It started in the greenroom under the stage – seemingly caused by a careless act by one of the company – and soon the entire building was ablaze. Ten or twelve houses nearby were also gutted. Only the previous evening the directors were in discussions with an insurance company to insure against such a calamity but terms could not be agreed, thus the whole loss fell on the proprietors.

1845_04_28c ABERGAVENNY (Cwmreigyddion).   COLLAPSE OF GALLERY

It was benefit night for Mr J W Cooper at the town's public hall and a bumper audience was there to enjoy the show. After the first piece, there was a sudden crack, a crash of timber, shrieks and screams as the entire gallery collapsed taking over 100 people with it. The show was halted and the company and audience members rendered assistance. There were a great many sprains, cuts and bruises, but no serious injury. The performance was continued the following evening with a refixed balcony. This was a hall that had been fitted up as a theatre, but neither the management nor the fitter-up was to blame as the gallery had been installed as a permanent feature by the owners of the hall.

1845_04_25 NEW YORK, USA (Bowery).   DESTROYED BY FIRE FOR THE FOURTH TIME

I said at the start of this section I would not mention any of the many fires that plagued the Victorian era except ones that actually broke out during a performance. This is an exception.

The fire started in the carpenter's shop, immediately adjacent to the gas works of the theatre. In under an hour the theatre was completely wrecked. The reason why I have singled this out for attention is that it was the fourth time this theatre had been destroyed within seventeen years!

Built originally in 1826 it was destroyed and rebuilt in the years 1828, 1830, 1838 and 1845.

1845_05_25c CANTON, China (Theatre).   FATAL FIRE SPREADS TO ADJACENT BUILDINGS

A theatre in the Chinese part of the city, housed within a square, caught fire and the only access was via one narrow lane. It appears that people fighting to get out via this lane were met by people trying to get in – it is not clear why – and there was a total jam of bodies in this narrow passageway. The fire spread to nearby buildings, and as a result the loss of lives was considerable with total numbers given varying between 800 and 1400.

1845_08_20c WEST BROMWICH. (Temporary).   COLLAPSE OF GALLERY

The show was being given in a temporary theatre, the audience numbering around 180 persons. Five minutes after the curtain rose, the gallery fell with a sudden crash and the air was filled with the screams of men, women and children. In spite of the number of people fallen among benches and the framework of the structure, only one woman appeared mildly hurt with a few scratches and bruises. However, when the debris was lifted away, a crouching body was found with hands and knees on the ground and his head forced between his shoulders. The body was identified as Benjamin Rubery (24) who, it is supposed, crawled his way under the seating clandestinely to avoid paying the admission charge. In his efforts to see the play he had dislodged some of the supporting posts which led to the whole balcony falling, crushing him to death.

1845_09_18 LONDON (Adelphi).   ATTEMPTED SUICIDE

At the Adelphi Theatre, London in September 1845 Miss Elizabeth Millington (18) was in the company of friends sitting in the pit. She gave a loud scream and was promptly taken out in a state of insensibility followed by her friends. She was taken to Charing Cross Hospital where it was ascertained she had "swallowed a small quantity of the oil of almonds" (ie cyanide). A half-ounce phial of the poison was found in her possession but as it was nearly full it followed she had taken no more than three drops. "She possesses great personal attractions, and unrequited love is said to have been the cause of the somewhat peculiar but rash attempt she made at self-destruction."

1845_10_07 LONDON (Drury Lane).   FIRE IN THE BOXES

Just before midnight as the opera *Der Freischutz* was drawing to a close, smoke and flames were seen issuing from the back of the boxes. The occupants of the boxes immediately rushed along the passages to the exit, and in the rush the iron gate of the check-taker was broken and several ladies and the check-taker were knocked down. On investigation, it was found that Mr Carter the Check Inspector had lit a fire in his room, and somehow it had communicated with the stage box. It was with some difficulty that Mr Harley calmed the audience and the opera was allowed to end.

74

1845_11_27 LONDON (Adelphi).   MYSTERY SMOKE ISSUES FORTH

During a performance of *The Green Bushes* a quantity of smoke was seen to emerge, apparently from under the stage. It was accompanied by a strong smell of gunpowder. Loud shouts of fire, screams from ladies and a mass rising to make for the exits followed. However, the sole occupant of the stage at the time was Madame Celeste the manager who came forward and said "There is no danger – pray keep your seats." Others of the company then entered assuring the audience there was no cause for alarm, but some time elapsed before order was restored enabling resumption of the play. "The cause of the smoke did not transpire".

37. *Madame Celeste*

1846_01_30 GLASGOW (Royal Hibernian).   SEATING COLLAPSE IN PENNY GAFF

['Penny gaffs' were a form of popular entertainment for the lower classes in the 19th century. They were set up anywhere big enough to cram in an audience – empty shops, back rooms of pubs – any old ramshackle place would do, as the admission charge was only one penny. Tales that were well-known to the audience, and the deeds of famous highwaymen, robbers and murderers, were popular subjects for the plays. The stories of the 18th-century robber *Jack Sheppard* who escaped from prison on numerous occasions, and the gory *Murder in the Red Barn* were among the most enduring. The established penny gaff theatres were feared as breeding grounds for criminals by the Victorian moral reformers, as, in the words of one city missionary "no respectable person goes, so they have it all their own way, and corrupt the minds of youth without rebuke". The shows were popular from about 1830 to around 1870, by which time they had largely disappeared.]

At 10pm in a penny show booth that rejoiced in the name of The Royal Hibernian Theatre, the play was the popular *Jack Sheppard*. The place was so crowded that several seats in the pit gave way causing alarm and confusion. The shrieks of females, the curses of males and the wailing of children accompanied a rush for the doors.

Many people were injured, two so seriously they had to be sent to the Infirmary. "As soon as the excitement was a little allayed, the immoral performance of *Jack Sheppard* was resumed, and finished without further interruption. Such a place of amusement, being a den of the lowest vice and infamy – the resort of thieves, pickpockets, and other disreputable characters – ought surely to be suppressed by the Magistrates. We have been informed that a more fruitful nursery of young criminals does not exist."

38. *A typical Penny Gaff*

1846_02_16 AIRDRIE (Town Hall).   FLOOR COLLAPSE AT TOM THUMB SHOW

[General Tom Thumb (1838–1883), was the stage name of the diminutive Charles Sherwood Stratton who, under the guidance of P T Barnum, achieved great fame and fortune. At birth in Bridgeport USA to parents of medium height, Charles weighed 9 pounds 2 ounces. By the age of four, Charles was only one inch taller than he was at six months, but otherwise a normal, healthy child, with a body proportionate and functional. Signing up with Barnum at $3 a week, he was taught how to act, sing and dance. Making his first tour at the age of five, he had progressed to $7 a week, and by the end of the year he was earning $25. The following year, Barnum took General Tom Thumb, as he was now known, on a tour of Europe ($50 a week) which lasted three years. Returning to the USA he became the biggest star of the day. (Ho! Ho! Ho!)]

General Tom Thumb was only eight years old and 26in tall when he visited Airdrie under the auspices of P T Barnum. He had toured all over Britain, met Queen Victoria, and was a huge (Ho! Ho! Ho!) attraction. He exhibited himself during the day at the Town Hall but, so that the working classes could see him at a cheaper rate, in the evening he moved to the Trades Hall for greater room. Even so, the place was full to overflowing.

After his demonstration of 'Grecian attitudes', the General went off to garb himself as Napoleon. In his absence, the crowd pressed round the platform and the entire floor collapsed into the tinsmith's shop 12ft below, taking 300 people with it. There seems to be a difference of opinion as to injuries, one paper saying "one man had his leg broken", while another claimed "there are a few broken arms and legs and a great many bruises, but no deaths". Many commented on the fact that the platform that the General had been performing on only two minutes previously crashed down with the rest of the floor.

39. General Tom Thumb

1846_03_30 MANCHESTER (Theatre Royal).   ONSTAGE FIRE

At a fire which happened at this new theatre the previous year shortly before opening, the chief loser had been Mr Graham who lost a number of costumes valued at £100. This performance, a benefit for the actor, had attracted a bumper audience, as knowledge of his loss was added to the ongoing popularity of the performer. All had been going well until around 10pm. The curtain was down and the audience was astonished to see two gentlemen jump down on to the stage from the nearest box. One man, peering behind the curtain, exclaimed: 'Good God! The theatre is on fire!' At this there was consternation as people rose and were making for the exits, when Mr Wallack the manager stepped on to the stage and assured them there was no danger. The fire, only a small one, was at that moment being extinguished, and they should resume their seats. Most obeyed though a few continued on their way out of the theatre.

Within a few minutes Wallack returned and said the fire was more serious than they had thought and recommended the audience now to leave the building in an orderly manner. Most left speedily but calmly, except for the pit where there was much pushing and jostling, with people ending up on the ground and others trampling over them.

The cause of fire was a perennial one, a draught had been caused by moving scenery flats, this had flapped one of the borders which had touched a gas jet in the nearest batten. With one border alight, the flames spread to adjoining ones until some five borders above the stage were all ablaze. A feature of the new building was a tank of water on the roof containing 20,000 gallons of water with pipes going to taps in several parts of the building. A flexible hose was attached to the nearest water point and a jet of water soon quenched the flames. The stage was, of course, drenched with water so the performance had to be abandoned at that point.

1846_08_31 HAMBURG, Germany (Theatre). FATAL FALL OF CHANDELIER

From London, the theatre had ordered a splendid new bronze chandelier for gas lights. This magnificent piece weighed 10,800lbs. While it was being hauled up, the rope broke and the whole enormous mass fell, smashing all to pieces and fatally crushing two Englishmen who had come with the chandelier to supervise the suspension.

1847_02_28 CARLSRUHE, Germany (Grand Ducal). FATAL PRE-SHOW FIRE

The fire broke out around 5pm before the start of the performance while the audience was still assembling. The cause was a draught of air in one of the Court boxes wafting drapery on to a gas light. The blaze spread rapidly and the people in the gallery were suffocated by smoke where they sat. The lower tiers struggled to get out, having to break through doors that were locked. By 10pm the fire was extinguished but only two walls were left standing. The final death toll was 62 plus 200 injured.

1847_03_21 COPENHAGEN, Denmark. FATAL FALL OF CHANDELIER

[In the mid 19th century it was not the practice to have the auditorium in darkness while the play was being acted, such as is the norm today, but there were attempts to dim the auditorium to enhance the stage effects in certain scenes. Richard Wagner was a pioneer of getting the audience to sit in the dark. Alternatively, sometimes it was necessary to raise the chandelier in a theatre because it blocked the view from the gallery. The easiest way to solve both these problems was to raise the central chandelier, in some cases a recess in the ceiling could enable it to be hauled totally out of view. It is possible that something of the sort was being attempted here.]

The "ponderous chandelier" was drawn up after the second act of *Don César de Bazan*. Suddenly the lustre descended at a rapid rate as far as the uncovered boxes where it hit eleven people with such violence they were all stunned and carried out "in a lamentable state" to hospital where three subsequently died. On immediate investigation it was found that when the time had come for the lustre to be lowered only two of the four-man team had been present. The pair decided that they would not hold up proceedings searching for the two absent colleagues and attempted to lower the lustre between them. This was a grave error as the weight was more than they could manage and the chandelier descended rapidly in an unchecked run.

There were several cases where chandeliers crashed to the ground in the Victorian period, so the scene in *Phantom of the Opera* was not just a stage effect but true to life.

1847_12_08 LONDON (Strand).   AUDIENCE MEMBER FALLS INTO PIT

During a performance of *Valentine and Orson*, a gentleman was observed sitting on the edge of his box with one foot on the seat. Losing his balance, he fell head first into the pit, striking the orchestra partition rail with great force. Mr Fox Cooper the manager stopped the show and had the man conveyed backstage, to await medical attention after which he was taken home in a cab .

1847_12_29 LONDON (Sadler's Wells).   FAULTY GASLIGHT IN THE GALLERY

For some time, a gas light at the back of the gallery had needed attention and repair. It was the manager's intention to have it seen to in due course. After 8pm every part of the house became crowded to excess. One of the check-takers, unaware that the light was out of order, simply thought it had gone out so put a match to it. The flame rushed out with alarming force so a cry of 'Fire!' was instantly raised. There was some disorder, but calm was quickly restored allowing the play to proceed.

1848_03_18 LEEDS (Temporary Circus).   COLLAPSE OF SEATING

[Pablo Fanque, a "man of colour", (1810–1871) was born William Darby at Norwich. Apprenticed at the age of 11 to circus proprietor William Batty, he made his first appearance at Norwich in 1821, as Young Darby. He was versatile, performing equestrian acts, rope walking, tumbling, etc. Once established as a young adult, William Darby changed his professional name to Pablo Fanque. He left Batty and joined Ducrow for a spell, returning to Batty before starting his own show in 1841 which he ran for some 30 years. Pablo married Susannah Marlow and they had two sons.]

Pablo had moved into a temporary circus building for a season in Leeds and on this night the show was a benefit for William Wallett a clown known as 'the Queen's Jester' having once appeared before Victoria at Windsor Castle. Wallett was a good friend and colleague and, on occasion, also a business partner. Wallett being a popular performer, the circus was packed with 3000 for his benefit.

Pablo's son was performing on the tightrope when there was an enormous crash and a huge section of the seating collapsed throwing down 500

40. *Part of Opening Night bill at the new venue*

people. Many were bruised and maimed, around 50 being injured. There was only one fatality – that of Mrs Pablo Fanque. She had been in the pay box which was placed under the gallery, chatting to Mrs Wallett. Mrs Fanque, hit on the head by a falling timber, died instantly; Mrs Wallett, seriously injured was taken to a nearby pub. The building had been erected in November for Charles Hengler's circus. It was constructed to the plans of Hengler's surveyor who supervised the work of William Britton a local joiner. At the inquest, Joseph Woodhead, a joiner and builder, stated he had been the recognised builder of such places, having built every one in Leeds for the past 20 years except the last two. His examination of the debris led him to deduce that whilst the longitudinal beams were strong enough in themselves they had mortise holes in them which weakened them. They were old roof beams, dry and brittle, taken from a disused chapel and should have been supported by upright props, presumably with tenon tops to slot into the mortise holes. The excessive weight of the crowd caused the unsupported lateral beams to snap.

Britton said he recalled that there were such props, Woodhead stated he did not see any in the wreckage and if there had been props there would have been no collapse. He expressed surprise that anyone should have built the place without. Britton said that there had been props, there was positively a prop at every bearer, he would not have left any without. He agreed that inspecting the wreckage did not reveal any such props. He then stated that Hengler had used the part under the gallery for storage and the likelihood was that Hengler's men removed them when getting their things out and away. He then went on to say he was intending to dismantle the building, but when Mr Pablo offered to hire it he let him have it as it stood, free to make any alterations at his own expense. Mr Pablo's own surveyor had inspected the building and declared it satisfactory. Pablo had been operating there for 14 days before the accident occurred.

The coroner said despite the death of Mrs Pablo, and injuries to some 40 people, he could see no grounds of culpable negligence, though commented on the practice of packing in more people than a building could safely hold. The verdict was 'Accidental Death'. In June 1848, widower Fanque married Elizabeth Corker, a 22-year-old circus rider, and with her had two further sons.

1848_04_17 LIVERPOOL (Adelphi). RIOT

The lessee of this minor theatre was one J Corbet Cooke (no relation to the circus Cookes). Among his promotions was a three-night engagement of the opera singer Madame Anna Thillon. He was warned that while there would be great interest in seeing this star – who had appeared in the town the previous year – they would not turn out to see her at the Adelphi. Heeding this warning, Cooke arranged to transfer the show to the upmarket Theatre Royal where, in spite of all, the whole night turned out to be a fiasco.

The first piece was an opera called *The Young Guard* but there were no band parts as the star had forgotten to bring them with her, so a concert was substituted. No notice had been given of this apart from flyers at the door which only a few persons had received. There was an outcry at this so Cooke offered money back to anybody choosing to leave; 219 people preferred this option. After the concert there was a ballet which was again poorly received as it used old well-known scenery, lacked props and was patently under-rehearsed. This was followed by an operetta in which only Madame knew the words, so the curtain had to be lowered. Mr Rice the stage manager came forward and said anybody who wished to leave without seeing the rest of the entertainment could leave now, and get tickets for the next performance when all would have been sorted out. There was a general rush for the doors at that point, after which the operetta was tried again with scripts in hand, but even then one actor was so inept he was mocked, and walked off in high dudgeon.

41. *Anna Thillon*

Even on the last of the three nights when all the music had arrived and things had settled down, there was a problem as the operetta was performed without any songs at all. More uproar when Mr Rice had to explain that M. Thillon had left town and inadvertently taken the music with him. All this would have been reprehensible at the Adelphi but was outrageous at the Theatre Royal.

I assume as a result, Cooke was plunged into debt, because back home the Adelphi company started operating on a sharing basis headed by Charles Rice. On this night, the performance had been scheduled as a benefit for Mr Cooke who was variously described as 'lessee' and 'late lessee'. After the first piece ended, the place was plunged into total darkness with the audience at a loss to know why. After a few minutes a voice from the pit asked them all to be quiet for a while, and no doubt the management would make an announcement. The people waited in the dark but no explanation was forthcoming. After 20 minutes restlessness set in, with the gallery audience tearing up the benches, throwing them into the pit, starting smashing all the non-functioning lights and generally setting out to wreck the place. The problem was simple. Cooke had not paid his gas bill so had been cut off.

1848_10_03 YORK (Theatre Royal).   DRUNK FALLS DOWN STEPS

William Dobson, "was in the gallery of the theatre in a state of intoxication" clutching a bottle of rum. Attempting to leave for a few minutes, he got to the top of the gallery stairs, lost his balance and tumbled head first down the flight of 20 stone steps severely bruising all parts of his body and cutting the side of his head. He was immediately lifted up by two policemen and taken to York County Hospital where he rapidly recovered. Proof that the Lord looks after children and drunkards.

1848_12_26 LONDON (Victoria).   FRENZY

42. *Note the excessively crowded gallery and pit in the Victoria's panto audience*

It was Boxing Day when new pantomimes made their debut. During the afternoon a great many people gathered early at the gallery door to ensure their seats, some arriving at 2pm for doors opening at 6pm. As soon as the door was opened a huge surge forward rushed up the gallery steps which in a very short time were jammed tight. Men, women and children were packed together and cried for those below to back down, but those below were reluctant to give place. In the upper part, in spite of cries of "Oh, save us!" and even "Murder!" there was no sign of easing, and the weaker people were thrown to the floor and trampled on. A hand rail collapsed under pressure, resulting in about 30 people hurled underfoot. Several men tried to pass children and weaker folk to safety over the heads of others. There is a witness report of one man literally picking up a boy and throwing him downstairs as the boy cried "Murder!" On landing, the lad cried out "Oh I am killed."

Eventually, the stairs were cleared and the wounded were taken to Mr Sewell's surgery where two boys were found to be "quite dead". These were William Phillips (11), and John Costello (15). Several seriously injured were taken to hospital. It seems incredible in the circumstances, but the evening's entertainment, including the pantomime, went ahead as normal.

With the post mortem revealing the two boys had been suffocated, the inquest jury said there should be additional ventilation on the stairs, and the doors should not be opened so early. An interesting sidelight to this affair was press comment that the English system of opening gallery and pit doors allowing crowds to flock in fighting their way to the pay box, then once in the auditorium all clambering for the front seats, was considered by foreigners to be totally bizarre for a civilised nation. It was a system that had been customary since theatre patents were first granted in 1662. Readers may be as surprised as I was to discover that France and other continental theatres had a queuing system much like the present-day one at post offices and airports with zig-zag barriers controlling an orderly movement. Now the situation is reversed, the British queue and the continentals indulge in a free-for-all.

1848_12_28 CHESTER (Theatre).   RIOT

[Charlotte Cushman (1816–1876) made her first professional appearance in Boston, USA in 1835. She went on to play leading roles including Romeo to her younger sister's Juliet. She became known for this duet, and also for her portrayal of Lady Macbeth. Cushman became involved romantically with several women before meeting the journalist, writer and part-time actress Matilda Hays in 1848. For the next ten years the two would be together almost constantly. They became known for dressing alike, and in Europe were publicly known as a couple.]

The name of Mr Corbet Cooke will be familiar from the riot at the Adelphi Theatre (*see above* 1848_04_17). It appears that gentleman after leaving Liverpool then essayed a season at nearby Chester. Unfortunately, "the speculation has been a losing affair." In an effort to turn things round he engaged the star American actress Charlotte Cushman and Matilda Hays to appear as Romeo and Juliet respectively in the well-known tragedy.

While Cushman was almost a guaranteed attraction in major cities through her dubious private reputation, she obviously did not mean much in Chester, not even when appearing on the public stage with her new paramour. The house was meagre with little more than £18 taken at the doors. The play proceeded as usual until the love scene in Act II when any audience may have enjoyed the titillation of two real life lesbian lovers enacting the most romantic lovers in all fiction. But that was not to be, as all the actors suddenly went on strike. They had not been paid for some time, and had only continued on the hopes of getting a share of a decent house because of Miss Cushman. Finding out that the entire takings had been taken by Mr Poole the printer to pay outstanding unpaid bills, the actors refused to continue. Miss Cushman offered £5 of her own money if the players would continue but they were adamant. On hearing this, the audience

43. *Cushman and Hays*

rioted, the pit people smashing up the benches, the box customers tearing up the cushions from the boxes and throwing them about the house, while up in the gallery benches were torn up and thrown into the pit below. These major assaults were accompanied by the hurling of fruit and vegetables. The lights were gradually extinguished and the audience induced to leave.

1849_02_05 LONDON (Strand).   RIOT

At 11pm there was a major disturbance at this theatre when it was realised that only three of the four items were to be given. By way of compensation, Miss Terrey sang some songs and danced, but this was not sufficient to quell the rage of the gallery which took the usual form of ripping up the benches and hurling them into the pit. The ringleaders who were all arrested were Randall, Harrington and Carroll. The first two were ordered to find £20 for bail and Carroll was fined 10/-.

1849_02_17 GLASGOW (Theatre Royal).   NEEDLESS PANIC

There were some accidents like the Ring and Exeter theatre fires of such enormity or infamy that they still live on today. This is such another that took place in a theatre less than ten years old.

At 7.45pm in the Theatre Royal, a most reprehensible act occurred that led to a major panic and a multitude of deaths. A man sitting at the front of the upper gallery (admission 3d) lit his pipe and threw down on to the floor the blazing paper he had used in the process "in a most culpable and careless manner." The sight of the smoke raised a cry of 'Fire!' and immediately panic seized the entire population of the gallery and a mass exodus took place. This was thwarted by the gallery doors which opened inwards, so that the force of the panicking people was holding them fast. The accumulation of bodies built up in the fetid staircase with more and more piling into, and on to, those already stuck fast in the stairway. Most of the victims dying from suffocation were young men and girls under the age of twenty.

Meanwhile, the small fire that had started the panic in the upper gallery had been put out by staff with a few buckets of water. The audience in the lower gallery, boxes and pit had remained calm and in their seats throughout. Once that had been dealt with, attention was given to the horror in the stairs to the upper gallery. The stage became a charnel house as dead bodies were laid out there when retrieved. When the full tally of deaths was made there were – age in brackets – 1 [3], 1 [10], 1 [11], 8 [12], 2 [13], 4 [14], 7 [15], 12 [16], 12 [17], 4 [18], 2 [20], 1 [21], 1 [22], 1 [43], 8 [Unknown]. In all 65 dead. It is particularly distressing to learn that "Mrs McEwan lost three promising boys in the catastrophe". All these deaths were caused by the initial act of a stupid man dropping a small piece of burning paper which he could have merely stamped on.

The victims were all of a decent industrial class – trades people and apprentices – although it was the case that some of the latter would have been there without the knowledge of their parents. Proof of this was given by the fact that, without exception, all the funerals were private ones, paid for by the families. No parochial aid was sought, though would have been forthcoming if requested. The gallery was always the haunt of the "thriftless rabble" and it is not supposed that there were none of these present. They would have been there all right but occupying the front seats which they always managed to achieve by being selfish and uncouth. The gallery entrance was always at the back – at the highest point of the gallery – so on entering there is naturally a desire to charge down the steps to bag the front seats. Therefore the people at the back, nearest the exit, get out first, as the front rows have to climb back up the stairs. On this occasion these front people were totally safe because they could not attempt to get out even if they tried.

This anecdote vividly illustrates the position at the time of the panic: "A boy, an apprentice to a smith and edge tool maker in the eastern part of the city, was seated in the upper gallery, alongside of a man who had a child in his arms, of which he was understood to be the father. When the panic got up the man handed over the child to the boy desiring him to attend to it till he saw what all the noise was about. The man then bolted. The boy sat still, nursed the bairn, and finally made his way quietly out of the house after the panic was over. In Dunlop Street, he found the cowardly father and presented him with his child. We scarcely know whether most to commend the coolness of the youth, or shudder at the heartlessness of the parent."

Two evenings following the tragedy were devoted to benefits in aid of the families of the stricken and dead. Only £50 was raised from the two.

1849_05_10 NEW YORK, USA (Astor Opera).   INFAMOUS RIOTS

These infamous riots, known as the Astor Place Riots, have been very widely written about ever since they occurred, so the words here are little more than a précis. The leading Shakespearean actor of the day in Britain was William Charles Macready who, like many of his confreres, also toured America. The principal home-grown American actor was Edwin Forrest, a tragedian who played much the same repertoire as Macready. He, in turn, toured in the British Isles. By this date, each had appeared twice in the other's country. Forrest becoming jealous of Macready's success, on the latter's second US tour, followed him from date to date, deliberately playing the same roles in opposition. Some newspapers – especially in America – seemed to delight in presenting the two actors as rivals in a contest. Forrest was gratified when the American newspapers clearly preferred him to Macready. On his second British tour, less successful than his previous one, Forrest mistakenly became obsessed with the idea that Macready had somehow raised an opposition against him.

44. *Edwin Forrest*

45. *William Macready*

So we come to Macready's third and final USA tour. Apart from the partisans of Forrest, a greater hostility came from the policy of Nativism which, standing for 'the American way of life' was the creed of various secret and overt organisations with a hatred of all things foreign and a background of rioting whenever a suitable occasion arose for protest. Macready's farewell performances at the Astor Opera House were the ideal catalyst for these malcontents.

On 7 May, Macready gave his Macbeth, but not a word was heard. The audience was well supplied with pockets of Forresters and Nativists making such a racket and throwing such an assortment of things that the whole thing was like a mime performance. Macready stood his ground throughout, but after the curtain finally fell he declared he would perform no more in America. On the following day, Macready received a formal request from a committee of prominent New York citizens, asking him to continue with his planned performances, assuring him that the good sense and the

83

goodwill of respectable citizens would quash the rioters. The Nativists, though having some good and sensible men among them, were really a collection of working class rabble rousers who thought anything English was aristocratic and 'snooty'. Macready acceded to the requests and his next performance was scheduled for 10 May. It is clear from Macready's attitude that he was placated by the sight of police out in full force, while not understanding the underlying hatred was not only for himself but more for what he represented to the organised gangs of the Bowery class of workers; the whole set up being a sort of extra virulent form of extreme trades unionism mixed with a dash of Mafia.

Macready's Macbeth sailed through the play with chaos outside, hooligans breaking lights and windows, fracturing water mains so that parts of the theatre became flooded, and similar vandalism. The chandelier was shattered and battering rams pounded the doors. Still Macready played on as did the whole cast, and at the end he actually went on for a call and made a short speech of farewell though not a word could be heard. At last, he must have thought, it was over and he was not going to risk performing any more. But how was he going to get out of the theatre, now in a state of siege? None of the audience could attempt to leave in safety. Unknown to Macready, the police chief had admitted that the full force of his men would be inadequate and the New York Guard was standing by. The police had been withdrawn at 9pm with the military now in charge. It was estimated that 10,000 people were in the streets surrounding the theatre. The military fired guns into the air and when that proved futile fired into the crowd. Many of those killed were innocent bystanders, and almost all of the casualties were from the working class; seven of the dead were Irish immigrants. Between 20 and 30 rioters were killed, and 48 wounded. 50 to 70 policemen were injured, as were 141 militiamen.

46. *The Astor Place riots*

1850_04_20 LONDON (Drury Lane).   AUDIENCE MEMBER FALLS FROM GALLERY

A man in the dress of a baker, somewhat inebriated, bought a seat in the upper gallery. On entering he ran down the steps to the front, and unable to stop himself rolled over the front, falling below. At this theatre, the fronts of the galleries were not flush to one another, the lower gallery protruding forward further than the upper gallery, so that the man did not fall right down to the pit but merely into the lower gallery. As it was, he had to be taken to King's College Hospital by stretcher. It was fortunate there were not as yet any persons in that part of the lower gallery, thereby avoiding injuring anybody else in his fall.

1851_09_15 LYONS, France (Celestins).   DIABOLICAL MURDER COMMITTED AT THEATRE

Professor and Madame Ricard were watching a performance of *Adrienne Lecouvreur* in the Theatre des Celestins when the young man sitting behind her reached over and stabbed Madame in the breast with a large knife causing her to cry out and blood to spurt forth over people near her. Her husband at her side, not seeing the knife or blood, simply thinking she had been struck by some lout, demanded "What have I done, that you strike my wife?" The murderer replied with great *sang froid* "Nothing I don't even know you." Madame Ricard was immediately removed to a salon and medical attention sought, but all efforts were fruitless and she died. The man who had done this foul deed, called Jobard (20), was promptly arrested as he made no attempt to flee.

The bizarre story behind this was that Jobard, having embezzled money from his employer and fearing detection, resolved to do away with his life. However, being a person of strong religious upbringing, he could not condone suicide and decided that if he committed a crime that would send him to the scaffold there would be sufficient time between the perpetration of the crime and the punishment to make his peace with the Almighty. After buying a suitable knife he considered various persons as his victim including the President, a priest, and a prostitute in a brothel, all of whom he rejected for one reason or another. Finally he decided to kill a woman totally unknown to himself, hence the carnage at the theatre. Jobard wrote all this down in a lucid, detailed and methodical manner in a letter which he sent to his parents.

Apparently, two years previously Jobard's elder brother committed suicide by blowing his brains out at a dinner to celebrate his conclusion of law studies. While in prison, Jobard was visited by his mother who talked to the chaplain and said in the last three years no fewer than seven members of her family had committed suicide. At his trial several doctors who had examined Jobard came to the conclusion he was suffering from monomania, but another expressed the opinion that he was fully conscious of what he was doing when he carried out the crime. The jury brought in a verdict of 'guilty of murder under extenuating circumstance.' The judge condemned him to hard labour at the hulks for life. Jobard heard the sentence without showing the slightest emotion. The conclusion must be that insanity ran rampant in the Jobard family.

1851_12_01 WHITEHAVEN (Theatre).   RIOT

It was announced in advance by Dr Darling that Mrs T L Loveless would give a talk on "the novel and attractive subject of Bloomerism". Mr John Theophilus Jones arrived on the night to arrange matters and sell tickets. The theatre was opened and lit, while a respectable audience gathered. Alas, no lecturer made her appearance, neither was Mr Jones to be found. It appeared he, like the takings, had disappeared. After demanding their money back, several people then starting leaving, but when the money ran out others started wrecking the place. The police arrived and prevented further destruction of the property.

Jones was captured at Workington and arrested. He admitted to fleeing because the audience was angered, but had taken no money. On the contrary, Jones had not received his agreed fee for supervising the advertising and managing the evening. To his rescue came his principal Dr Darling who explained all. He had gone to Edinburgh, where Mrs Loveless had just spoken, to escort her by train to Whitehaven. The lady was taken ill and they were delayed in getting to the station, missing the train by a mere three minutes. As there would be a delay he sent a letter to Jones explaining the situation. Jones did not receive this in time, though it was produced in court the following day. Darling agreed to pay for the damage to the theatre which amounted to £7, and discharged all demands. On that basis the case was dismissed and Darling stated the lady would positively appear on the following day Wednesday. Adverts proclaiming the new date promptly appeared. Mrs Loveless and her advocacy of bloomers were very popular with free-thinking females of the day.

47. Bloomers

1853_03_19 HONG KONG, China (Theatre).   FATAL FIRE IN BAMBOO THEATRE
The Chinese theatre at Whampoa, Hong Kong, caught fire during a performance. The theatre was built of bamboo and matting so when a spark from a fire cracker set light to the mat roof, the combustible nature of the place meant within 15 minutes the whole was ablaze. No fewer than 60 females were burnt to death and many more severely injured.

1853_03_23 MOSCOW, Russia (Imperial).   FATAL MAJOR DAYTIME FIRE
Fire blazed out at the Imperial French Theatre at 10am when 60 pupils of the Conservatoire were attending dance classes. They were saved with difficulty, some being wounded and bruised. Several children were thrown from windows into blankets held below. The fire spread with such rapidity that within three hours the destruction was complete but the fire continued to burn for two days. All that was left of "one of the finest buildings in Europe" were blackened walls. The building housed two auditoria, wardrobes, library and everything necessary for the everyday running of two theatres. The on-site employees numbered 150, and the venue gave work to 1000 people. The number of known deaths was 11, and the financial loss estimated at 3 million roubles (12 million francs).

1853_11_26 LIVERPOOL (Royal Amphitheatre).   AUDIENCE MEMBER FALLS FROM GALLERY
A young man named Connolly fell over the front of the gallery into the pit, landing on a rare empty bench. There was great consternation in the house, and Mr Copeland the lessee was immediately on the spot. The distance from gallery to pit was great, and severe injury, if not death would be expected. Astonishingly, apart from being a little stunned, the man was unhurt. He was taken to the nearby chemist shop of Mr Sutton, where examination showed no external injuries. A few minutes later Connolly re-entering the theatre, watched the show to the end. He was intoxicated.

1854_02_15 LONDON (Drury Lane).   AUDIENCE MEMBER DIES IN SEAT

On this evening a respectably-dressed young man, his brother and two friends were sitting in the pit, watching a performance of *Hamlet*. Suddenly the young fellow fell forward off his seat and on being picked up was found to be dead. "The melancholy occurrence cast a gloom over the occupants of the pit, which was not dispelled during the evening."

The play is hardly a bundle of laughs at the best of times so the gloom that night must have been really gloomy. A heart attack was assumed to be the cause, with the young man suffering some disease of which he was ignorant.

1854_02_26 NEW ORLEANS, USA (French).   DROPPING OF GALLERY

During a show at the French Theatre, two galleries, "set aside for persons of colour", fell a distance of three feet resulting in many persons and lots of chairs being showered on the people sitting below. The cause of the collapse was that the galleries were held up by suspending iron rods from the roof, rather than supported from below by columns. These rods broke near the roof and the reason that the fall was not greater, or the destruction of lives wholesale, was the presence of further side supporting iron rods from the walls to the galleries. This unusual arrangement was the builder's worthy desire to omit pillars which would obscure the view of the stage from the dress circle.

The human damage was fairly small considering what would have happened if the galleries had crashed immediately down on to the pit. Two deaths occurred - Florian Malus, a notary's clerk, was killed instantly by being hit on the head by one of the iron bars, and also Fergus Toledano a youth of 14 years.

87

1854_05_30c PARIS, France (Grand Opera).   SUICIDE

This is another example of a suicide in the auditorium, which seems an odd place to do such a deed. This one was successful in May 1854. "A tragic circumstance took place on Monday evening, at the Grand Opera, Paris. During the latter part of Myerbeer's opera of *The Prophete*, a shot was fired in one of the side boxes. The greatest alarm instantly prevailed throughout the house, under the impression it was an assassination, but it turned out to be a suicide. The unfortunate man was a Prussian officer." *Norfolk News* 1854_06_03.

1854_08_28 BOLTON (Temporary theatre).   STAGEHAND SETS LIGHT TO HIMSELF

A stagehand, attempting to light a naphtha lamp, managed to set fire to his hand and clothes. To rid himself of the naphtha he threw it at the scenery which immediately combusted, causing the audience to rise as one and flee for the exits. In doing so, several people were injured and many items of loose outer clothing shed. Two nights later some miscreants destroyed part of the wooden walling.

1854_12_23 LONDON (Queen's).   AUDIENCE MEMBER FALLS FROM GALLERY

The gallery side-slips had the railings a yard higher than the gallery itself and it was handy for youths to climb over the bars to get access to the front seats in the gallery proper. On this night a young man, attempting the manoeuvre, slipped and fell, passing both upper and dress circles and a further 20ft to land in the pit. Astonishingly, nobody in the pit was injured, and even weirder the man himself, though shaken, had no injuries and remained in the pit to watch the show.

1855_04_28 BIRMINGHAM (Spread Eagle). NEEDLESS PANIC

This venue was a lofty brick erection at the rear of the Spread Eagle Tavern and on this night some 800 people were present in the 1200 seat venue. Around 9pm, a person in the upper gallery noticed smoke rising from the floor. Afterwards it was found that the smoke was caused by a piece of lighted paper igniting a small quantity of sawdust, but that was not known at the time. The alarm of fire spread immediate terror, and the audience in the gallery, collectively rising, fled towards the exit. As in many places at this time, entrance to the gallery was via a narrow staircase with a single door at the top.

Those in the rear rushing forward pushed those in front, causing them to stumble and fall in the narrow passage at the foot of the stairs. The falling bodies were immediately covered with another lot in a similar predicament, as the rear pressure forced more and more casualties. The narrow passage was choked up with prostrate bodies. People trying to help had to lift up the top layer and get them out, only to find they had been replaced by another layer. Dragging people out from the middle of the stairs was very difficult to achieve, thus it was a long time before all could be removed. It was then that three dead bodies were found – Pc Balance who was on duty at the hall, a young woman of 18, and a youth named Cressday. Seven people were injured severely enough to be sent to hospital.

There had been no cause for alarm. The small fire could have been efficiently quashed without anybody even being aware of it. If all had remained in their seats they would have been safe. It was the panic that killed them.

1855_09_18 LONDON (Garrick). AUDIENCE MEMBER FALLS DOWN STEPS

"On Tuesday night, a respectable female named Mary Sullivan, aged 43 years, while in the act of descending the stone steps leading to the pit saloon, by some means lost her equilibrium, and fell a depth of 15 feet, whereby she received a most extensive laceration of the scalp and fracture of the skull. She now lies in the London Hospital in a precarious state." *Morning Post* 1855_09_20.

1856_01_14 LONDON (Surrey). ALLEGED MURDER IN THE AUDIENCE

This is a most mysterious affair, and even after the trial that followed, circumstances are unclear. This entry is pieced together from subsequent statements. Henry James Cornwell (11) went with his mother, a neighbour Mrs Frances Jones, and Sergeant Salter of the City Police to the Surrey Theatre on Monday evening. Mrs Jones and Henry could not see the stage so both stood on their seats. Behind them were Thomas Sydenham (40) and another man, who asked them to sit down as they also were then obliged to stand to see over them. Mrs Jones said if they sat down they would see nothing whereupon one man said "Knock her down". Sydenham then pushed Mrs Jones aside and forced Henry out of his place. Mrs Jones remonstrated with "Don't push the boy about".

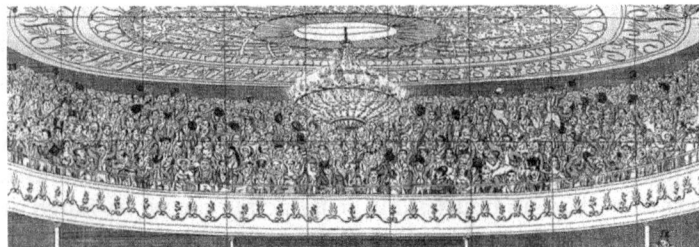

48. *A crowded gallery. Seating was in continuous benches with no aisles. The sole entrance was in a back corner. Also see cover picture.*

Things seemed to have settled down for 45 minutes after that, then the boy started fidgeting about. Mrs Jones said "Harry, stand quiet." Henry replied that he couldn't because the man behind was pinching him. Mrs Jones saw that Sydenham had his hands between the boy's thighs. Henry pointed at Sydenham and said "This is the man who pinched me" and started crying. Mrs Jones then called for Salter who was sitting a short distance away, and said to Sydenham "What did you pinch the boy for?" The reply was "My dear woman, I have done nothing of the kind." Salter now took over and had the two men removed. Sydenham was brought before magistrate's the following day and fined 40/- for assaulting Mrs Jones. There was no charge for assaulting the boy.

However, on the way home from the theatre after the pinching incident, Henry had complained very much of the pain and shortly afterwards become very unwell. Mrs Jones, who lived nearby, went to see the boy several times and reported he was not as cheerful as he was wont to be. On 19 February, Henry became much worse and was confined to bed, where Salter visited him. The lad uttered these words "Mr Salter, I am dying from the injuries I've received from that man at the Surrey Theatre." Salter said he would go and see the magistrate and tell him about it. The boy then said "That will not save my life; but have me opened after I am dead, Mr Salter." Henry died the following morning.

An inquest was held and a verdict of manslaughter was returned against Sydenham. At the Old Bailey, Sydenham was tried before a jury and further details of the post mortem were aired. Mr Saunders the pathologist suggested death was from peritonitis caused by violent pinching. When asked by the judge if peritonitis could have been caused by anything else, the surgeon replied it might have been "brought on by other things, such as a cold etc." When asked by the judge if the witness could say positively that "the act of the prisoner was the cause of death." The surgeon's reply was an emphatic "Certainly not, my Lord." After the judge's summing up, the jury took only a few minutes to pass a verdict of "Not Guilty".

1856_03_05 LONDON (Covent Garden).   FIRE DESTROYS COVENT GARDEN THEATRE
[This majestic building was one of the two original patent theatres in London. Its history went back to the Restoration. However, it was an expensive house to manage and the old system of keeping a repertory of plays together with all the scenery and costumes for a long period, to be brought out for a day or two at a time, was now long past. It was a nightmare to cover the daily expenses of simply keeping the place open, so as well as opera and ballet seasons, the desperate directors were willing to try anything just to keep afloat.]

Thus it was that when Professor Anderson, the Wizard of the North offered £2000 for a ten weeks season from 26 December 1855, they practically snatched his hand off. Many were the howls of derision at the managers for allowing this noble theatre to descend to a home of a fairground charlatan. But being the man who had to find box office draws, manager Gye agreed to the contract.

Anderson offered his usual repertoire of magic and entertainments following a month of loss-making pantomime. After a six week season of magic he decided to close his tenure in grand style with a masked ball. On hearing of this, Gye immediately vetoed the scheme. It was not extraordinary to use theatres for other purposes; both patent theatres had held balls before, as well as promenade concerts and other things. Many of the smaller country theatres were designed so that the pit could be floored over, linking with the stage, thereby creating a large floor area for dinners, dances, auctions etc.

Gye thought the idea was not included in the contract he had made with Anderson, and did not want further obloquy descending on his head. Gye was in Paris at the time, having arranged everything for his new opera season due to follow soon after Anderson had gone, but swayed by the persuasion of his board members, reluctantly gave way and permission.

So the ball went ahead. It was a splendid night and a glittering occasion, continuing into the early hours of the morning. Most dancers left between 2am and 3am, but there were still around 200 stalwarts at 5am when Anderson decided to end the evening by calling for the National Anthem.

49. *After the Ball is Over. Theatre Royal Covent Garden on fire*   image© The British Library Board

It was at this point that a man in conversation with Castle the theatre fireman noticed a bright light through the chinks in the floorboards of the carpenter's shop high above. Like most theatres in the land, the scenery dept was situated above the ornamental ceiling and under the actual roof. At Covent Garden it was a very large open area because of the great dimensions of the auditorium. An open space in the centre of this floor gave access for lighting the grand chandelier.

On investigation, the two men found the place full of black smoke. They could make out a smouldering heap and Castle, attempting to crawl towards it, was defeated by the choking smoke. He retreated, descending a level to open the fire-main on that floor, but was not able to attach a hose before beaten back by pieces of flaming material dropping from above. Again he retreated to a lower deck to try once more there. By now he realised that the fire had a major hold, so he cut away hanging scenery to make a gap where he thought the fire would spread next. The National Anthem had not finished when scenery dropped on to the stage, and Anderson, realising the peril, himself gave the fire alarm. Tumult and chaos began. The few remaining dancers fled, as did anyone else able to do so. There was time to get out a lot of Anderson's magic gear as it was stored near an exit, and the takings were safe. Theatre workers evacuated much of the material from Gye's office.

A great number of fire engines were summoned and the entire fire-fighting forces of the capital were employed. After all, this was one of the grandest buildings in all Europe, the theatre that was the wonder of the world when it opened on 13 September 1809 with *Macbeth*. When at 6am it was clear that all was lost, it was decreed that Mr Gye should be telegraphed in Paris. Professor Anderson does not seem to have had much luck with his theatres – in 1845 his brand new theatre in Glasgow was destroyed by fire within months of being opened, and he also lost one to fire in New York when he was a lessee there. His insurance was limited to £2000 which did not cover his loss. The loss of this venue was thought to be a minimum of £250,000.

1856_10_19 LONDON (Surrey Gardens). NEEDLESS PANIC AT SERVICE

The Rev C H Spurgeon was a popular preacher who attracted thousands of followers, much like the 20th century Billy Graham. There were few religious venues that could accommodate all his audience, the regular Exeter Hall being too small. Thus on Sunday nights when entertainment venues were closed he was able to hire large capacity halls in which to preach. Spurgeon was the foremost of the speakers but there were several others.

On this night he had hired the Surrey Gardens Music Hall (not to be confused with the Surrey Theatre) which had taken as many as 13,000 for Jullien's concerts. The building had three tiers of galleries all packed to capacity, and the ground floor could not accommodate all who wished to be present. It was estimated that 2000 were standing in the aisles and passages, with hundreds more outside hoping to hear the service through the windows.

50. *Surrey Gardens Music Hall*

In the midst of all the preaching and singing, a voice shouted 'Fire!' At once there was a rush for the exits. In vain did Spurgeon announce a hymn which the choir took up, but were all fleeing for the exits. Spurgeon carried on while his audience screamed and scrambled to get out. The platform party assured the audience that all was safe, there was no fire, but the top gallery was where the mischief arose and which suffered the most as, in spite of three exits, people went to the one where they had entered. Men broke windows to leap from, convincing the ignorant that the fire was real. Steps and passages became jammed tight as people were trampled underfoot by the pressure from those behind.

When all was over, there were seven dead and 300 wounded. At the inquest the question arose whether the panic was deliberately concerted by rivals of Mr Spurgeon but that was dismissed. Also quashed was the suggestion it was the work of thieves as the hall was so full they could not gain admittance. It was believed that three youths on the ground floor had made for the door shouting 'Fire!' and it was highly probable that it was meant as a prank.

1857_03_12 HUDDERSFIELD (Theatre Royal).   BOXES COLLAPSE AT POLITICAL MEETING

At a political meeting to hear Mr Cobden, 2000 people, many of them boys, crowded into the theatre. During his speech there was a loud crack and investigation showed that one of the wooden supports to the left side boxes had split. The occupants were approached and advised to vacate the boxes but they refused claiming it was only the noise of a bench breaking that had been heard. Then there was a tremendous crash as the right side boxes gave way, precipitating 20 people into the pit below. Several were injured and "the meeting was abruptly terminated." When the building was cleared it was found that the left hand boxes and the stage had sunk nine inches. This venue had started life as a lecture hall and converted into an unsatisfactory theatre around 1841.

1857_02_17 HUDDERSFIELD (Theatre Royal).   RIOT

The town had been peppered with bills advertising an entertainment by Mr Henry Russell *"The Far West, and Sketches of Negro Life"*. At 7pm the man who had hired the theatre and posted the bills opened the door and the people flocked in. By 8pm the place was full, the takings in the region of £30. The audience getting impatient started stamping and shouting as there was no sign of anything happening. The man decamped, the takings going with him, the regular money taker being left to deal with any further customers.

The audience, now realising they had been conned by a swindler, started wrecking the auditorium and police had to intervene. The gas was turned off plunging the place into darkness enabling the police to empty the theatre. While all this was going on, the con-man took a cab to Elland. Opening the cab door at the address given, the driver found his passenger had disappeared, and so had to return unpaid.

1857_05_23 WOOLWICH (Theatre).   RIOT

On Saturday night, after the first piece, the actors gathered backstage and informed the manager William Holbrook that they would not continue with the performance until they were paid their week's salary. Even in these modern times, actors put up with being owed money, optimistically believing promises that it will all be sorted out and settled, so blithely continue giving their services until even the densest thespian realises that no money is ever forthcoming. Holbrook's actors were made of sterner stuff, and when Holbrook said he would pay them after the performance they did not believe him. One of the actors went onstage and announced that the curtain would not rise again and they should all go to the entrances and demand their money back. This did not please the audience and a riot ensued. Every window in the place was smashed, doors taken off hinges and destroyed, benches torn up and thrown about, and gas pipes broken. The damage to the venue was estimated at £50. Holbrook narrowly escaped being injured and applied to the magistrates for summonses against several named persons, and two people were arrested for stealing property during the confusion. He would have been wise to pay his actors.

1857_06_07 LEGHORN, Italy (degli Aquidotti).   PANIC

Another major disaster. Some 3000 people were assembled at the Theatre degli Aquidotti in Leghorn to see the spectacle of the *Siege of Sebastopol*. One of the rockets, let off to imitate the bombardment, set fire to a piece of side scenery. This immediately caused the audience to rise and flee for the exits, many in the boxes and galleries leaping down into the pit. Windows were smashed through as people jumped to save themselves. Officials vainly tried to get the people to leave in an orderly manner saying they were in no danger, but panic overtook common sense and those exhortations were ignored. Later, rumours claimed it was first thought to be a political uprising and that doors were locked, thus delaying the audience getting out. I can find no confirmation that is so.

In fact, there was no need for the audience to attempt to leave, as the fire was contained to the stage, no other part of the theatre damaged in any way. As is often the case in theatre fires, it is the mass stampede that causes deaths and injuries, which in this case numbered 106 dead and about 300 severely injured.

1857_12_15c PARIS, France.   PRIVATE DUEL

This was not an accident but a duel with pistols in the Bois de Vincennes between M Vieyra, auditor of the council of state and M Gay, a clerk in the foreign office. Gay lost, being seriously wounded but expected to recover. Why am I telling you this? Because the cause of the duel was a squabble over a theatre seat!

1858_09_13 SHEFFIELD (Surrey).   NEEDLESS PANIC

This is a record of yet another horrendous panic wherein several died. On this day the Surrey Music Hall in Sheffield re-opened for the third day after an extensive improvement scheme which included magnificent chandeliers. It was a large hall seating some 3000 people, one of the largest of its type in the country. The name Surrey Music Hall will inevitably remind readers of the disaster at the similarly named London hall detailed at 1856_10_19. In fact, the circumstances are indeed comparable. Little has been written about this disaster over the years, this entry being a digest from contemporary newspaper reports.

The audience was fully enjoying the entertainment when at 8.20pm there was a disturbance. It appears a person shot off a pistol in the gallery. The proprietor Mr Youdan immediately took to the stage urging people not to panic and offering £5 reward to anybody identifying the malicious person. Shortly afterwards, three young men in the gallery shouted 'Fire!' and made a hurried exit. Immediately, the shout was taken up and people rushed from the gallery to the exit. The stairs and corridors got jammed, people stumbled, the pressure from those behind forcing them on. Thus it was that five people were crushed to death. The five fatalities comprised four young men – aged between 16 and 18 – all with the typical Sheffield profession of grinders, and an 18-year-old female.

The following investigation was immediately muddied by the fact that Mr Youdans, when going to assist the crush on the gallery stairs, found a woman's velour mantle burning there, and two different opinions arose about the cause of the pistol shot. Another odd aspect was the statement from Inspector Linley that he received word "about 8 o'clock" that the Music Hall was on fire and he went straight there with Detective Officer Brayshaw. When they arrived, Linley made his way up the steps to the first gallery where he heard a shout of 'Fire!' and encountered the rush of people descending the

93

steps. He was in the melee that caused the deaths and injuries. Therefore the message of a fire was sent before the cry of 'Fire!' had occurred.

Taking the incidents in order, the first was when a man went down from the gallery to complain of a smell of gas. A search was made but no evidence of gas could be found. Next came the pistol shot which, it was assumed, was meant to cause terror and panic in the audience. However, Mr Youdan successfully stopped that with his reward announcement. These two ploys failing, the third and most successful attempt was the age-old frightener – the shout of 'Fire!' It was assumed (again, there was a good deal of assuming and little actual fact on searching) that the flaming mantle on the stairs was a belated attempt to verify the warning shout. At this point chaos prevailed as people tried to flee from the supposed fire.

So we come to the inquest. The coroner said he was only concerned with evidence about the five dead bodies, however two youths came up with an alternative story about the pistol shot. William Henry Greaves (19), accompanied by his pal Wilfred Ledger, said he had found a bit of a cigar in his pocket and proposed to smoke it. He struck a match to this end, then there was an explosion. He stated he had smelt gas ever since entering, the noise was a gas explosion not a pistol shot. The following day, Greaves went to Mr Youdan to explain about the gas explosion, claiming he had fled before Youdan made his speech. Greaves was directed to Inspector Linley who, after listening to his tale, then went with the gas inspectors to the gallery where Greaves had been sitting. Ledger was also with the group. No evidence of any fire could be seen, the nearest gas pipe was to a chandelier some four yards away from the indicated spot, and the pipe to it ran under the gallery. The two lads were adamant that a pistol had not been fired and the noise heard was a gas explosion. The coroner adjourned the inquest for two weeks.

Mr Youdan, now confident there was nothing wrong with his gas system, it having been thoroughly checked by experts, re-opened his hall on 17 September with the same company. At the resumed inquest the coroner heard 31 witnesses and still could not declare whether the noise was from a pistol shot or a gas explosion. However, he said that any person bringing a pistol into a crowded public place was either foolish or wicked, but the matter was not really material as the panic had arisen from the later cry of 'Fire!'. Undoubtedly, a person crying out such a thing without due cause was culpable of a criminal act and would have to answer before another tribunal. But nobody could identify such an individual, and neither Mr Youdan nor the police had been able to elucidate the matter. Thus an open verdict must be given, until further evidence be forthcoming.

And that was that. It seems pretty clear to me that for some evil reason, or merely as a prank, this cabal of lads had decided to cause trouble in the newly opened hall. Perhaps they had been paid to do so by a rival? I consider that the gas suggestion was a first attempt to frighten people, the pistol was a second attempt, neither of which worked. The shout of 'Fire!' worked a treat and caused chaos, but Greaves, worried that blame might be attached to him, concocted the far-fetched alibi about a gas explosion. It all seemed so weak, the sole purpose of it being to deflect attention from the truth that he and his cronies were the only ones responsible for the whole farrago. They wanted to empty the place, then took fright when five people were killed as a result.

> "The theatre is the only institution in the world which has been dying for four thousand years and has never succumbed." John Steinbeck (1902-1968)

1858_03_19 BLACKBURN (Theatre Royal).   BAILIFFS RAID THEATRE

This night, the final performance of the season, was a benefit for the lessee Mr C P Plunkett. In the playbill for the evening Mr Plunkett made a desperate appeal for liberal support as, in spite of suffering great losses through poor business, he wanted to leave the town in a "creditable manner". The response to his appeal was good with the house well filled for the event.

The audience was seated, the show about to begin when William Charnley & Son bailiffs stormed in, charged with recovering goods and chattels from Plunkett in lieu of unpaid debts. They behaved in a violent and disruptive manner, bursting into the ladies' dressing room where four actresses were getting ready. The ladies were bare-breasted and Mrs Plunkett asked her dresser to pass her coat so that she may preserve her modesty. John Charnley is said to have put his hand on her breast and squeezed it replying "You don't need, you have a beautiful form; you are all beautiful forms. You don't need covering."

The place was in uproar, as the bailiffs had tried to seize all the box office takings but found only a few coppers left, and the audience knew they would not get their money back. It was also apparent to all that the bailiffs, especially John Charnley had been drinking. During all the chaos, as goods were dragged out, with the audience supporting the actors and vilifying the bailiffs, John Salisbury the owner of the venue arrived with a summons for £9 rent owing. The police appeared and eventually restored calm as the disgruntled audience left without show or refund. The bailiffs were then able to take everything.

Mrs Louisa Plunkett took John Charnley to court for assault which being proved he was fined £5 or two months in prison. "The decision seemed to give great satisfaction to the crowded court."

1858_10_04 LONDON (Surrey).   FATAL FALL FROM GALLERY

Around 6pm an unknown man was seen to run down from the back of the gallery to the side-slip. It seems he thought there was an empty seat and was rushing to gain it. However, a boy had his legs out as he was saving it for a pal. The man jumped over the boy's legs and placed his hands on the protection in front, presumably to steady himself. Nobody could say how it happened that the man toppled over and fell from the gallery to the pit below, as the panelling at that point was 4ft 6ins high and came up to chest level. He was taken to hospital but died within six hours. There was a likelihood he had been drinking. He was never identified.

1858_12_26 LONDON (Victoria).   NEEDLESS PANIC

[The Victoria Theatre which has been mentioned several times previously still exists as the Old Vic and is London's oldest and most historically important theatre. In its long lifetime the building has seen many alterations both inside and out but the roof and exterior shell are original as can be seen in the very early picture on page 69.]

This is another major horror story similar to examples previously mentioned and exactly ten years since a previous tragedy at this venue (*see* 1848_12_26). It was Boxing Day and the new pantomime was a 'must see' attraction. This theatre had an afternoon performance for the first show, followed by an evening one. The attraction was so great that people started queuing for the evening performance hours before to have a chance of getting near the front of the gallery. The gallery entrance was at the top of four flights, each of 16 steps 6ft 6ins wide, with a landing between each flight. Three

95

of these flights were packed tight with waiting customers who had already been there for two hours when a slight leak of gas occurred around 4.20pm. The leak was from a small split in a pipe some 9ft above the floor. The theatre gas man said if ignited it could have burned harmlessly for hours, nevertheless this immediately caused yells of 'Fire!' and attempts by the people at the top of the stairs to escape back downwards. The ones below, not realising that a fleeing mob was about to descend, were sticking fast to their long held places. The inevitable happened – a total wedge of bodies on top of one another, the underneath suffering physical damage and suffocation. Local residents who had heard the news swarmed like flies round the entrance, dragging people out with drunken chants of "More to come! More to come!"

All this was going on unknown to the audience and players inside, who blithely carried on with the matinee performance. A boy in one of the boxes accidentally set light to a packet of fusees (an early form of match) in his pocket without realising it until neighbours cried out he was on fire. This cry was taken up by some in the gallery who tried to exit. They were not allowed to go out by the usual door because of the waiting crowd. Past experience had brought in a system whereby when the matinee finished the audience were released via other exits, the gallery people going via boxes, pit and even over the stage. It is thought that this cry, communicated to the waiting stair crowd, was the cause of the stampede, rather than the leaking gas.

Whatever the initial cause, the tragic result was, apart from the injured, no fewer than 15 youths between the ages of 13 and 18, and a man of 21 were dead. The evening performance went on as normal.

1859_01_01 GLASGOW (Parry's).   AUDIENCE MEMBER KILLED ON LEAVING
Parry's Theatre was a licensed theatre but operated much like the notorious penny gaffs that were mainly frequented by children of the lower classes. About 1pm, at the end of the second show of the day, the audience was rushing out. There was only one step at the door but several people stumbled including 15-year-old Rebecca Montgomery who fell. She was trampled on by the pressing exodus behind. Although rescued as soon as possible, she was insensible when taken to the shop of a surgeon, where she shortly expired.

1859_01_03 LONDON (Polytechnic).   COLLAPSE OF STAIRS

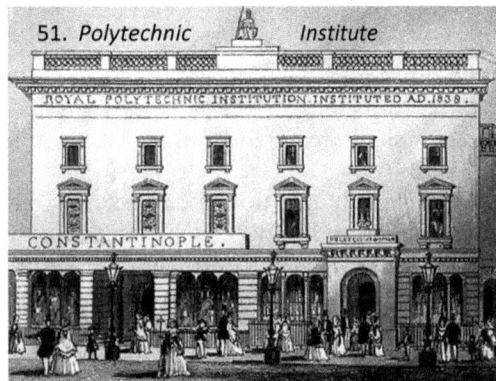
51. Polytechnic Institute

This was a popular venue, especially at Christmas time, as it provided scientific wonders for the common man. The audiences at the festive season were families above the lower classes going to see *Childe's New Phantasmagoria* (a sort of lantern slide ghost show) and *Dissolving Views of Don Quixote*. On this night, the audience of some 800 or so were coming out of the theatre around 10.30pm and descending a staircase to the entrance hall. Most had reached the bottom but there were still people on the stone steps when one flight suddenly collapsed on to the flight below which then also collapsed taking people with it, falling on to those who had reached the ground floor. The steps appeared to have simply broken off at the wall where they were keyed in. Some 40 or 50 people, comprising many women and children, were flung 30ft to the well of the stairs to land on a pile of jagged stone, and have a similar lot of stones fall on them. Around 40 persons were injured, six of them seriously, and Emma Pike (8) was killed.

The reason for these apparently solid stone steps – that had survived for 20 years – suddenly giving way was easy to find, yet it took four adjournments of the inquest to get to the bottom of it. The steps having been traversed by thousands of feet were quite worn down after two decades. Four months prior to the accident, levelling repairs had been carried out in the form of an iron grid laid on each individual step then filled in with concrete. A cutting was made on each step to recess the edge of the grid into the wall, the other end floating unsupported. The weight of this increased each step by 1cwt, making each one 2½cwt. When the steps collapsed it was seen that each individual step had snapped off the wall in the same place leaving 4" only protruding.

The jury did not apportion blame but made several recommendations, the principal one being that all steps should be supported at both ends.

1859_05_20c PARIS, France (Opera Comique).   WOMAN HANGING FROM GALLERY

A young woman climbed over the front of the Upper Gallery and remained there hanging by her hands. People below scampered away in fear of her falling on them and people in the gallery tried to drag her back in but failed. It was soon clear that her strength was fading fast and she would have to let go, but at that stage a powerful man seized her by the arms and dragged her back to safety. She was taken to the commissary of police where it was ascertained she was insane. She must have been!

1859_12_10c NANTES, France (Graslin).   AUDIENCE MEMBER FALLS FROM GALLERY

Rene Tessier (17) was watching a new play called *Le Chateau de Clisson* from a seat in the fourth gallery of the Salle Graslin. Coming back after the interval to resume his seat he lost his balance and fell over the front of the gallery. As each successive gallery was set back from the one below, his fall should have been limited by the third gallery, but there he struck a soldier Alphonse Bretel, bounced off, falling down into the second gallery where he fell against the head of Madame Hortion, thence brushed past a person at the end of the boxes and into the pit. In his fall he is said to have been spread-eagled like a diver. He landed on a front bench that had just been vacated, merely grazing the foot of the person sitting alongside.

The only damage in this bouncing flight seems to have been that the soldier bit his tongue and Madame Hortion had a bump on the head and a bruise on her neck. Tessier had a pain in his thighs and when attempting to walk fell back so was stretchered to hospital.

1861_02_04 DUBLIN (Fishamble Street).   PARTIAL COLLAPSE OF GALLERY

There was an old building known as the Fishamble Street Theatre which, in its past glory days, had been fashionable with eminent actors playing on its boards. I am not sure if this was the same building as the Music Hall which opened in 1741, saw the premier of Handel's *Messiah* the following year, turned into a private theatre in 1793 and was still in use during the early years of the 19th century. But whatever it had been, by 1861 this building had "for many years past been consigned to desolation".

97

On this night however it was the first night of a new venture by one Mickey Free who had taken on the old place and renamed it somewhat grandiloquently as the Royal Lyceum Theatre appealing to amateur societies to rent the place and he also offered a host of theatrical artefacts for hire.

52. *Fishamble Street Theatre*

The place was packed for this new attraction, especially in the gallery where admission was only 3d. Shortly before 10pm the audience were startled, nay, terrified to see the front part of the gallery collapse on to the pit below. The pressure of the unwonted bodies on the rotten timbers had caused them to give way. Some people in the collapsed area managed to cling on to parts of the boxes below, but many were precipitated directly on to those sitting on the pit benches. Remarkably, only one person required hospital treatment, a boy called Michael Walker, whereas all the other battered and bruised people were helped home by friends.

A letter on 6 February from The Secretary of the Oddfellows Dramatic Society assured the public that the "slight damage" had been repaired and their charity show would go ahead as planned that night.

98 **1861_10_28 LONDON (Adelphi).**   QUEUING WOMAN FATALLY FAINTS

A middle-aged woman named Ann Burrows went with a friend to see the popular play *The Colleen Bawn* at the Adelphi theatre. As will have become obvious to readers by now, admittance to the gallery and the pit depended on waiting at the door, and to be sure of getting a decent seat the earlier you were there the better. Thus, for a popular attraction such as a new pantomime or a very successful melodrama crowds formed long before the doors opened. So far so good, but when the doors opened, in place of a queue moving in a proper orderly manner, there was a mad rushing and pushing with rough and rude people at the rear forcing themselves forward with elbows and fists at the ready. This was a nightly occurrence at theatres throughout the land, and had been so ever since the first theatres opened. We have noted many examples of people knocked down and trampled on in the narrow passages and stairs that led to gallery and pit.

53. *Scene from The Colleen Bawn*

On this night, Ann and her friend tried to avoid this scramble by arriving very early, and were at the front when the doors opened. Ann promptly fell down in a faint. It had been a long wait, and by now the entrance way, full of people, was hot and fetid. In spite of press reports at the time, she was not left on the floor for people to trample over, she was actually helped to a chair, and as she did not seem to be recovering was taken to hospital where she died. The post mortem indicated she had a heart fault, and it was assumed that she had died through the excitement of going to the theatre.

1863_06_10 FLORENCE, Italy (Politeama).   FIRE AT CELEBRATION BALL

The theatre was a new elegant open-air amphitheatre which seated 6,000 people. It had opened on 17 May 1862 with a production of *Lucia di Lammermoor* and soon became hugely popular and well attended. A ball was to be held on this day to celebrate the Battle of Solferino, but shortly after the doors were opened, a man passing with a flaming torch on a pole near the proscenium arch decorated with cloth banners brushed against it causing a fire to start. This soon spread to the rest of the building and despite all efforts raged for 20 hours. Three lives were lost. After closure caused by the fire, the theatre reopened in April 1864 and acquired a roof in 1882. By 1911 it had both electricity and heating.

1863_11_23 LONDON (City).   YOUTH FATALLY INJURED IN QUEUE

A youth named Wilkinson (16), a shoeblack, was intending to see the performance at the City Theatre on Monday night. He was early in the queue for the gallery and when the door opened he had a crowd of 40 or so behind him and he was pushed against the door-post. He complained of back pain and could hardly get his breath, but managed to reach the second landing where he again complained. The check-taker Carslake saw the youth doubled up in deep distress on the stairs, and Stainbridge the money-taker seeing him on the floor in agony told him to come up and enter the pay box. He crawled up five steps, and then rolled over, dead.

1863_12_05 LONDON (City).   FATAL ACCIDENT TO CHECK-TAKER   99

The City Theatre, not content with one death on the gallery stairs shortly after suffered another – this time Mr Carslake the aged check-taker. On Wednesday evening the interval was cut short because of the over-running of the first piece, and the gallery audience – keen to get out for refreshment – rushed out, knocking the old guy down stairs with a dozen or so falling with him. He was picked up as soon as possible, but that was after 40 or 50 people had trampled over him. Taken to the nearest surgeon, it was found he had several broken ribs and a broken arm. Transferred to his own home, he had local medical advice, but getting steadily worse was moved to St Thomas's Hospital. He remained in a dangerous condition because of internal injuries later discovered, dying at the "advanced age of 73".

1864_01_29 BRESCIA, Italy (Theatre).   "A strange accident happened at the theatre at Brescia by the falling of the chandelier attached to the ceiling into a crowded pit below, in which many were seriously wounded and several killed." *Stamford Mercury* 1864_01_29.

1864_09_09 LONDON (Adelphi).   NEEDLESS PANIC

Smoke seemed to have appeared in the auditorium, possibly only somebody lighting a pipe, but it caused "some scoundrel in the gallery" to shout "Fire!" at the top of his voice, repeating it four times. Females around also took up the shout, and soon the audience was in turmoil with people crying "Escape for your lives", and running for the doors where they had entered. In doing so they met people still coming in, and a deadlock was caused at every entrance. Women were knocked down, some swooned and had to be carried out into the fresh air, and Mr Prater a man in the pit was forced to the floor and some 30 people trampled over him while rushing for the exit, many stumbling and falling themselves. Police were soon on the scene led by Inspector Bannon who rescued Mr Prater and had him taken to Charing Cross Hospital suffering from a broken arm and internal injuries.

While this panic was in progress Mr Anson was on stage trying to assure the fleeing audience members that there was no fire. The manager Mr Webster offered a handsome reward for information leading to the scoundrel who instigated the panic, the audience returned and the show resumed. All this chaos was simply because some person unknown shouted 'Fire!' when there was no such thing.

1864_10_26 TUSA, Sicily (Theatre).   "A part of a tier of boxes fell into the pit during the performance, carrying with them the persons by whom they were occupied. Two men were killed, and several received serious injuries." *The Scotsman* 1864_10_26.

1864_11_03 LONDON (Surrey).   NEEDLESS SMALL PANIC

George Riley and William Bowdery two sailors who had been drinking on a spree in London went to see the show *The Orange Girl*. Sitting in the gallery lighting their pipes they threw the still lit lucifers over the front into the pit shouting 'Fire!' which they presumably thought a great joke. However, one match burnt a woman's dress on landing and many people hearing the shout accepted it as a genuine warning and started fleeing. Ann Day, a young woman attending the show, was injured trying to escape from the theatre and a scuffle arose in the gallery as sensible people seized the malefactors. The pair, handed over to the police, came before the magistrate. They were asked to provide bail for their future good conduct but unable to do so were sent to Horsemonger Lane Jail.

100

1864_12_26 LIVERPOOL (Adelphi).   NEEDLESS PANIC

The house was crowded in every part for the annual pantomime. Around 9.30pm somebody in the pit cried out 'Fire!' whereupon a large portion of the audience commenced to flee the premises. The crushing was terrible and many were trodden underfoot and injured while confusion reigned. When order was eventually restored it was found that the alarm was entirely spurious and no fire had occurred anywhere. Several people, mainly boys, suffering contusions and bruises, received attention at St Anne's Dispensary. The pantomime continued and the only suggestion for the alarm was that some person, unused to theatrical effects had mistaken optical water effects as flames.

1865_01_02 DUNDEE (Springthorpe's).   FATAL FRENZY

Springthorpe's Music Hall was a popular venue for holiday entertainment and on this New Year special night very many people were waiting for the gates to open. The hall was situated beneath ground level under a church. Access was by a 6ft wide staircase descending about 10ft; a pair of iron gates closed the top of the staircase; at the bottom was a 7ft space, the width of the stairs where the pay box was situated. Mr and Mrs Springthorpe catered for the working class as admission was 6d for ladies, gentlemen and tradesmen, but only 3d for others.

It is estimated that 1000 were crowded waiting to gain access, so to relieve the pressure Mrs Springthorpe decided to open an hour earlier than planned. Her method was to have an attendant at the gates, one gate securely fastened, the attendant opening and closing the other as required to allow three or four people at a time to descend, pay, then pass into the auditorium. This procedure progressed until the hall was around a third full, but the waiting crowd's impatience was wearing thin and pushing the attendant aside, thrust the ajar gate wide open and a young man undid the fastenings on the other gate, thus the widest possible entrance was gained and the crowd poured in, tumbling down the steps. Those at the bottom were felled by the people behind, who in turn were crushed by people descending on them. That narrow passageway 6ft x 7ft was wedged with sprawling bodies to a height of five feet, and people were still trying to gain entrance, in spite of the few upright people urging everybody to back off. It was fully 20 minutes before the stairs could be cleared and the gates locked closed. Then the grim task of sorting through the bodies began. Dozens were injured to a greater or lesser extent, and 20 were either brought out dead, or expired shortly afterwards.

To add to the distress, a sickening number of people already in the hall refused to leave until their admission money was returned. The hall was closed immediately after clearance.

1865_01_23 LONDON (Haymarket).   FALL OF CHANDELIER
Without any warning, the large glass chandelier fell from the ceiling and crashed down on the people seated below. A man from Newcastle injured his arm and a Londoner had slight injuries whereas everybody else escaped scot free.

1865_01_30 LONDON (Surrey).   THEATRE COMPLETELY DESTROYED BY FIRE
The pantomime of *Richard Coeur de Lion* had reached the final scene at 11.40pm when Rowella the clown while playing his comic tune on the trombone, discerned a bright light in the aperture above the chandelier. Suspecting it was a blaze, he left the stage to inform the acting manager

101

Mr Green, who immediately despatched some staff to investigate. At that moment smoke began to pour from the opening and the cry of 'Fire!' arose. Green dashed onstage and asked that the audience should make their way out quietly and orderly, and the curtain was lowered. As it was very late, the audience – which had not been numerous earlier – was now quite scanty, thus evacuation was swift and easy. As the carpenters' and painters' rooms were, as customary in theatres of the time, between ceiling and roof, the fire was sure to have originated there. As the last of the audience cleared the interior, flames burst through the ceiling spreading to the boxes and

54. *Fire blazing onstage with Rowella the clown rescuing young dancers*
image© The British Library Board

proscenium. Backstage the half-dressed cast were in dark turmoil as Mr Hinkley, the theatre's gas man, had turned the main gas tap off to avoid an explosion. The ballet girls were screaming and panicking and it was only the bravery and forcefulness of Green, Rowella, Evans the Pantaloon, Mr Vivian the Sprite and other principals who succeeded in propelling the girls through the flames to the stage door and safety. The last to be brought out were several children who acted as fairies in the transformation scene. Rowella and Vivian, having reported that all the cast were out, made their own escape still dressed in their panto costumes as it had been only ten minutes since the first alarm to the entire interior being ablaze. Fire engines, rapidly on the scene, were not early enough to stop the fire from reaching adjacent buildings. By 3am the fire was still smouldering but further danger was over. The loss to the lessee was around £12,000, his insurance was for £2000. The destroyed building had opened at Easter 1806 as a replacement to the former circus which had been built as a rival to Astley's in 1782 and destroyed by fire in 1805.

1865_02_06 LIVERPOOL (Croueste's Circus).   COLLAPSE OF GALLERY FRONT

On a Monday evening, there were about 150 people in the 1d gallery which ran around three sides of the building. Many of these were children who at that moment were watching a comic routine by Delavanti, a French clown dressed as a monkey, and Jennings, another clown, who was to be placed in a box. The box was positioned on the west side of the ring, so the audience in the gallery at that side could only see it by pressing forward to peer vertically downwards. The pressure on the balcony front – made of wooden boarding about 3½ft high – caused it to give way along its 15ft length and some fifty bodies were hurtled into space falling down with the broken boards on to the people sitting in the pit 15ft below.

The crash and screams frightened the rest of the house, and a rush was made for the doors. To add to the confusion a gas pipe had broken and the gas ignited. Fortunately the circus gas man turned the main tap off and fire damage was trifling, although a fire engine was speedily in attendance. Of the sufferers in the fall – mainly children – 16 were taken to hospital where they were attended to, 14 then allowed home while two more seriously hurt were kept in.

1865_02_24 LEEDS (Theatre).   RIOT

[The Davenport Brothers were Americans who presented a séance type entertainment. They had started this act in 1854 in the wake of the new fad for spiritualism. After ten years of fooling the American public they came to the UK. In the Davenports' most famous stunt the brothers were tied inside a double box which contained several musical instruments. Once the box was closed, the instruments would sound. Upon opening the box, the brothers were tied in the positions in which they had started the illusion. This was supposed to indicate the presence of spirits.]

While a long sojourn in London proved successful, the Davenport Brothers met with so much opposition and derision in the provinces that their staging was regularly invaded. They

55. *The Brothers in their Cabinet*

must have got fed up with having to constantly build new cabinets. "Notwithstanding their recent discomfiture at Liverpool and Huddersfield" the Davenports arrived at Leeds with a newly made box which was placed on a platform over the orchestra pit. Two men from the Engineer Volunteers were to check the ropes and tie the brothers up while another two men from Leeds Infirmary were on hand to ensure there was no injury to the spiritualists' wrists. This palaver went on some time and William Davenport caused uproar when he complained the rope was tied too tightly round his wrist. Dr Smith from the Infirmary checked them and said the séance should continue as planned.

Dr Ferguson, who was part of the Davenport entourage, said the ropes were too tight and adjustments should be made. At this a riot ensued with the musical instruments destroyed as they were mauled by the crowd, the new cabinet was pitched off the platform into the body of the hall and smashed to smithereens. The Davenports fled, the police arrived, the lights were turned off, and all the audience trooped out. Sadder and wiser men?

It is of interest that in Manchester the young Henry Irving and two fellow actors put on a spoof version of the Davenports' act with Irving made up like Dr Ferguson and aping his mannerisms. They exposed the whole tawdry gimmickry to much mirth.

1865_03_17 WALSALL (Touring theatre).   SUDDEN HEART-ATTACK TO ACTRESS
On Friday night, the play was *Othello* and at the end of the third act, the actor playing Iago came forward saying there would have to be a temporary pause in the performance because of an unexpected incident. He then left the audience buzzing with rumours but very soon afterwards the actor playing Othello entered and declared that unfortunately the evening must terminate at that point, as it was morally impossible to continue. The explanation was most unusual: a boy had attempted to gain entrance without paying and had been chased away by Mrs Howell, one of the company acting as an attendant. During the chase Mrs Howell suffered a heart attack and dropped down dead.

The manager came on to request that the audience should leave in a quiet and orderly manner and suggested that in the circumstances the admission charges paid that night should be given to the local hospital which was universally agreed. Mrs Howell (30) had been under the care of doctors at a Birmingham Hospital for an ongoing heart problem. She had only joined the company on Wednesday, performed on Thursday, and was dead on Friday. A shutter was found and the deceased was carried to a local pub to await the coroner's inquest.

1865_09_01 LYONS, France (Theatre).   DIRECTOR ATTEMPTS TO FLAUNT TRADITION
Raphael Felix the director of the Lyons Theatre, brother of star actress Mdlle Rachel, took it upon himself to cancel a long standing tradition in the French theatre. On the opening night of the season under the new regime the audience expressed its displeasure by hisses, whistling, groaning and throwing things at the stage. An iron grill at the front of the stage was lowered to prevent the stage being taken over. Having damaged as much as they liked at the theatre, the mob-like audience marched to M Felix's house, smashed his windows and tore up the paving. The military was called out and order was restored by clearing the street by the early hours of the morning. And M Felix's offence? Trying to abolish the long-held custom whereby the audience is allowed to hiss any actor off the stage during the first night of his or her appearance on a new stage, by which the contract is cancelled.

1865_09_17   MENILMONTANT, France (Temporary).   "An accident attended with loss of life occurred on Monday evening at the fête of Menilmontant. A temporary wooden theatre erected there, suddenly fell down while nearly 300 persons were in it. Only two of the spectators, however, were slightly bruised, but on removing the planks of the outside platform a dead body was found, supposed to be that of some houseless wanderer, who had crept in there to pass the night. The body was carried to the Morgue, as there was nothing on it to prove the person's identity." *The Era* 1865_09_17.

1865_09_29 SUNDERLAND (Theatre Royal).   RIOT
          Charles Dudley was the lessee and manager; on the last night of his tenure for his benefit he produced *The Lady of Lyons*. All went well for two acts, when there was a lengthy wait with the curtain down. The rumour went round that the actors had struck for non-payment of their wages. This caused uproar in the house and all kind of missiles were hurled at the stage including fruit and copper coins. Some adventurous youths climbed on to the stage to gather up the coins, capering about to the hoots and jeers of the crowd. Mr Dudley appeared trying to appease his dissatisfied customers, but unable to get a hearing, had to dodge a new hail of coins and vegetables. He tried to be whimsical by picking up some coins, but fled when he was hit on the head by a loaf.
          Eventually, Mr Morton Price and Miss Lucette appeared and sang some songs and duets which were listened to and appreciated. Dudley, taking advantage of the calm audience, announced that the two actors would appear in a piece called *Perfection* but that started the rioters off again and the racket continued until the actor and actress walked off the stage.
          Those in the gods swooped down, respectable people fled, and the rioters had a jolly time ripping up seating and throwing it about, "creating a scene of confusion and uproar" until the theatre was closed.

1865_12_09 PARIS, France.   "Two youths in Paris were admirers of an actress at one of the Boulevard theatres. The other night, as ill-luck would have it, they were both at the theatre, and both flung one franc's worth of flowers to the object of their affections. The young lady took up only one of the bouquets, whereon the slighted swain called out the favoured one and ran him through the body with a rapier. The wounded youth is not expected to survive. His assailant is in custody." *Leeds Times* 1865_12_09.

1866_01_12 LONDON (Standard).   EXPLOSION
          During the pantomime at the Standard Theatre in Shoreditch immediately prior to the transformation scene, a large explosion took place, shaking the building, filling the auditorium with smoke and plunging the place into blackout as the gas went out. The theatre was "extremely full" and there were the inevitable shouts of 'Fire!' as the audience members blundered their way to the exits. The chaos in the dark may be imagined, but fortunately it did not last long and the lighting was restored. However, the gas pipe to the lights at the front of the circle had somehow become detached and when the gas came back, on lighting, a jet of flame shot out for several feet thus giving vent to a second panic. The blaze was immediately put out, so calming the sparse audience that now remained. Once order was restored the manager came onstage dragging what he explained was a rubber bag used for the limelight, which had exploded. No damage had been done, neither was there a report of any injuries, so the show continued to its close.

1867_01_19 LONDON (Drury Lane).   "A youth, named Crouch, 16 years of age, member of the Marylebone Temperance Society, went with some companions to Drury Lane Theatre on Tuesday night. After the theatre he was induced to break his pledge, and got so drunk that his companions, afraid to take him home, locked him in a room at a friend's house. Half-an-hour afterwards a loud crash was heard. The young fellow had precipitated himself from the window on to the flags below, fracturing his skull. He died very shortly afterwards." *Hereford Times* 1867_01_19.

1867_06_19 PHILADELPHIA, USA (American).   FIRE DESTROYS THEATRE
While the performance of *Black Crook* was under way, at the rear of the theatre a stable was on fire. This part of the theatre comprised wooden boarding so the back of the stage too was soon alight. Ballet girls fled to the dressing room to reach their garments but before they got there they could see it was on fire, so they rushed down and joined the actors who had evacuated into the street. James Pilgrim the stage manager went onstage and calmly announced that the show had to be adjourned, please leave as soon as you can – and quoting *Macbeth*!! – 'stand not upon the order of your going'.
Some of the audience went, but most remained seated. Pilgrim, returning, repeated his request, which caused others to leave, while some mounted the stage to ask what was amiss. Again Pilgrim merely asked them to leave. Presumably he was trying to prevent a panic and the resulting horror of crushed and trampled bodies. But when the smoke started filtering through, the rest got the message and fled. Everybody escaped without injury before the fire burst from the stage to the auditorium.
The fire raged, and the building was lost. The firemen's efforts were fruitless, but they kept on playing water until the blaze was subdued. The front wall was badly curved and warped causing spectators to shout warnings to the firemen to watch the wall. "The firemen were reckless of the danger" and soon the wall did, indeed, collapse. When the debris was shifted, there were 30 wounded, many severely, and 13 dead bodies.

1867_12_27 LONDON (Victoria).   FRENZY
Edward Fleming (16) went with his brother Peter (11) to the pantomime *Charles II and Pretty Nell Gwynne.* On arrival they found a great crowd waiting to gain entrance to the gallery. Edward suggested taking a walk down New Cut, returning when the crowd was not so large. At 6.57pm they returned to find people still climbing the stairs and so took their place among them. As they neared the top there was consternation as the money taker called "The price is 6d. No seats under 6d!" The normal price had always been 3d, and on the playbills for the panto the price of the gallery was 4d. Many theatres charged extra for the few days over Christmas (they still do). The bills proclaimed the price of the gallery as 4d in large letters, only in smaller type underneath were the prices for the Christmas period. As many could not read, or were poor readers, this was interpreted as a seat in the gallery for the panto was 4d. An indication of how managers cashed in on the popularity of the new pantomime was a special door where people could enter for 9d prior to the normal admittance doors being opened. This system was known as 'Early Doors'.
The people at the top of the stairs, hearing they were expected to pay 6d, protested that for that money they could go to Drury Lane, not a hick venue like the Victoria. There was then a general exodus back down the stairs where leavers clashed with the rest of the queue still coming up. A melee followed in which many bodies were knocked to the ground and trampled over. One of these was Peter

105

Fleming. Brother Edward trying to get to him to haul him upright and out, could not get near. Peter was taken to hospital where he was diagnosed as suffering from inflammation of the brain caused by being trampled on. Peter seems to have been the only fatality in this frenzy. He remained in hospital and died two weeks later.

The accident happened on a new stone staircase opened by order of the Lord Chamberlain's surveyor. A juror pointed out that the accident would not have happened if money was paid at the foot of the staircase rather than the top. Mr Towne the manager stated the Lord Chamberlain had made the instruction that he had obediently followed. The brothers' aunt said they had gone to the theatre because the pictures on the walls outside looked so beautiful and grand.

1868_01_18 LEICESTER (Theatre Royal).   ACCIDENT IN GALLERY SLIPS

On Saturday night, Henry Payne (12) went with his father to the pantomime *Little Red Riding Hood*. As the gallery was very full, about 30 people were sent into the side slip. Slips were against the wall, stretching from the ends of the gallery to the proscenium, and thus a wretched place to watch from as it meant either leaning out or standing up or both. Some ingenious boys, finding a heavy door, hauled it into the slip so they could stand on it, thus improving their view. Alas, the door was so heavy and cumbersome that they lost control of it and it fell forward on to the back of Henry, crushing him up against the front of the gallery and causing serious internal injury. He was taken home and doctors arrived with treatment, but on Sunday whilst at dinner Henry fell back and expired.

1868_07_31 MANCHESTER (Victoria).   NEEDLESS PANIC

The Victoria Music Hall, known locally as Ben Lang's, occupied three levels of a four storey building and the admission charge was only 2d to the gallery, 3d to the pit. It was frequented by young people of the working class. On this night the place was packed with 2000 people as it was the benefit of Mr Clifford a local favourite. The show started at 6.30pm and all went well until around 10pm, at which point sack races on the stage were organised. Youths at the back of the pit – who had the lower gallery above their heads at a distance of no more than six feet – to see better, stood on the benches and, to keep their balance, held on to a gas pipe that was fastened to the under surface of the gallery. This pipe broke away enabling gas to issue out. The smell of gas becoming immediately apparent caused some people to cry out 'Fire!' resulting in an immediate mass scramble for the exit. Heyward, one of the performers, jumped off the stage, and screwing up some paper stuffed it in the end of the pipe. The curtain was lowered and Mr Clifford came before it to ask that all should retain their seats, there was no fire, there was no danger. He was totally unheeded in the panic to flee the building.

Many at the front of the pit mounted the stage and made their way out via a backstage exit. People in the upper gallery rushed down to the lower gallery then jumped down on to the people struggling in the pit. The pit itself was on the first floor with steps leading down to the entrance. An iron rail which divided the stairway gave way under the pressure, hurling over a hundred people down the stairs in a mass. The stairs and passages were now blocked with wedges of humanity all trampling over each other in their desperation, as it was believed that an explosion was sure to follow escaping gas.

Those who had not made it to the stairs and passages were breaking windows and trying to climb out and down on the outside, a lot desperate enough to jump. Outside crowds had gathered as the news had spread of the calamity. Police had arrived and some sort of order imposed. The process of carrying out bodies began, the less injured, who had friends and family searching for them, were helped to their homes, the unconscious and injured were loaded into cabs waiting in an ever growing line, and taken to the infirmary.

When the dust had settled there were 23 bodies in the morgue, three were females between the age of 12 and 15, the rest were males – four young adults, and youths between 13 and 17. There was no fire, there was no explosion, there was only an escape of gas that had been stopped by a twist of paper.

1868_08_20c DURHAM (Theatre Royal).   RIOT

A concert by several artistes was advertised and on the night an ample audience gathered for the entertainment. The first two or three songs were satisfactorily delivered and then there was a long pause. The singer who had last sung came forward and said that the "other gentlemen in the undertaking" had gone off to the pub and he asked for the audience's indulgence while he went to bring them back. After he made his exit, the audience, smelling a swindle, attacked the stage, whereupon everything portable was taken up and smashed. One hoodlum went into a dressing room and severed the gas pipe, but fortunately somebody with more sense turned the gas off at the main tap, plunging the whole place into darkness. Thus forced into the street, the audience went rampaging round town searching the pubs for the miscreants. It needed the police to come out in force to prevent "wanton mischief", eventually clearing the streets by 10.30pm.

107

1868_08_22 LONDON (St James's).   RIOT

It was announced that the Mexican tragedian Don Edgardo Colona would appear as Richard III at this theatre which, having suffered a turbulent time, had recently closed, and was now reopening with this unusual attraction. A respectable crowd attended, but as the play wore on and it became obvious that a) the man was not a foreigner, and b) that he was not very good, the audience started dribbling away. Some reviews were polite but dismissive, some saying he was just imitating Barry Sullivan – a popular star, but a personality rather than a subtle Shakespearean – others that he was nothing better than a competent amateur.

The tepid reviews did nothing to attract custom but – also adding *Othello* to his programme – the Mexican tragedian plodded on through the week. Then came the rumours that he was not a Mexican at all but an Englishman named Edgar Chalmers who had been in last season's Drury Lane company playing Second Murderer in *Macbeth* and other roles of a similar low standing. This was denied by the management, but it meant the man lost any credibility he might have gathered so business slumped even more. Chalmers (1846–1904), the son of a Scottish mining engineer had, in fact, grown up in Mexico and had become an actor at the age of 18.

When *Richard III* came round again on Saturday night the meagre clutch of visitors watched until the end of Act II when the play stopped. The supporting actors, fearing they would not get paid for their week's work, refused to continue unless they got their pay. It was not forthcoming, which displeased the audience who then started booing, barracking and shouting. The manager came before the curtain to make excuses and apologies but the explanation was clear – he had no money to pay the actors. The gallery started tearing up the seats but were stopped by theatre staff, which indicates how few there were if they could be so easily controlled. The theatre closed at 10pm and "the audience saw only the Great Mexican Tragedian to the second act of *Richard III*".

This was just another case of an over-optimistic manager launching an underfunded enterprise, expecting that the first week's takings would pay for the next week's expenses. The only novelty aspect was the attempt to hoodwink the public as well. The "Mexican tragedian" persisted in his profession to the end of the century.

1868_12_28 LONDON (Britannia).   FATAL ACCIDENT TO BABY

Mrs Wright took her children – one a baby of six weeks – to see the pantomime. There was a large crowd at the doors, so for an extra payment the family was allowed to cross the stage to a private box. Owing to the inclement weather, Mrs Wright had previously wrapped a cloak around Mary Elizabeth the new baby. Having gained their places in the box, Mrs Wright, removing the cloak, found her baby was dead. At the inquest, the examining doctor Mr C Benley MRCS deposed there was "blood issuing from the mouth and nose, the hands were clenched and the legs drawn up". The face was bruised by pressure, and the child had died from violent suffocation.

1869_04_12 ALNWICK (Theatre).   FATAL TUSSLE WITH ATTENDANT

108

One of the most popular solo performers of the day, Charles Mathews, engaged at the Alnwick Theatre attracted the customary full house. At the end of the show a young man named Turner tried to move from the gallery to a side box and so leave via that exit. Apparently being a common procedure, some had gone prior to Turner, others were following. He was forestalled by a theatre attendant named George Craster who said this was not permitted, insisting people should exit the gallery by the gallery exit. A struggle took place, with other audience members egging Turner on at the expense of Craster, urging him to throw the official into the pit. Both men fell into the box, Craster underneath with his arm round Turner's neck. Craster got to his feet, Turner, unable to do so, was carried out and propped against the wall. A friend said he did not look well and helped him home where he died. Craster was remanded in custody.

No doubt many of us at some time have exchanged angry words with a 'Little Hitler' theatre official but I doubt if any of us have been killed by them. The post mortem by two doctors agreed that Turner had died by asphyxiation, not by deliberately putting hands on the windpipe with that intention, but rather, during the struggle an arm, or other part of the body may have put pressure on the windpipe without any malicious intention. The coroner pointed out to the jury that Craster was an official carrying out his duty, and had every right to stop people taking that way out. On Monday, not only were people disobeying the theatre man's instructions, they were goading his opponent to throw him from the boxes into the pit, which, if Turner had succeeded in doing, would have been a very serious matter. Many witnesses concurred that the squabble had been brief, only three minutes or so, and the men had fallen down together twice. The jury agreed with the doctors' verdict leaving in the air the question whether Craster was to be charged. That was deferred for a future decision when the magistrates, unable to convict Craster on such evidence as had been shown, therefore discharged him.

1869_04_17 LONDON (Surrey).   INTERVAL MELEE IN STAIRCASE

The play was the popular attraction *True to the Core* and, as it was also a Saturday night, the gallery was particularly crowded. When the interval came at around 10pm, a large percentage of the men and boys made for the exit to seek refreshment. Admittance to the gallery in those days was by buying a metal token at the bottom of the steps and handing it in to the checktaker near the top. At the interval, people leaving with the intention of returning were given a similar token which allowed them to return. To facilitate this there was a barrier across the stairs so return checks could be handed out in an orderly manner.

On this night, a boisterous crowd of 200 were rushing and pushing to be first out. The ones at the front were pressed onwards by the bulk behind, with the result that the wooden barrier gave way and a mass of bodies fell forward down the stone steps below. One man had a broken arm, another a broken leg, a third had fractured ribs. A dozen others were bruised and battered around the body. The incident was caused entirely by racing to get out before anybody else and "the thoughtlessness of a lot of rough fellows who considered it a good lark to push about in a crowd."

1869_04_19 BRADFORD (Theatre Royal).   AUDIENCE MEMBER FALLS FROM GALLERY

The play was *Red Hands* and seemingly not a particularly crowd-pulling piece, as the gallery must have been fairly empty when Greenwood Raistrick (16) and a pal entered. Raistrick going to the left of the gallery, rapidly jumped from seat to seat down the rows, gaining such momentum that, when he got to the front, he pitched over, grabbed the metal rail, but losing his grip, he turned over and fell about 25ft, bouncing off Mr Cooke the violinist and coming to rest on an empty seat. He was taken into the ladies cloakroom and tended to by Dr Taylor who declared no bones were broken. The boy came round and must have felt all right because he demanded to go back to the gallery and watch the play. The doctor forbade that and had him sent home. The boy then demanded the return of the 6d he had paid, which was given to him. This was Yorkshire after all!

1869_05_18 LEEDS (Amphitheatre).   AUDIENCE MEMBER FALLS FROM GALLERY

The production was the pantomime of *Cinderella*. The manager Mr Weston had a real hit on his hands with full houses night after night. This night was no different with every seat taken, and around 9pm a group of lads was enjoying the show from the right slip of the upper gallery. The slips at this venue were very narrow, having room for one row only between wall and the front rail. The height of the slip from the pit floor was around 50ft. While fooling about, William Ballard (15) overbalancing, fell over the front rail into the pit below, striking the cello, the boarding round the orchestra, and a woman seated in the front row. The boy was picked up unconscious and taken to the Infirmary where little damage was found, as he recovered. The lady who was struck was taken to her home, where her injured neck rapidly improved.

Weston had dashed on stage at the accident, calming everybody, and supervised the removal of the two inflicted people. An hour later he reappeared to assure the audience that both were fully recovered and no permanent damage would be manifest. "On this assurance being given, the performance proceeded." I have to wonder if the audience was left sitting idle for an hour between the manager's entries, or had the show carried on anyway? I assume the latter.

1869_05_25 LONDON (Royal Alfred).   CRÈCHE PROVIDED AT THE THEATRE

This is not an accident as such but a news item that seems very modern for its period. The managers of this theatre had resolved not to allow children under the age of five into the auditorium. They set aside a large room in the theatre where mothers could leave their babies at a charge of 2d per baby, whilst they enjoyed the play. Included in the charge were nurses, milk, feeding bottles, and all the impedimenta of a nursery. What a brilliant and foresighted idea!

1869_05_29 LONDON (Royal Alfred).   BABY CRÈCHE A FAILURE

The cloakroom for babies, proving a dismal failure, was immediately abandoned after the theatre's management was left with a number of unclaimed babies on its hands. A warning was issued that if these unnatural parents did not collect their children immediately they would be passed on to the workhouse as the theatre had no facilities to prolong their stay. Ghastly as it seems to us today, many poor Victorian families had so many children they leaped at the opportunity to shed one of them for 2d, no questions asked, in this very convenient way.

1869_11_15 MILWAUKEE, USA (Gaiety).   LIGHTING BY NAPHTHA OIL

On this night a new company under Mr J C King had just started a series of performances and the building was crowded. An innovation was lighting by naphtha oil instead of gas, which had been turned off. Lamps loaded with this new oil were scattered throughout the building. Naphtha is the first stage in distilling oil into petroleum. One of the actors caught one of these lamps with his sword and it fell to the stage. The man, thinking swiftly, grabbed a coat that was hanging up and threw it over the flame. The oil ran out of the lamp, started spreading over the stage, and instantly ignited. Soon there was a wall of flame and backstage people ran out through the stage door, while the audience rushed to the exits. Once achieving the exits some lingered, looking back to see the flames, thus preventing people inside from getting clear. People were escaping out through the windows in the upper floors. Fire engines arrived and quenched the fire within an hour of it starting.

Two bodies were found, a man and a boy William Brewer an apprentice at the local newspaper. A thorough search was made but no more bodies were found. Between 20 and 30 people were seriously injured.

1869_12_20c PHILADELPHIA, USA (American).   NEEDLESS PANIC

The theatre was crowded with many would-be customers turned away. The show proceeded successfully until around 10pm when, for some reason, one of the gas brackets snapped off allowing gas to escape, this being ignited by a nearby lamp. The resulting flame was the size of a man's arm, but this was enough to start up a cry of 'Fire!' which set the entire audience on its feet, some running stagewards, some for the exits. Boys in the gallery slid down the columns into the pit.

A small gang of theatre workers appeared, with bucket, hose and tools and within 20 minutes a repair had been effected. Seeing all was now calm, the scattered audience sheepishly returned to their seats and the performance continued. Fortunately, nobody had been harmed in the panic, but again gave proof that a theatre audience at the slightest hint of danger "acted like a lot of foolish children."

No doubt the reader will be astonished at how often unexpected flames appear through broken pipes and the like and it is no wonder people so readily flee.

110

1869_12_26 BRISTOL (New Theatre Royal).   TRAGIC FRENZY

This is another major horror story but not of panic but of eagerness. The New Theatre Royal had been built as recently as 1867, and the biggest attraction at Christmas for miles around was the new pantomime. On this, the opening night of *Robinson Crusoe*, as early as 4pm there were 2000 people waiting to gain admittance to the pit stalls, pit and gallery. The entrance to these parts was at the bottom of a slope. Because of the crowd, it was thought advisable to open the doors early, to relieve the pressure. When this was done the people at the front of the crowd – queuing was unknown to theatregoers at this period – paid their money and went in.

56. *The frenzied crowd trying to gain admittance*

image© The British Library Board

As soon as it was realised further back up the slope that the doors had opened, the crowd pushed forward and in the crush strong men, weak women and weaker children were all thrown down and literally trampled to death. "To expatiate on the horrors of the scene would be a heartless profanation." Two things then happened. The pantomime started as normal with the people seated inside totally oblivious of the scene of human devastation outside; and somebody shouted 'Fire!' at the struggling mass. This was in fact a policeman on duty, his thinking being that this would cause the people to flee from the area, and to some extent that worked. The manager's rationale for carrying on with the show was to save further panic as, when the audience emerged at the end, there was still a massive clear up in progress as many bodies had lost shoes and clothing, others clad in mere rags, making identification particularly difficult. The newcomers were aghast and starting enquiring about family and friends. Identification went on for several days before a complete account could be given.

This was another of the terrible tragedies that resound through history, as 18 lives were lost plus untold numbers of injuries. The ages of the dead mainly ranged between 13 and 18. Again, the fatalities were caused by the thoughtless antics of ill-bred louts who relied on brute strength to get their way. It was the third similar major frenzy that happened at ten year intervals. On 17 February 1849, 65 people perished at Glasgow, on 27 December 1859 at the London Victoria 15 young lads were trampled to death, and now this outrage at Bristol. Not before time, this particular tragedy was a deciding factor in new rules about entrances and exits, and for the first time came suggestions on how to deal with the nightly animal scramble for places. In the oppressed city of Paris, regulations were in place for queuing at the doors, whereas in libertarian Britain it was devil take the hindmost.

1870_08_09 GLASGOW (Theatre Royal).   MAN FALLS CLIMBING FROM WINDOW

William Wilson went to the Theatre Royal and fell asleep in the amphitheatre – the show must have been pretty dull. He awoke at 2.30am in the dark and silent building. He groped his way to a window and opened it, climbing out hoping to reach the ground, presumably forgetting how many flights of stairs he had ascended at the beginning of the evening. He fell from two storeys high and hit a ledge projecting from a wall. Rescued after his cries were heard by two patrolling policemen, he was taken to the police office and thence to the Royal Infirmary.

1871_02_27 CORK (Theatre Royal).   EXPLOSION

On this night there was a loud explosion backstage causing alarm to all. Fortunately, the damage was slight, mainly comprising some displacement of woodwork behind the scenes and a small portion of the roof blown off. As in most explosions, the cause centred on the limelight apparatus. Rubber bags containing the necessary gases were used, and on this night a little boy got on top of one of the bags, his weight causing it to burst, and the gas coming in contact with a light resulted in a shattering explosion. It has to be said that as the gas was used up small boys were often allowed to sit on the 'wedge board' to help force the lowering pressure.

1871_03_04 BOLTON (Adams's Circus).   FATAL ACCIDENT BUILDING CIRCUS

Mr James Rigby and his team of carpenters had been contracted to build a wooden circus in Bolton market place from the design of Mr Harrison, the architect of Adams's circus buildings for 30 years. All was proceeding well, with the walls erected, and the roof currently being built. The roof relied on ten principal beams, and these were in situ but not fixed. A rope was used as a temporary measure to hold them in place as they were all interconnected by purlins. During work on the roof a carpenter, finding the rope was tied such that he could not fasten down the plank he was working on, untied the rope. Immediately, like a row of dominoes the main beams collapsed, crashing inwards to the ground. Eight men were working on the ground and six men on the roof when it caved in.

Two men were killed, including a 17-year-old apprentice, and three injured, including John

Rigby (42) brother of the contractor and his son John Rigby Jr (20). Of the men on the roof, a deaf and dumb joiner and a 20-year-old apprentice were seriously injured.

1871_12_27 LONDON (Variety).   FATAL PINT POT FALLS ON WOMAN
      [It was the Christmas attraction and, as often at holiday time, the poorer people flocked to the cheap galleries of the London theatres and music halls in abundance. As has been shown on many occasions, the now commonplace British method of queuing had not been introduced, and people seeking admittance to the gallery had to endure scrambling in a scrum while climbing stairs.]
      Mrs Waldron and her sister-in-law laundress Susannah Waldron (17) went to the theatre this night, waiting at the foot of the gallery stairs, with above them a seething mass of closely packed bodies. An impatient and cocky boy decided to get to the head of the crowd by clambering up the balustrade, and in doing so knocked a pint pot out of somebody's hand. The pot landed on the head of Susannah causing an injury, and she was taken home. Two weeks later she died from "inflammation of the brain". The inquest was obliged to pass a verdict of "accidental death", as the pot was obviously not dislodged on purpose, and the boy had not been identified.

1872_01_13 YORK (Theatre Royal).   AUDIENCE MEMBER FALLS FROM GALLERY
      Charles Dillon the eminent tragedian was giving his Hamlet to a crowded house. John Bell (15) an ironworker, entered the gallery between the first and second acts and seeing a friend nearer the front made his way forward through the benches. Some of the audience gave him a lift, passing him forward over the heads below. He rolled over the front rows and finally dropped over the iron guard rail at the front of the gallery, into the pit below, a distance of around 25ft. Landing across the knees of two or three people seated in the pit, he escaped with very little injury. He was taken out and home, but whilst great consternation arose in the theatre, "no delay in the performance took place."

113

1872_10_19 LIVERPOOL (Adelphi).   AUDIENCE MEMBER FALLS FROM GALLERY
      The boy was Dominick Bradley. Around 9pm, two men, jostling each other and larking in the gallery, lurched violently against Dominick sitting on the front row, knocking him over the railing into the pit 30ft below. There he landed on a child of 17 months called Mary Fannon who was sitting on her mother's knee. The doctor who attended said Mary was "in a dangerous condition". Dominick, shaken up but uninjured, was able to walk home. Lino Courtney the lessee offered a reward of £5 for information leading to the two men, but "nothing could be ascertained of them."

1872_10_21 SHEFFIELD (Hengler's).   FATAL COLLAPSE OF GALLERY
      Mr Hengler had a new wooden circus built in the town and when opened it attracted full houses for the excellent shows presented. On this night – the circus having flourished for some ten days – in mid-show, without any warning, a side gallery collapsed shooting around 40 people downwards to the ground some 14ft below. Panic seized other spectators and they rushed to the exits while Hengler and his staff set about rescuing the fallen from a tangle of boards and beams. Seven people were taken to the General Hospital and seven to the Public Hospital, some very seriously injured. Business at the venue did not suffer, and Hengler gave the proceeds of several shows to the afflicted. One of the worst cases, Richard Kneeshard, who had his back broken, died from his injuries.

1873_02_24 BLACKBURN (Theatre.)   EXPLOSION

During the play *The Jewess*, a loud explosion from the stage was heard and all the lights in the theatre went out. Instant panic ensued with people making for the exits. However, Chief Constable Potts happened to be present in the boxes and, believing the danger to be over, calmed the boxes, then went to those in the pit and then into the gallery. In the latter place the ticket taker and a policeman were manning the door, not allowing anybody through. This was a wise precaution as the exit door led to a flight of narrow stairs, and a mass of people fleeing in the dark would have brought inevitable serious accidents, as happened on several similar occasions.

The explosion was caused by one of the limelight bags, apparently in the fly gallery and under the charge of a youth named Whittaker. An escape of gas from the bag ignited with a bang when it came into contact with a gaslight. The result was that part of the fly gallery some 5ft wide and 10ft long was blown down, Whittaker falling with it on to the stage 18ft below. The light restored, medical aid was summoned and Whittaker was found with wounds on scalp and neck which were dressed and he was taken home. The performance continued after the delay.

1873_04_07 HANLEY (Foottit's Circus).   COLLAPSE OF SECTION OF SEATING

[At this period we have to still distinguish between temporary wooden circus buildings (as Hengler's *above*) that are built on the lines of permanent theatres and expected to stand for some time, often years, before either demolished or converted into permanent buildings, and the 'new' canvas big top type of marquee referred to as a pavilion which was erected for a day or two on waste ground or field such as in this entry. The seating in the latter was formed on a 'slot together' basis of A frames of varying heights linked by beams, these stepped to take plank seats. When the ground was soft or loose, there was a danger of some of the A frames sinking, thus causing a section of seats to twist out of the proper alignment and liable to collapse.]

During the performance in a 'big top', a section of the seating collapsed throwing a number of people to the ground. Several were severely injured, one fatally. The tent was packed to excess, and the accident caused a panic which brought the show to a close. The local council passed a motion that any future use of such structures had to be certified as safe by the borough surveyor.

1873_02_15 BIRMINGHAM (Theatre Royal).   FATAL FALL OF BOY FROM GALLERY

Thomas Millbanks (13), at the back of the crowded gallery, wanted to be at the front so, emulating the regular antics of older fellows, scampered down over the heads of the rows of occupied benches. He was so successful he rolled over the iron guard rail and plummeted 40ft down into the pit. He was lucky as he landed on two women with a boy which broke his fall. They were lucky too, being only slightly injured. Unfortunately, Millbanks was not lucky enough as he was taken semi-conscious to Queen's Hospital suffering from contusions to the head and died at 1am.

1873_06_09 LONDON (Alexandra Palace).   DESTROYED BY FIRE

[This venue was created from the materials of the 1862 Exhibition buildings, just as the Crystal Palace was built in South London from the dismantled 1851 Exhibition, and was intended as a northern counterpart. Alas, the company failed and further ideas came to naught until finally at Whitsuntide the new conception opened with great éclat on Queen Victoria's 54th birthday. The building was 900ft long and had cost £500,000 to build on its new site. It housed art galleries, concert halls, refreshment rooms and a theatre.]

Alas, within a mere 16 days of opening the building caught fire. It was a Monday, and in spite of being a cheap 6d day, there were few people about at 12.30pm as the new venue had not yet really caught on and people tended to roll up later in the afternoon. This was a blessing as the place was speedily evacuated. The fire broke out in the magnificent dome towering over the mighty organ which was a feature of the theatre. The ironwork of the dome structure warped and buckled in the heat, sending it crashing down. Being of highly combustible materials, the theatre was instantly engulfed in giant flames, which then swept along the whole length of the building.

A message was telegraphed to Captain Shaw the head of the Metropolitan Fire service. He set out with nine steam fire engines, seven manual engines, and 120 of the most experienced firemen in London. The engines were, of course, horse drawn and having 7 miles to travel from base to fire, by the time they arrived destruction was almost complete.

[Captain Sir Eyre Massey Shaw (1830–1908) was the first Chief Officer of the Metropolitan Fire Brigade from 1861 to 1891. Born in Ballymore, Co Cork, he served in the army before becoming Chief Constable of Belfast in 1860. He was an influential thinker, publishing at least one book on fire fighting, and many articles and reports. He introduced modern fire fighting methods to the Brigade, and increased the number of stations. He is noted for implementing uniforms and the famous brass helmets, and for creating a ranking system. He also introduced the use of stand pipes and fire hydrants, and the electrical telegraph for communication between stations.

115

Shaw was a well-known figure and a personal friend of the Prince of Wales. He lives on today in a lyric in Gilbert and Sullivan's *Iolanthe*

57. *Capt Shaw*

>Oh, Captain Shaw!
>>Type of true love kept under!
>Could thy Brigade
>>With cold cascade
>Quench my great love, I wonder!

Shaw was present in the stalls at the first night of *Iolanthe* in 1882, and the actress playing the Fairy Queen, addressed herself directly to him. Legend has it that he stood up and took a bow.]

1874_01_19 KING'S LYNN (Theatre).   FALL OF BOY FROM GALLERY

Mr Callender's Company was performing *True as Steel* when a boy, in the usual endeavour of worming his way into a front seat in the gallery, fell over the rail into the pit, landing on Mr and Mrs Holland. The boy crashed through the chandelier at dress circle level, so the smash of glass, falling body, and the cries of the seriously injured Hollands, was accompanied by the shrieking and fainting of women. The rush to the doors "is said to have been indescribable".

1874_08_17 BOLTON (Museum).   COMEDIAN SHOOTS AUDIENCE MEMBER

The performer was Walter Marrion who fired off a blunderbuss which, although only loaded with powder and paper, hit Lambert Fletcher seated in the pit. This innocent viewer, receiving a serious wound to his temple, was instantly conveyed to the Infirmary where the wound was expertly stitched.

1874_10_15 LONDON (Covent Garden). PISTOL FIRED IN AUDIENCE

About 9pm during a concert, a pistol was discharged and a subsequent scuffle took place wherein one man – Hiram Thompson, an American newly arrived in London – was arrested. Like many Americans he was accustomed to carrying a loaded pistol in his pocket, and as he was fumbling for his handkerchief, the trigger had accidentally fired. A man named Stewart who had been near Thompson was very fortunate as the bullet had passed by his legs and burrowed itself in the floor.

Brought before magistrates, Thompson claimed that he had forgotten guns were not carried in England (though it was not illegal to do so) and it was mere accident that it went off. The magistrate agreed, though made the point that Americans sometimes shot an opponent through their pockets. He asked the prisoner for £40 from himself for surety, and £20 surety from one other.

1875_04_10 BIRMINGHAM (Theatre Royal). BOY THROWN OVER FRONT OF GALLERY

It was a Saturday night and the gallery was crowded. John Kelly (11) a boy who had been several times to the theatre, keen to get a seat near the front, had already been passed over people's heads to reach the fifth row where a man called Dayus, handed him forward to the man in front, John Collings (23) a butcher. Seizing the boy, Collings threw him with such impetus to the front of the gallery he flew over the balcony rail "like a bird".

When considering the case in court on Monday morning, Mr Cheston, defending Collings, persuaded the witness who used those words to agree to temper it to "gave him a push" though the witness added he could not say whether it was deliberate or not. The magistrate snorted "Of course the man did not intend to do it." Cheston then said he had several witnesses to call, but ventured to suggest before he did that, some compensation should be paid to the boy. The lad was not hurt much or he would not have been able to be in court. The magistrate stated the deed was most recklessly done, though not, of course, intentionally. Constable Townsend said the boy was discharged from Queen's Hospital the previous morning after having been kept in overnight. Again Cheston mooted that £2 compensation should be paid, and the magistrate concurred, saying that the prisoner had been extremely careless and rough in his conduct, and that it was a great pity that theatre managers allowed boys under 12 in at all, and better control should be taken in the gallery. This was the third time people had fallen from gallery to pit. Kelly's father being dead, Inspector Robinson was placed in charge of the compensation money with orders to spend it on the boy.

116

1876_02_05 CINCINNATI, USA (Robinson's OH). TRAGIC NEEDLESS PANIC

58.

The Opera House, was built by retired circus impresario John Robinson and opened in 1872. The theatre seated 1800 with standing spaces for almost as many again. The attraction on this day was a charity show called *The Great Republic Allegory and Tableaux* with a huge cast of local performers including many children. As a result the audience also comprised mainly children and their parents. It is estimated that some 2,500 people were attending the matinee with standing areas and staircases full.

The show had barely got under way when some idiotic fool cried "Fire!" which immediately started a stampede for the exits. Many in the upper tiers jumped down on to crowds milling on floors below, while stairs were jammed with fallen people who were trampled on as others fought for safety. Chaos and panic ruled. Everybody was fighting to get to the huge front doors to make their escape. The fatal stampede that day became known as "The Horror." Men who should have behaved bravely scrambled over women and children in the choked hallways of the theatre. It was a crazed mob blindly rushing for the exits when there was no cause at all, there was no fire, and the horrendous result was 30 injured and 11 dead all as a result of the cry of an unknown mischievous moron. *(see also 1897_10_15).*

1876_07_23 HAMBURG, Germany (Central Halle). ONSTAGE FIRE

This venue – a theatre and pleasure garden combined – was crowded on a Sunday when the fire broke out. Panic sent the crowds rushing wildly about with "women fainting, and children crying piteously". The fire – caused by the familiar curtain blowing into a gas light – rapidly spread. Some of the actors and ballet girls received burns before they got out, and a dozen members of the public had limbs broken in the fleeing melee.

1876_12_05 BROOKLYN, USA (Conway's). MAJOR TRAGEDY WITH MANY FATALITIES

[Some accidents were so horrific in their own time that they live on in history. The Brooklyn Theatre fire was one such. This theatre with a seating capacity of 1,600, opened on October 2, 1871. As the theatre was only five years old it had adequate exits, wide doorways and passages, and had been approved on the grounds that the entire place could be evacuated in 5 minutes.

Alas, none of these attributes proved much of a success when a fire swept through the building during a performance. A long entry about this fire appears in the companion book *Perils of the Victorian Stage.*]

Although the UK had had its share of horror stories of fire, panics and frenzies, it was often the reports from abroad, USA in particular, that made the authorities sit up and take notice. This major conflagration with appalling loss of life had some effect in London's theatreland. It was, of course, widely reported, with many newspapers giving the wisdom of their readers and editors. One particular point that had never been much made of was the practice of managers packing in as many people as possible. The suggestion was that more space should be created in galleries by removing several rows of benches. Also the Lord Chamberlain who was responsible for London theatres put pen to paper again reminding managers of his instructions sent in February calling particular attention to the absolute necessity of the following first four rules being attended to — "1. All doors and barriers to open outwards, or to be fixed back during the time when the public are within the theatre. 2. All gangways, passages, and staircases intended for the exit of the audience to be kept entirely free from obstructions, whether permanent or temporary. 3. No part of the auditorium to be without at least two means of exit, in case of need. 4. All doors not habitually used for exit, but available as additional means of escape in case of alarm, to be indicated by printed placards in plain characters. The Lord Chamberlain regrets that many complaints have reached him of extra chairs and seats being still placed in the gangways; a practice not only inconvenient to individuals, but extremely dangerous in case of an alarm of fire. He therefore gives notice that he has desired to be specially informed from time to time, and particularly during the ensuing Christmas holidays, whether this practice is continued, and if any flagrant case is detected of the rules being evaded." *Pall Mall Gazette* 1876_12_22

117

1876_12_20 NEW YORK, USA (Wallack's).   FIREPROOFING SCENERY

Dion Boucicault actor, manager, playwright and impresario had been banging on about the way to deal with theatre fires was not via iron curtains and wider passages etc that tried to deal with the effects, but to strike at the root cause by fireproofing the scenery. He had been saying this for some 16 years without getting anywhere. The recent Brooklyn tragedy was an ideal opportunity for him to demonstrate the efficacy of his theory and he organised a demonstration on the stage of Wallack's theatre and invited local fire chiefs and theatre managers to attend.

A piece of scenery was centre stage, a flame 5ft long and "the thickness of a man's body" was directed at it and held "in close proximity". Equal to the force of one hundred and fifty of the ordinary stage gas-jets aimed at it, the scenery did not catch fire – the canvas did not blaze or even smoke. Boucicault was asked if a prolonged flame would cause it to take fire, and he answered they had better try the test. The flame played on the scenery but all that happened was a large hole appeared and black powder fell to the ground. At no time was a spark or flame to be seen. The fire chiefs declared themselves convinced and went away.

Boucicault was interviewed by the *New York Herald* and said he was used to this – everybody was impressed and convinced, but nothing was done. He said nothing would happen unless major newspapers took up the cause that all lessees be required to adopt this fire precaution under pain of losing their licences. He made no secret of his 'magic solution' which comprised of tungstate of soda in which canvas and ropes are soaked for half an hour. After drying, the canvas is primed with a solution of silicate of soda. Boucicault stated: "There are three well-known resisting agents to flame, they are tungstate of soda, phosphate of ammonia, and sulphate of ammonia. There are two agents used as dressing to the above; these are silicate of soda and chloride of calcium."

118

59. *Fire Prevention*

Many people had come forward with 'patent potions' but all had necessarily been combinations of these chemicals. A recent more effective addition was tungstate of molybdenum. If theatre timbers were treated with the same stuff, the risk of fire was negligible. The whole scenic stock of a theatre could be treated for $100 (£20).

1876_10_30 SAN FRANCISCO, USA (Royal China).   NEEDLESS PANIC

The place was packed with an audience of 2,000 people for the benefit of a popular actor when around midnight some person unknown shouted the dreaded word 'Fire!' A man in the gallery had thrown down a cigarette which ignited some matting. A Christian Chinaman named Adam Quinn had stamped it out, removed his coat and covered it, but the gallery audience had already started stampeding. The exit was down a flight of stairs with a bend to two doors 12ft high opening into the vestibule. The gallery folk rushed to this exit and the sudden increase of weight by so many people brought down the stairs with a melee of bodies that were tangled up and trampled on. At the bottom the crush caused the doors to collapse from their hinges, falling on to the people who had just passed through, knocking them to the ground. The following mass trampled across the doors as if they were a drawbridge. The noise alerted police who, entering the building, took control of the chaos. There were many injuries and a total of 19 dead.

1876_11_18 SACRAMENTO, USA (Moore's).   FATAL COLLAPSE OF UPPER FLOOR

The Opera House opened for the season on this night, and the upper floor collapsed precipitating the audience on to those seated below. There were many casualties and seven deaths.

1877_04_02 LONDON (Crystal Palace).   FALL FROM MAKESHIFT BOX

It was Easter Monday, and Mrs Brickett and a friend went to the pantomime. From their original seats Mrs B found it difficult to see, so moved forward to a box that had been assembled from planks resting on girders. The height of the surround of this makeshift box was 32". Leaning against a girder at the rear she was pushed by people in front and toppled backwards out of the box. At the same level as the plank floor of the box was a canvas awning, and Mrs B fell through this into the refreshment room below, a distance of 20ft. Her head coming into contact with a marble table, resulted in injuries to head and face, a broken arm and other lacerations. She was immediately taken to St Bartholomew's Hospital where she remained for seven weeks, and was an out-patient until November.

In court the following March, when Mrs B sued for damages, the defence was that the accident was caused by her own want of care. Witnesses claimed that she had been standing on a chair, or even on the girder itself and losing her balance toppled backwards. Furthermore, an attendant cautioned people entering the box to be careful of the drop behind it being covered by the canvas. Mrs B said this man had never spoken one word to her. The jury decided for Mrs B and awarded damages of £100 – about £8200 in today's money. Good for her, the set-up sounds very peculiar and quite rackety for a professional entertainment.

1877_10_26 CHELTENHAM (Theatre Royal).   FALL THROUGH CEILING

The play *Fron Fron* was nearing its conclusion when a young man crashed through the ceiling of the promenade into the stalls, startling everybody around by the suddenness. Luckily, he fell between the seats. The ladies, finding this unwelcome visitor from above alarming, feared the likelihood of an injury, so were relieved when a hearty laugh issued from the intruder who had suffered nothing worse than a severe shaking.

1878_02_03 CALAIS, France (Priami & Pierontoni). TROUBLEMAKERS CAUSE NEEDLESS PANIC

This was an Italian circus from Milan built up on the Grande Place for the annual fair. The building – entirely of wood – was capable of holding some 3500 people. On this night the place was packed out, with another 1500 turned away. During the performance a crowd of young workmen in the gallery was creating a noise and being a nuisance. Finally, when the pantomime *Le Médecin de Campagne* was under way, this gang of troublemakers came clattering down the ramp from the gallery and some irresponsible person shouted "Fire!" or rather "Au feu!" immediately causing others in the audience to make for the exit.

Panic ensued, the two main trouble spots being at the base of the two ramps where people stumbled and fell, with those behind trampling over them to get out; and at a designated fire exit where the doors stupidly opened inwards. In spite of police officials present attempting to keep order, the people in the cheap seats broke through the expensive seats into the ring itself, and out via the performers' entrance. Four firemen, permanently on duty in the stables, assuming the cry of fire was correct, themselves took it up, and outside the circus the watchman in the adjoining belfry rang out the warning bell rousing the entire town and garrison to emergency measures, including the despatching of fire engines and the military.

Though not needed for quenching a fire, the forces were invaluable in bringing order to chaos, and clearing the trapped people. Twelve people died in the panic – including seven children – and some 20 injured. A mass funeral with expenses paid by the municipal authorities was held three days later.

1878_01_07 LIVERPOOL (Alexandra).   FALL OF PIECE OF CEILING

About 9.15pm at the theatre, a small portion of ceiling at the extreme edge of the gallery nearest the stage suddenly fell. Immediately some malevolent person shouted "Fire!" and a few people fled. Fortunately, the vast majority believed Mr Roberts the stage manager, Mr Wilkinson the treasurer, and leading actors Mr and Mrs Saker when, taking to the stage, they all assured the audience there was no cause for alarm, and no danger. Order was speedily restored and the performance continued without the slightest injury to anybody. It was claimed that the fire precautions, and the means of exit "are not surpassed by any other theatre in the kingdom."

1878_06_01c AHMEDNUGGAR, India.   FATAL FIRE IN THEATRE MARQUEE

The entertainment at this town was given in a large marquee housing 1000 people. The performers were from a well-known Parsee theatrical club in Bombay. The show was very well received and at the end around 10pm the audience was chattering excitedly and still laughing from the farce they had just seen. Suddenly a fire burst forth, apparently from nowhere, and in minutes the whole canvas erection was ablaze. A rush was made for the tiny door, which would indicate that the marquee had solid sides and the entrance was the only exit. The burning canvas was falling on the people struggling to get out, and in the panic the crowd at the door became a solid wedged mass of bodies. European residents, who had not been part of the audience, rushed to the rescue and managed to pull out bodily the nearest at the door. The whole fire occupied no more than five minutes, but in that time there were a great many suffocated, burnt and wounded people.

When the flames had died down, and the rescuers were able to drag out the victims from the centre of the tent, it was found that around half the victims were native soldiers suffocated by smoke.

It appears that the flimsy edifice was not a help, as the falling roof entangled around 100 people in canvas and ropes. The final death toll was 49; there was no figure given for the injured. The indigenous people immediately blamed the players for the misfortune then, seeing the nonsense in that, equally stupidly accused the military officers who had done their utmost to help in the calamity.

1878_09_16c BIRKENHEAD (Theatre).   COLLAPSE OF CLOAKROOM FLOOR

The final item in this all Welsh affair was a new dramatic cantata *The Fairy Tribe*, which was well received "though in the Welsh language and somewhat long". I think this was a polite way of saying 'As boring as all get out.' Anyway, why am I mentioning this event at all? Because at the end when the ladies were thronging the cloak room, the floor gave way and 20 ladies fell 8 to 10 feet. Several were seriously injured, medical aid promptly summoned, and they were dispatched home in cabs – some in a fainting and/or insensible condition

1878_09_28 CAMBRIDGE (Barnwell).   RIOT

[The Barnwell Theatre itself is of particular interest as it is extant and has a unique history. It was built in 1814 with a typical Regency auditorium. In 1926, it was bought by the theatre pioneer Terence Gray who adapted it by removing the proscenium and adding a cyclorama. He also created a revolving stage. These alterations were carried out to test the modern theatre theories of Edward Gordon Craig who had been propounding them for 25 years but which had never actually been tried out. Gray gave up the theatre in 1933 to breed racehorses and took up Taoism. In 1996, there were hopes that the theatre could come back to life, as the auditorium was still intact and the stage pretty much as Gray had abandoned it, but it was sold to a Buddhist organisation. However, the building is Listed Grade II so there should be no drastic alterations.]

The Barnwell Theatre is on the outskirts of Cambridge and was outside the University authority, the lessee Alfred Parry. The play was *Jessy Vere,* and halfway through, Parry walked on and stopped the show. There had been some dispute between the owners of the theatre and himself, during which a representative of the owners had seized the night's takings. The audience, not accepting whatever explanations Parry offered, started trashing the place. Destruction went on for some time in all parts of the house. Although it was very near the end of the season, Parry had negotiated a four-day extension that may have been the cause of the dispute, but in any case the building was due to become a mission house after closing, which it duly did until reverting to theatrical use at a future time.

1878_10_11 LIVERPOOL (Colosseum).   FATAL NEEDLESS PANIC

This venue had been refused a licence by local magistrates but somehow kept functioning as a concert hall on the 'twice nightly' system. This meant that after the performance, one audience left, and another different audience was admitted and the show repeated. This became the norm in the 20th century with shows typically at 6pm and 8.30pm, but still unusual in 1878. Holding between 4000 and 5000 people, with admission charges from 3d to 6d, it was therefore frequented by the working classes.

On this night at 8.15pm, a comic vocalist Fred Coyne, was singing the last verse of a song when a fight broke out in the pit. This in itself caused a minor disturbance, but some foolish and/or misguided person shouted the dreaded word "Fire!" Panic arose immediately, with everybody rushing

121

for the exits. There were four large exits, but people naturally turn to the way they enter, and within but a few minutes the stairs passage was packed tight with a mass of writhing bodies, those underneath "struggling in death, while the upper layer struggled for life". While the street entrance provided an outer door giving on to a ten foot wide passage, this narrowed to around 5ft with a pair of swing doors. Then a pay box intruded, and a turnstile arrangement with narrower passages leading off to the pit, and a staircase leading to the boxes and gallery. Thus people rushing out in the reverse direction all ended up in a confined space, heaping themselves on top of one another as the early ones stumbled and fell, all trying to get through the obstacles at the same time.

Many, realising the staircase mentioned above was pointless to attempt, and finding their way to other exits, got out easily and safely through wide passages and doorways, though it appears the doors of these opened inwards, and one exit, actually bolted and barred, had to be broken down with an axe. People in the front seats of the pit, mounting the stage, escaped easily as there were doors leading directly from the stage to outside. More adventurous boys and men, finding themselves trapped, smashed through windows and made an exit not knowing what was beyond.

It has to be stressed that none of this was at all necessary. There was no fire. There was nothing but a brawl between two men in the pit. Perhaps the shout had actually been "Fight!" Though the place was large, the manager was able to prove that a full house could be cleared in an orderly fashion within nine minutes using all the exits. This was done to prove to the watch committee when doubts about licensing the place arose.

The total of dead was 37, mostly young working men with fit and strong bodies, only two females and two boys were among the number. The following night the manager Jacob Goodman placed bills up saying performances as usual – with a footnote of £20 reward to anyone who could identify the person who cried "Fire!" This outrageous intention caused great ire throughout the town, and Goodman was told not to press ahead with the performances. Fred Coyne declared he would not take part, and Goodman backed down saying his proposal was to give the proceeds to the sufferers in the calamity of the previous night.

The inquest revealed the shortcomings of the building, and Goodman was found wanting in the matter of keeping the place in good repair, and lacking a social and moral responsibility, although not transgressing any legal obligation. He continued to run the place as a concert hall.

It has astonished me when recording the many fires, panics and other death-causing disasters that there never seemed to be any legal examination as to criminal culpability. However, following on from this tragedy there was an attempt to pin responsibility. On the 7 January 1879, five separate actions were placed against Jacob Goodman by relatives of people who had lost their lives. The first case was brought by Mrs McIntegart reduced to widowhood in a helpless state with four children. She claimed compensation for damages because of the death of her husband. The judge, at the beginning, said he did not know of a precedent for this case, that there had been panics in other theatres, churches and buildings, and, if an action was possible in such circumstances, one would have been brought, but he knew of no action having ever been done so.

The lawyer for the plaintiff based his case on the state of the building, particularly the restricted exits. The judge said the question regarding that was in two parts – were the exits sufficient under normal conditions, and were they sufficient in an emergency? The crucial point in this particular case was whether the death of the plaintiff's husband was caused by a lack of egress, or whether he died by his own imprudence or negligence. Goodman's lawyer argued that the death was caused not by any fault in the building, but the panic of the audience. Mr Goodman did not cause the audience to panic, he had no more idea of what was going to happen than anybody else.

After much discussion of these points it was left to a jury to decide, and they found for the defendant on all points. The cause of the death was the false shout of "Fire!" and the defendant could not be held responsible for that. The judge was satisfied with the verdict, adding that if no agreement had been reached he would have directed the same. The decision in this case would apply to the other four waiting to be heard. Horrendous.

1878_12_09 NORTH SHIELDS (Northumberland).   COLLAPSE OF ROOF
There had been several days of snow in the area, and around 3am during a further severe snowstorm the weight of the unusually heavy load of accumulated snow caused the roof of the Northumberland Music Hall to collapse with a tremendous crash. Inside the building the fittings, scenery and all the contents of the auditorium were ruined. The damage was so great that repair was not feasible, and the venue had to be dismantled for future rebuilding, while in the immediate interim the lessee Mr Chisholm transferred his company to the Odd Fellows Hall.

1878_12_27 SHEFFIELD (Theatre Royal).   SMALL NEEDLESS PANIC
Shortly before the close of the pantomime on this evening, an alarm of "Fire!" resulted in the large audience showing "signs of excitement and terror". Around 50 people rushed for the same exit door, thus immediately blocking it. Fortunately, before the panic could spread, the lessee Richard Younge came onstage and stated the cry was false, there was no fire, and even if there should have been they had more than adequate equipment to deal with it. The cry had been raised during the transformation scene when it was said that a costume momentarily caught fire. Costumes catching fire were astonishingly frequent and over 150 cases can be found in the companion book *Perils of the Victorian Stage*.

1879_10_04 EXETER (Theatre Royal).   AUDIENCE MEMBER FALLS FROM GALLERY
Remarkably, people were still falling from the gallery into the pit below. This was a man named Mudge who, in a hurry to occupy a front seat he had spotted, missed his footing and fell over, striking the front of the dress circle and plunging into the pit where he snapped a seat in two on landing. He got away with nothing more than a badly bruised thigh.

1879_11_10c PARIS, France (Gobelins).   AUDIENCE MEMBER FALLS FROM GALLERY
"An accident, of a happily unusual character, which might have been attended with serious results, occurred at the Gobelins Theatre, Paris." As we have seen, this type of accident was not so unusual and, what is more, the result was very often remarkable as here. A man fell from the gallery into the *parterre* (UK pit) just as the curtain had fallen on Act I. This caused much excitement and agitation, as the poor chap was expected to be lying there injured or dying. In fact, he was nowhere to be found, and it was thought he had joined the mass leaving to spend the interval. "A shoemaker and a young girl who were immediately beneath the spot where the unlucky victim of the force of gravity alighted were less fortunate, for he struck against them as he fell, and inflicted some slight injuries."

123

1880_01_09 HULL (Alhambra).   AUDIENCE MEMBER FALLS FROM GALLERY

The spectator in the gallery was trying to reach a light from one of the gas chandeliers, presumably to light his cigarette. He overbalanced and fell into the pit. The unnamed man was uninjured and able to walk home, leaving the two people he had fallen on "somewhat seriously hurt" which necessitated their taking a cab home. If somebody fell on to me at the theatre and caused serious hurt I think I would expect more than somebody summoning a cab to take me home, wouldn't you?

1880_01_09 WORKINGTON (Theatre).   NEEDLESS PANIC

At around 9pm in the middle of the show, an actor rushed on to the stage and "peremptorily ordered all the gas out" ensuring a cry of "Fire!" was immediately raised. The manager's brother jumped up on the stage and extinguished all the lights. Thus panic ensued with everybody in the dark rushing to get out of the doors. The means of egress were insufficient for a mass emergency exit and several people were cut and bruised in the melee. Many ladies fainted and were taken in at adjoining houses, others were given smelling salts in the dark theatre. Eventually it transpired that a workman had left a gas tap partly on, "but there was no cause for alarm at all".

1880_01_31 LONDON (Haymarket).   SMALL RIOT

This was not actually a riot more an angry disturbance. Squire Bancroft was the lessee of the theatre at this period and after closing for refurbishment he reopened to face mutinous pittites. He had

done away entirely with the pit and replaced the old benches with separate stall seats. He expected the pittites to now find their place in the gallery. It was a move that had been imminent for some time. Previous lessee Ben Webster had in 1843 put backs on the pit benches – an improvement that had been neglected since Shakespeare's time – and had also changed the first few rows into orchestra stalls. Other theatres had also taken this step as it was necessary to not only provide better comfort for patrons but to raise the admission charges which had been slumping lower for many years due to the growth of additional theatres with much bigger capacities. Somewhat

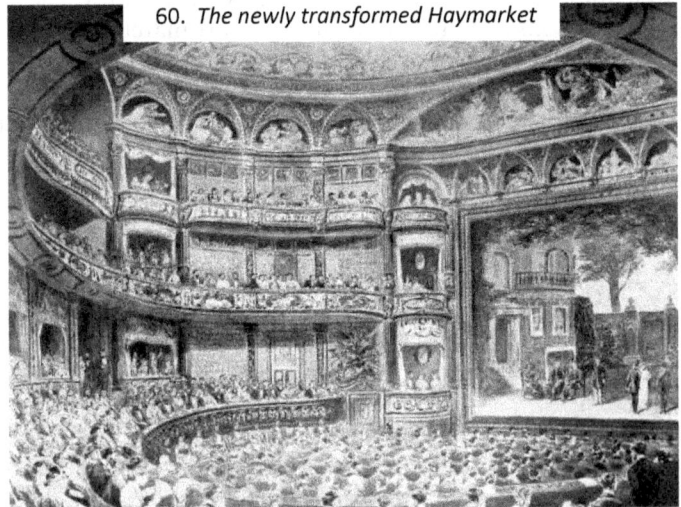

60. *The newly transformed Haymarket*

belatedly (like 300 years!) it was realised the best view was from the front of the pit, so these were upgraded to individual chairs called stalls, and priced the same as the dress circle. These seats were very popular with the upper classes so more and more rows were converted until Bancroft was the first to complete the process by abolishing the pit altogether. Instead of 2/- for a place in the pit, a person had to pay 7/- for a separate bookable stalls seat.

1880_04_17 SHEFFIELD (Alexandra).   FALL OF DRUNK YOUTH

The play was called *Rescued* and, though billed as a sensational drama, perhaps it was a dull play, as James Tankard (17) sitting in the corner of the gallery decided to provide his own excitement. Whatever his drunken reasoning – for the youth had over-supped – he announced he would "do a Blondin" and, climbing on to the metal screen erected to prevent accidents, attempted to balance on the top rail. He toppled over, struck the front of a box which broke his fall, and ending up on the stage promptly rolled into the orchestra pit. He was insensible when picked up, badly cut and bruised, and his shoulder was dislocated. Apparently, the appropriately named Tankard was a regular customer at the theatre as the leader of a gang of noisy youths.

1880_07_27 WREXHAM (Circus Big Top).   FIRE

A chandelier with a tank of benzoline (a fuel mixture made from coal gas and petrol) was hauled to the top of the tent king pole. However, the thing fell and oil, running out, caught fire, causing a spreading blaze in the whole place. Seeing the danger, the audience fled.

1880_12_18 ST HELENS (Theatre).   RIOT

The play was mid-way through when a dispute arose between the manager of the company then performing, and the owner of the theatre, as a result of which the actors refused to carry on. When this was announced there were cries from the audience demanding their money back. The answer to that was that the "cashier had gone away". The angry audience, now infuriated, started tearing up the benches and hurling them about. The barrier that protected the orchestra was torn down, the music grabbed and thrown around, light shades taken off and broken. Finally, the police arrived and took control, dispersing everybody from the premises. An angry detachment hung about outside throwing stones at the doors, but the manager wisely stayed inside until the street had cleared. Between £20 and £30 of damage was done.

1881_03_23 NICE, France (Opera House).   EXPLOSION AND FIRE

The audience was still assembling to see a performance of *Lucia di Lammermoor* when a loud explosion rocked the theatre and all the lights went out. Worse was to come as flames quickly burst forth, causing the gathered people to grope their way to the exits. By a quirk of good fortune, theatre-goers in France who occupy the boxes and the front stalls take their seats at the very last minute, presumably because they have been reserved in advance. This meant that the theatre was not yet at full capacity, which it would have been only a few minutes later. That was the only blessing, as the fire spread with mounting speed and fury. "Even in London, with all our excellent appliances, the difficulty of mastering the fire would have been great, but at Nice, as in so many foreign cities, there was practically no method of extinguishing the fire. The sailors of the fleet behaved nobly, as sailors always do. To their brave efforts and humanity it is due that the loss of life was not greater."

The sailors provided pumps from the ships, but water was low in the river. It would appear that a town fire brigade did not exist. The fire was under control by around 10pm, mainly because it was burning itself out. Also, by this time, there were fatalities among the frightened mass of people clamouring to get out in the pitch dark. As is usual in these horrendous conditions, the poorer folk in the gallery bore the brunt as they had to get down flights of steps and along passages far too narrow to cope with a crowd of people striving to get out urgently. In the panic people fell and were trampled over by others who feared being trapped by the fire.

Most casualties by far were from the top gallery audience who were suffocated by smoke as they jammed themselves at the bottom of the narrow stairs. In contrast, there was a solid wall behind the stalls on the ground floor and the boxes level which divided the auditorium from the front of house facilities, salons, staircases etc. The fire never touched anything beyond this wall, and anybody seated on those levels of the theatre would have been perfectly safe once they had passed through it. The total number of dead numbered 73, mostly local working people.

It was thought no English or USA citizens were present at the Opera House. In fact, three Scottish musical siblings lost their lives – James (23), Kate (19) and Lizzie (17) – children of David Kennedy a well-known Scottish singer – who were in Nice studying under Signor Lamperti, and in the theatre at the time of the explosion. An English lady called Mrs Magnay also died. An old gentleman was discovered crouched in a lobby as if sheltering a little girl from the flames. His back was burnt but his face recognisable. When a sailor took hold of her, the child fell to pieces in his hands.

1881_06_18 NEWCASTLE (Tyne).   FATAL FALL OF BOY FROM GALLERY

John Baston (13) had been sitting on the gallery rail as the show ended shortly before 11pm. As the audience made its way out of the theatre, John overbalanced and toppled from the gallery into the pit 30ft below where he crashed with great force on to a wooden seat, breaking it and exposing a metal piece that pierced his body. He was immediately rushed to the Infirmary where he died at 2pm the following afternoon.

So far I have recorded twenty such falls from gallery to pit, this being the fourth fatal one. Astonishingly, though new theatres were now better constructed, in the remaining 19 years there are many more still to come!

1881_08_23 LONDON (Crystal Palace).   FATAL FALL ON TO COFFEE STALL

The accident took place in the central transept where an organ recital had just finished. George Ogburn, who had been sitting in the orchestra stalls, was walking alongside the gallery. He saw what he thought was solid flooring at the other side of the railing and vaulting over it landed on the canvas top of a coffee stall. This immediately gave way and he fell with such force on to one of the large coffee urns that he broke his back. He was taken to Guy's Hospital where he died the following morning. The layout of the place must have been very odd and deceptive as this was the second time somebody had fallen through the top of a refreshment stand (*see 1877_04_02*).

1881_10_08 CHELTENHAM (Colosseum).   "A man, partially intoxicated, overbalanced himself in the course of an altercation with the checktaker, and he fell to the bottom of the gallery stairs, breaking his neck. The verdict at the inquest was Accidental death." *The Stage* 1881_10_14.

1881_11_23 NEW YORK, USA (London Variety).   NEEDLESS PANIC

It was Thanksgiving Night, the busiest night in the USA showbiz calendar. At the London variety theatre, a favourite resort of young men and boys of the lower classes, it was a packed house of 2780 people of whom 1152 were in the upper gallery. The auditorium was heated by steam pipes and radiators and, in attempting to get a better view of the stage, people were climbing on these fitments resulting in a pipe giving way allowing steam to escape. Immediately some imbecile (there is always one) shouted "Fire!" and started a panic. Nellie Richards who was singing at the time, bravely carried on until manager Donaldson ran on to try and quell the stampede, shouting until he was hoarse. Some sensible men took up his cause, and the panic subsided somewhat in the more expensive seats. Meanwhile the galleries had emptied without anybody getting hurt because the exits were wide and the men young and tough. They were all in the street outside and went back into the theatre when the danger was over.

1881_12_27 BRIGHTON (Oxford).   FATAL CANNON ACCIDENT
     "The judge declared it was not an illegal act to fire a cannon in a theatre." What on earth had happened for such an unbelievable statement to be uttered?
     The performer, a Chinaman named Ling-Look (34) a self-styled 'Lord of Fire, Cannon and Sword', was performing a series of sword-swallowing and fire-eating stunts. His climax was the astonishing feat of balancing a cannon on a sword poised in his mouth. The performer gestured to the

61. *Ling-Look*

image© The British Library Board

gallery 22ft away to sit back while the cannon was fired, and the Chairman rose to amplify his request.
     The cannon was fired and the charge struck a boy, George Smyth, sitting in the gallery who had his skull and brains completely blown away. There was a great commotion but no panic, and the house was immediately cleared. It appears that on the previous night – the first time the man had performed the trick – the charge blew out five gas lights in the roof.
     On the 2 January, an inquest was held and a jury gave a verdict of manslaughter against Ali-Ling-Look and his wife who pulled the trigger on the cannon. Mrs Botham the lessee of the hall was censured for allowing the dangerous stunt. All three were sent for trial at the Lewes Assizes, where the Grand Jury decided Mrs Botham had no case to answer and was dismissed, but the Ling-Looks had to stand trial.
     The judge declared it was not an illegal act to fire a cannon in a theatre. (Really?) As they had fired the cannon previously in the same way without any accident (the blowing out of gas lights seems to have been disregarded) they had no way of knowing that it might be dangerous. (again – Really?)

They were found 'Not Guilty' and discharged – which seems to me an unbelievable and appalling verdict.

Together with Holtum – who also had trouble with the law over firing a cannon (*see* 1880_02_13) – Ling-Look faced some adverse publicity with several newspapers deploring the fact that innocent members of the audience could be maimed or killed by the performers' dangerous antics. The *London and Provincial Entr'acte* (a rival showbiz paper to *The Era*) opined that had these two accidents happened in London, rather than the provinces, both perpetrators would have been banged up in jail, and certainly theatre and music hall managers would not risk booking them ever again.

1881_12_27 LONDON (Grecian).   NEEDLESS PANIC

The venue, the new Grecian Theatre, seating 5000 people, was packed for the new pantomime *Happy-Go-Lucky*. Shortly after curtain up a quarrel arose in the gallery. Theatres like the Grecian, situated in densely populated working-class areas, were no strangers to noise, arguments and even fights breaking out in the galleries. Whatever caused this fight, with husbands scrapping and wives screaming, it distracted attention from the stage. It was described as similar to "an Irish affray" where people – not immediately concerned – deemed it a good idea to join in on one side or the other, resulting in a couple of dozen creating the disturbance. The players on the stage paused, and at that moment some ignorant, stupid, or malevolent person at the back of the pit – on the ground floor under the Dress Circle who could not possibly know what was happening three floors higher up – shouted "Fire!" Immediately the audience, rising as one, made for the exits. Those inside boxes jumped down on to the stage and fled into the wings in a frightened manner, thus conveying to the pit audience that they were in danger from something they could not see. There were 1000 people in the crowded pit who moved *en masse*. It was reported a man was lying on a bench, his head thrown back, while panicking people crossed over him.

An actor still on the stage, looking out at the mayhem and melee, said he would never forget the sight of those faces ugly and agonising to behold. Of all the many panics noted hitherto, previously nobody had been onstage actually watching it take place. For there was no fire, no cause, just senseless panic. But it became unusual in another way; it all subsided within five minutes, and nobody was seriously hurt. Why?

The theatre was newly built in 1877 with six outward opening fire exits directly from the pit into the outside air, each allowing six persons simultaneously to pass through. The gallery had its own exits, and wide stone steps in shallow flights capable of taking eight people abreast. Similar set-ups provided for boxes and stalls, thus people could see and move easily, the outside was soon visible and had a calming effect. All this was in direct contrast to old theatres with few doors (that often opened inwards), narrow passages with bends, narrow stairs with steep descents, obstructions that narrowed them still more, all facets that induced panic.

The man who shouted "Fire!" – in danger of being lynched by those nearby – was actually caught by an officer, but escaped during the panic.

1881_12_12 LONDON (Astley's).   "During the performance at Astley's Theatre on Monday, one of the audience gave birth to a child, who, with the mother, was removed to the Lying-in Hospital." *Reading Mercury* 1881_12_17.

1881_12_27 LEEDS (Varieties). PAPER DECORATIONS CATCH FIRE

[Opened in 1865, at this period the theatre was known as Stansfield's Varieties but in 1893 became known as the City Varieties, a name it still bears today. It is one of the few music halls extant, largely due to its life as the location for the tv show *The Good Old Days* from 1953 to 1983. It is Listed Grade II and had a £9 million restoration in 2011. Located down a back alley, the picture (62) shows the entrance door as it is today.]

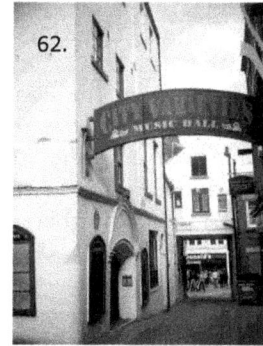

The paper decorations of a gas chandelier caught fire when a man lit his pipe from one of the jets. This immediately spread to other decorations, and the packed audience rose as one to flee. There was consternation when a main door was found locked. The first persons there tried to force it open, but without success, while those following poured down the steps, piling up on top of the ones already struggling. The passages were choked with shrieking people unable to progress to safety, many women fainted and several were injured. Sergeant Craddock of Leeds Police, forcing open the door from the outside, helped people out. Volunteers assisted, and medical men were called to minister to the wounded. Stansfield offered a £20 reward for the discovery of the man who started the fire. He was also summoned before magistrates and told "it was exceedingly dangerous to lock the main exit" and agreed to widen the aisles and corridors.

1881_10_22 AIRDRIE (Theatre). BROKEN WATER PIPE FLOODS THEATRE

During a performance of *Richard III* as two men were taking their seats in the gallery, a portion of flooring gave way and their feet, shooting down, came in contact with a water pipe which fractured under their weight. A great spout of water like a fountain burst forth high into the air, drenching the people in the gallery who rushed to leave. However, they reckoned without the duty policeman, Pc Lockhart, who closed the exit door and steadfastly refused to allow people to pass. This he did having knowledge of the many examples of panic and stampede. The water, gushing forth non-stop, found its way into the dress circle and the pit, causing people to clear those places. During the half-hour the water flowed, the steadfast company of Mr J B Howard ploughed on through the Bard's work, though it was really dumb show as the actors' voices were drowned out. (Ho! Ho! Ho!) The damage was considerable, and fears set in regarding the state of the thoroughly drenched plaster work.

1881_12_08 VIENNA, Austria (Ring). MANY FATALITIES IN THEATRE HORROR FIRE

[This is another of those horrendous accidents by fire that live on to this day in the memories of citizens. The theatre was not an old decrepit affair, it was built in 1873 at a cost of £90,000 and fitted with all the latest ideas in modern theatre including an iron safety curtain. A crowded house of 1700 people was eagerly assembling at 7pm when an explosion and a sheet of flame set all the stage house on fire. There were 384 fatalities. A long entry about this fire appears in the companion book *Perils of the Victorian Stage.*]

1881_12_19 VIENNA, Austria (theatre). FIRE

The Ring Theatre fire had a profound effect on the nation and the Emperor took a personal interest in visiting all the theatres in the capital to assess the fire precautions. In view of the recent disaster it seems hardly credible that a private theatre (ie not belonging to the state) in a suburb of Vienna caught fire on this night. It is not clear how many were attending the theatre, as in the aftermath of the Ring fire, theatre business had plummeted down to only 10% of normal. There was a chimney fire in a large saloon full of people, immediately creating confusion on the stage; the audience – ignorant of the cause and seized with terror – made for the exits. There were no precautionary measures in the theatre, and the stairs and much of the building were made of wood. Matters were made worse by the stupidity of the police and theatre officials preventing anybody from leaving the building until the fire engines arrived. Seeing the blaze, relatives outside were anxious to go in and save their family members but, quite sensibly for once, this too was forbidden. Fortunately, the brigade, arriving promptly, dealt with the fire efficiently, otherwise a further disaster in the city could well have occurred.

The Emperor decreed that all theatres not state owned would shortly close in order to carry out any necessary alterations, no matter how extensive, to improve safety. If this was not possible then such inadequate buildings would be torn down and rebuilt to a safe design. However, it must be reiterated that the very modern late Ring Theatre, although only eight years old, had been built with inward opening doors, and had a bewildering lot of passages that made moving from one part of the building to another a nightmare for the uninitiated. The Ring disaster, echoing round the world, had a major effect on future theatre planning.

130

1881 - THE FIRST THEATRE WITH ELECTRICITY THROUGHOUT

The Savoy Theatre, London was the first theatre lit entirely by electricity. It was furnished with 1158 Swan lights – 114 in the auditorium, 220 lighting rooms and corridors, 824 on the stage itself. The Savoy demonstration of the safety aspects has passed into history: On 28 December 1881 the theatre was for the first time entirely lit by electricity, and during the first interval of the matinee, manager Richard D'Oyly Carte gave a brief explanation of the electricity system, then Mr Keppler the electrician brought on a Swan incandescent lamp with wires attached but no kind of shade or outer protection. Unbelievable as it seems today, at this point one or two people actually made for the exit as the lamp was illuminated. Then Keppler wrapped several layers of gauze material around the lamp. It did not catch fire. Then he took a hammer and struck the bulb which shattered. There was no explosion or flames. The demonstration was greeted with loud applause.

63. *Savoy Theatre when newly built in 1881*

1882_02_28 LONDON (Astley's).   FATAL FALL OF CHILD FROM GALLERY

This was a particularly tragic event. A little girl was taken up into the flies by her father, who was a friend of one of the flymen. While holding her in his arms as he pointed out the wonders of the stage from that lofty position, she slipped from his grasp and fell on to the stage 25ft below. Her skull was so seriously fractured that she died shortly after, being dead on her arrival at St Thomas's Hospital. The same paragraph appeared in many papers up to 18 March.

However, this may not have been at all accurate as a very different report in the *Era* of 11 March concerning the inquest that took place on 7 March stated otherwise. A boy of 2 years 10 months, in the upper gallery with his father Frederick May, fell 40ft into the pit. Mr May stated he put the child on the floor to free his hands in order to pay an attendant for a programme, and in that instant his son fell into the pit. At the inquest, the father said no one was to blame, and the jury gave a verdict of 'Accidental death' recommending an additional rail should be installed "so as to prevent a repetition of such a sad affair." The difference in the stories is very marked. Unless two such accidents happened within a short time, one must accept that the inquest had the correct details, and the first paragraph was given out from a rumour, immediately after the accident had happened.

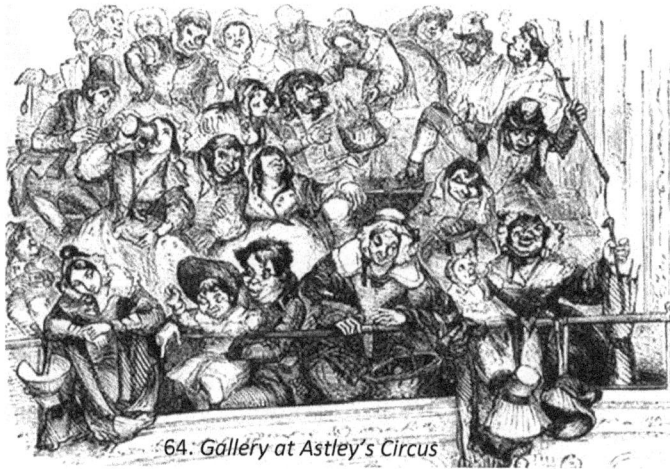
64. *Gallery at Astley's Circus*

1882_03_18 ST PETERSBURG, Russia (Winter-Livadia).   FIRE

The venue was housing the French Opera Bouffe, presenting the opera *La Perichole*. Around 9pm, when the show was in full progress, a fire broke out and the audience immediately panicked, rushing to the exits. The theatre, which had been recently constructed mainly of wood, seated around a thousand and was half-empty on this night. Fortunately, the exits proved adequate for the egress of the limited number, as only ten minutes elapsed from the alarm to a fully blazing building. It was entirely burnt down, but no lives were lost.

1882_03_27 BIRMINGHAM (Prince of Wales).   AUDIENCE MEMBER FALLS FROM GALLERY

The play was *Proof* and a popular attraction it proved, especially for pit and gallery which were packed. Around 10pm, Thomas Pope (27) a cooper, tried to make his way to the front of the gallery. He was "hustled about and lifted over the heads" of densely packed people, finally rolling to the front and over the rail, falling about 15ft on to the edge of the upper boxes. The accident was seen from the stage, and the curtain lowered while Pope was attended to. He, having fallen on his abdomen, was taken to the Queen's Hospital where he was kept while internal injuries were investigated.

In all the cases of people falling over the front of the gallery I have often wondered why they thought there would be space for them, and why other people were willing to pass them forward.

1882_04_01 PLYMOUTH (St James's Hall). COLLAPSE OF FRONT OF GALLERY

The show was something called a *Panstercorama* shown by Harry H Hamilton's company. This appears to have been on the lines of a painted diorama that illustrated recent events. Halfway through the show the left hand gallery collapsed, crashing some 50 people down 20ft into the body of the hall. Dr Pearce and Mr Steel soon arrived to attend to the sufferers. Seemingly the front of the gallery – removed for some former purpose – had not been replaced properly, and the excessive stamping of spectators' feet led to the collapse. A rush was made for the doors, and the groans of people wedged in the debris, mingling with the cries of fainting women, added to the confusion. Half a dozen were taken to hospital but, injuries being mostly slight, the people were allowed to go home.

1882_04_16 SCHWERIN, Germany (Court). FIRE

The play *Robert Bertram* was in progress when a fire broke out in the costume room situated at the back of the stage. The curtain was lowered and the manager walked on to explain the emergency, asking the audience to leave in an orderly fashion. The Grand Duke, seated in the royal box, also addressed the crowd urging them not to be alarmed. The firemen were all in place, and the orchestra struck up a waltz. Within seven minutes the house was clear without accident, "so perfect were the precautions which, since the Vienna disaster, had been taken to provide for such an emergency." However, the fire, raging on, reached the empty auditorium, gutting the place, leaving only the outer walls still standing.

132

1882_04_18 LONDON. *PROPOSED FIRE LEGISLATION FOR THEATRES-I*

In the light of recent notorious foreign fires, Mr Dixon-Hartland said there was an urgent need for Parliament to pass an act that would give legal control over theatres to prevent similar fires in London. Existing acts were too lax and frequently ignored. Parliament must be aware that fires such as the recent Ring Theatre fire in Vienna could easily occur in London, resulting in a similar horrendous death toll. A select committee should be formed to examine all the exits, passages and staircases and report the results of the investigations and the recommendations thereon.

In London alone there were 472 places of amusement providing a total capacity of 302,000 seats. These were divided as 57 theatres (126,000) and music halls 415 (176,000). The licences for these were varied and disparate, the authorities responsible for jurisdiction were several, including the Crown, the Lord Chamberlain, the Metropolitan Board of Works, Middlesex magistrates, Surrey magistrates and those of the City of London. There were five places holding around 5000 people that were not licensed at all. It was scandalous that even the authorities involved did not know where their responsibilities subsisted. Neither the Home Secretary nor the Metropolitan Board of Works had the power to close a theatre on grounds of lack of safety. From 1861 to 1877, 187 theatres had been totally destroyed by fire, and 13 each year since. The average life of a theatre was no more than 23 years.

Dixon-Hartland proposed that either the Home Secretary or the Chairman of the Metropolitan Board of Works should have complete authority over all, with the power to close theatres deemed dangerous on the advice of Capt Shaw of the London Fire Brigade. Capt Shaw's stringent fire fighting proposals for theatres were issued at the start of October 1882.

1882_04_21 LONDON (Court). EXPLOSION

The Prince and Princess of Wales graced the play *Parvenu* in a private box when, between the acts, an explosion was heard backstage. This was caused by the usual untoward mixing of gases before ignition for the limelight. The accident was widely reported because of the presence of royalty but, apart from the fact that presumably it did happen, the bare details of some reports were added to in a number of varying imaginative ways. The audience rose in panic and the Prince stood and calmed them with a gesture, or he said "Sit Still" in a loud and firm manner, clouds of debris settled on the stalls and boxes including on the royal pair, and even a person creating a panic by shouting "The Prince has been shot!" The most reliable was "The Prince and Princess of Wales attended a performance at the Court Theatre last night."

1882_08_20 CONSTANTINOPLE, Turkey (Hamadie). COLLAPSE OF THEATRE

As we have seen, quite often parts of buildings collapse in an alarming way, well the Hamidie Theatre was full for a popular comedy when the entire building gave way. The chandelier fell, smashing to pieces on the floor below, then the galleries followed, then the beams and rafters. The disaster was likened to an earthquake. The ruins blocked exits and 150 people were injured to some degree, though there were no fatalities. The audience comprised mainly "soldiers and men of good family". The theatre had been badly constructed and known to be dangerous but the authorities had refused permission for its reconstruction.

133

1882_08_31 OLDHAM (Theatre Royal). FIGHT LEADS TO MASS EXODUS

Only 18 days after an explosion at this theatre, another panic broke out with even less cause. The play, a new piece called *The Green Lanes of England*, filled the pit and galleries. For an unknown reason a fight broke out in the pit. This was by no means rare in industrial areas where low price admission theatres with huge pits and galleries presented sensational melodramas. Some person thought it was sensible to shout "A fight!" which was unfortunately misheard as a fire warning. The result of that was a mass exodus for the exits where theatre staff aided by two policemen, drove the people back from the doors, successfully persuading them to resume their seats without any injuries.

1882_10_27 FAVERSHAM (Institute). FATAL FALL OF AUDIENCE MEMBER

The venue was the Lecture Hall of the Institute, the company was that of Alfred Parry, the play *Queen's Evidence*. William Evans (50), a brick sorter, was attending the play – which must have been more interesting than sorting bricks. At interval time he went with pals seeking refreshment by jumping down the stairs "in a rough heedless way, jumping down two or three at a time". As a result he stumbled, and falling backwards down six or seven steps hit his head on the stone floor. His friends called out to him in a jocular manner but, getting no joshing rejoinder, went down to him to find he was already dead. He had broken his neck.

1882_11_16 GROSS BECS-KEREK, Hungary. NEEDLESS PANIC

A petroleum lamp used for lighting the lobby fell to the ground, filling the house with smoke. As usual, some helpful chap yelled out "Fire!" and the audience, rising as one, rushed for the exits. Some people jumped from the gallery into the pit, landing on spectators below causing many injuries.

1882_11_29c PARIS, France (Châtelet).   FALL FROM GALLERY

A carpenter named Decherbourg lost his balance when peering over the front of the gallery falling with a crash into the candelabrum placed above the dress circle. He was taken to hospital where "he lies in a precarious state."

1882_12_09 BARCELONA, Spain (Odeon).   "At the Odeon Theatre in Barcelona on Saturday night, a thief raised a cry of 'Fire!' and in the panic which ensued one person was killed and 18 others injured." *London Daily News* 1882_12_11.

1883_01_06 LONDON (Westminster Aquarium).   FIRE

At a variety show in the afternoon, while four girls were onstage dancing, the curtains on a box in the gallery caught fire. A bold man pulled them down to stamp on, but the next curtain had caught, flaming up as well. There was a moment of panic, the whole audience – comprising mainly women and children – rising. Several "ready-witted persons" shouted "Sit down!" while not only the blazing curtains but all the box curtains were torn down to prevent the fire spreading further. During all this the band continued playing and the dancers danced on. It is quite alarming how swiftly people try to flee and also significant when others – especially people of a superior station or class – command them to sit down they readily obey.

134 **1883_01_13** BERDITSCHEFF, Poland (Circus Ferroni).   FIRE

This fire was inexcusable if it was – as stated in the first report – started by a casually discarded cigarette as a stableman was lying on straw. Later statements blamed carelessly handled fireworks on the stage setting light to curtains. The building was entirely of wood with double walls infilled with straw for insulation. Inward opening exit doors and a dozen berserk horses trampling in the ring of fleeing spectators impeded attempts at clearing the building. The whole venue was ablaze within 20 minutes and the result was the loss of 268 lives.

1883_05_10 LONDON.   *PROPOSED FIRE LEGISLATION FOR THEATRES-II*

This was the Second Reading of the Theatres Regulation Bill which had been brought by Mr Dixon-Hartland over a year previously and he deplored the fact that nothing had happened since. In spite of massive agreement at that time, many had changed their minds. The Home Secretary was reluctant to add to his existing duties, the Metropolitan Board of Works already with sufficient powers in this regard, were insulted that they had been judged incompetent to carry them out. Various members spoke in favour and against the bill, those opposing saying it was poorly drawn up, "a garbled mess of indistinction", "crude and unworkable" etc. It was doubtful that the Home Secretary's Dept would welcome taking on the responsibilities for venues not placed in the metropolis. It was deemed that local authorities were far better placed to deal with such matters.

Dixon-Hartland said there had been 28 theatres in Europe destroyed by fire since he spoke on the bill a year ago, including the Alhambra in London. A vote was taken – For: 22; Against: 141; Majority against 119. It seems incredible to me that, in the face of the evidence, so many MPs were complacent enough to allow present conditions to continue, but they did.

1883_06_16 SUNDERLAND (Victoria Hall).   FATAL NEEDLESS PANIC

You will have already read of many people dying through foolish panics and stupid behaviour. This event was worse than any tragedy you have read in the book so far, and you will not read of anything else as dreadful before the end, because all the people who perished were innocent children.

The venue was the Victoria Hall, a large hall built in 1872, seating 3000, facing a park. The entertainment was a show given by Alfred Hutchinson (32) and his sister Annie (25). They were known professionally as Alexander and Annie Fay with an established music hall act featuring a séance with Annie as the medium and were currently appearing at Tyneside Aquarium. The two Fays also presented a show intended mainly for children consisting of marionettes, ventriloquism magic tricks, ghostly antics, and . . . prizes!

65. *Victoria Hall*

Victoria Hall, Sunderland
On Saturday Afternoon at 3 o'clock
SCHOOL TICKET

THE FAYS

From the Tynemouth Aquarium
Will give a Great Day Performance for Children,
THE GREATEST TREAT FOR CHILDREN EVER
GIVEN
Conjuring, Talking Waxworks, Living
Marionettes, The Great Ghost Illusion, &c.

This Ticket will admit any number of Children on payment of
ONE PENNY Each ; Reserved Seats, 2d, Nurses
or Parents with Children, 3d.

PRIZES!
Every Child entering the room will stand a chance of receiving
a handsome Present, Rocks, Toys, &c.
This Entertainment has been witnessed by thousands of
delighted Children throughout England.

Mr Fay had taken the hall on a sharing arrangement with Mr Coates who represented the owners. The admission charge was only one penny, reserved seats 2d, nannies or parents with children 3d. The entertainment had "been witnessed by thousands of delighted children throughout England." What could be more agreeable at 3pm on a Saturday afternoon?

We have no information about the show, no doubt it was satisfactory, and the children would have all left for home chattering with excitement. What we do know is that at the end the few adults presenting the show starting handing out gifts from the stage as the children left the stalls area. The children had paid the same throughout the building and there were over 1000 in the gallery who suddenly realised they were missing out on the presents. They were not going to stand for that! There was a mad rush down the gallery stairs for the free toys. At the bottom was an entrance door specially designed to bolt in a position that allowed only one person at a time to pass through, ensuring everybody paid, no sneaking past. This door opened inwards. It was normal in all the theatres of the time to have a barrier at the pit and gallery entrances, as seats in those areas comprising rows of benches, were neither numbered nor bookable in advance. BUT once the people were in and the show started, the barrier was intended to be opened to its widest extent and bolted against the wall in preparation for exiting which, of course, was far more uncontrolled. This door, on this afternoon, had been left in the narrowed position.

The children, thirsting for free toys, stampeded down the stairs, fell, tumbled and came to an abrupt halt sprawling at the bottom, the ones behind charging on until there was a massed heap of tangled bodies wedged against that infernal door. Adults, realising what was happening, ran to help. It was all clear on their side of course, but the bolt was on the other side of the door. The caretaker, knowing his way around got to the gallery and, like the Pied Piper, led 600 children out via another exit, then returned to pull back the ones jammed on the top of the stairs. Meanwhile, the poor parents who had arrived to meet their youngsters at the end of the show were plucking out children one by one through the narrow gap.

183 children between the ages of three and 14 died from compressive asphyxia in a flat area of 7ft x 7ft and the 14 steps of the same width leading down to it. The bodies were piled up as far as the 11th step.

As can only be imagined, as soon as the news spread, parents came looking for their offspring and many a dazed father was seen cradling a dead infant, not knowing what he should do next. Fortunately, authority in the shape of police, ambulances and volunteer doctors was soon on the scene. The Sunderland area might know how to cope with coal mine disasters, factory accidents, railway calamities and misfortunes at sea, but this was an unprecedented tragedy. Burying all the children was inevitably a drawn out procedure from Tuesday to Friday, as several different religious denominations were involved and all the funeral directors in the area together could not summon sufficient coffins quickly enough. The contributions, both in sympathies and cash, came from all over the country, eventually amounting to £5000. The Queen sent a wreath and asked to be kept informed. The government promised to send a barrister to assist at the inquest.

136

66.

It was then certain facts were revealed. Mr Fay had intended placing the 1d children in the pit, and the 2d children in the dress circle. He did not intend using the gallery at all. The owners of the hall forbad the use of the dress circle which was only used when the admission charge was at least 6d. This is understandable, as I recall when I was a boy going to the Saturday matinee at the cinema in 1950 – the best seats were always out of bounds. There were only five adults in the team: Mr Fay and his sister did the show, Raine and Wybert in the pit, and Hesseltine a floating dogsbody. Plus Graham the hall-keeper and his wife on duty in the gallery, these five were responsible for controlling admission, and other front-of-house duties. The gallery was capable of holding 1500 adults, and Fay stated 1050 children and "possibly 20 grown-up persons" were seated there.

At the end of the show, Fay pulled toys out of a magic hat, tossing them down to the children in the pit. Hesseltine was given a box of toys and told to distribute them to the gallery children. Fay had said at the beginning of the inquest that Hesseltine had come to him in a dazed condition, and after saying children were stuck on the stairs, and some were dead, promptly fainted. Fay dashed water in his face in an attempt to revive him. That was the first Fay knew of the disaster.

Hesseltine had stationed himself at the midpoint of the stairs – where on entrance admission money was taken – handing toys to the children as they passed on the way out. He stated that he had gone up to the gallery, and the fatal door – of which he had not even been aware – was fully open. At the top of the stairs children had started coming out of the gallery, so he went no further and gave out toys, walking down again as he did so, reaching the door to find it was now loose and half closed.

Several children said they had seen Hesseltine pull the door from its position against the wall and drop the bolt into a hole in the floor. One even stated she had seen him poke dirt out of the hole before putting the bolt down. Several said they had seen him press down the bolt with his foot.

The jury, out one hour and forty minutes, returned to deliver this verdict: "We find that Frederick Mills and others met their death by suffocation on the

67. *The fatal rush for presents*

stairs leading from the gallery in the Victoria Hall, on the 16th June, 1883, through the partial closing of a door on the landing, fixed in its position by a bolt in the floor, but by whom there is not sufficient evidence to show; that the managers of the entertainment be censured for not having provided sufficient caretakers and assistants to preserve order in the hall on that afternoon, and we believe that a partnership existed between Mr Coates and Mr Fay. We consider the modes of entrance and exit in the hall are sufficient, except the door at which the fatality occurred and we would recommend its removal at once. We attach no blame to the caretaker, but suggest in future the proprietor of the hall should instruct him to show to all persons who engage the hall all its modes of ingress and egress."

The Fays returned to the Tyneside Aquarium and carried on with their customary engagements into the 20th century. They did not attempt any more shows for children.

1883_06_28 EDINBURGH (Theatre Royal).   FIGHTING STUDENTS STOP SHOW

On this night, a party of 50 students was packed at one side of the gallery with the express purpose of making fun of *My Sweetheart*. This progressed from making jeering mock when the lovers kissed, to louder more objectionable interruptions. As a result another group of young men went out, returning with hard peas which they fired with pea-shooters at the students. An egg was also thrown, damaging a student's hat. As the melee increased, the play had to be stopped, and Heslop the manager together with his front-of-house staff and some policemen arrived to eject the whole mob of students. A fight broke out as the students tried to evade eviction, but they were overwhelmed and driven out to the exit, having to pass the gamut between two rows of protesting patrons who struck and buffeted them as they were marched past. The interruption went on for half-an-hour, an apology was made from the stage, and the play resumed. Nine of the students were arrested. One was fined £10 or 15 days imprisonment, seven were fined £5 or ten days in prison, and one discharged.

1883_08_28c KATAMOTOMURA, Japan (Govi Sanuki).   FIRE

"The building was filled with people during a performance, and being of a highly inflammable construction the flames spread with awful rapidity, and enveloped the theatre in a few minutes. In an instant after the alarm there was confusion, and desperate, though in many cases vain, attempts were made to get out of the theatre. Fifteen adults and sixteen children were killed, and over one hundred persons seriously injured." *Lancaster Gazette* 1883_10_10.

1883_09_18 PRAGUE, Czech R (German).   NEEDLESS PANIC

During the performance on this night a loud hissing and roaring could be heard, and the audience, fearing the place was on fire, headed for the doors. It is a fact, as observed previously, that even in an emergency, people tend to go out the way they came in. This theatre had several emergency exits which were largely ignored, people making for the main entrances. The director appeared before the curtain in the time-honoured manner to assure his patrons that there was no cause for alarm. The sounds they had heard came from a broken steam pipe, the theatre's firemen had already dealt with it, and the performance would resume as soon as all had returned to their seats. The hiatus had been no more than ten minutes

---

FIRE PREVENTION

At the Paris Opera House on 13 November 1883, it was reported that tests had been made of "M Gaspard Meyer's new invention" – another new compound for treating scenery and costumes. The Chief of Police, the Head of the Paris Fire Brigade and the Director of the Opera House were all present to see the demonstration. Various wooden frames covered with canvas and painted papers were subjected to the heat of a fierce wood fire and flames of gas for an hour. The materials survived intact, without even being "cracked or broken". M Meyer explained that wood so treated may become charcoal but would not burst into flame. The experiment was considered such an overwhelming success that orders were made for all the Opera House scenery to be immediately treated. The compound was not restricted to theatres – government offices, banks etc could adopt the new invention, as the paper of important documents could be made fireproof too.

1884_01_12 PLYMOUTH (Theatre Royal).   DRUNK STUDENTS ATTACK STAFF AND POLICE
Saturday night, and a group of 30 naval engineering students elated by winning a football match, and consuming "subsequent stimulants" behaved in an excessive unruly manner while in the theatre. They were remonstrated by officials and the police. At the interval they went out, presumably for more stimulants and, on return, were refused re-entry. Objecting to this, the students tried to get in by main force, seriously attacking police and staff. The fight lasted for several minutes until an officer present called out the names of several participants, and "the young men retired."

1884_04_20 BUCHAREST, Romania (Sidoli). "During the evening performance at the Sidoli Circus the roof fell in, extinguishing all the lights and causing a terrible panic, which was increased by the outbreak of fire. Five dead and nearly a hundred wounded, were carried from the spot. Great numbers of persons are missed." *London Daily News 1884_04_22.*

1884_04_22 WREXHAM (Public Hall).   NEEDLESS PANIC
The pantomime was *Robinson Crusoe*, the company that of Maggie Morton. Partway through the show "some miscreant raised a cry of fire". A panic instantly ensued, seats were broken, women and children screamed and a mad rush made for the doors. Some gentlemen in the front seats, retaining their presence of mind, aided the performers in trying to still the panic, but madly excited people continued fighting, struggling and smashing the seats in the hall. There were many torn clothes, bruised faces, "abraded limbs", and losses of watches and jewellery, but no serious casualty. A fruitless effort was made to locate the miscreant.

1884_08_23 LONDON (Holborn).   RIOT
A professional dispute between performers Thomas Coote, Miss Lizzie Coote and the manager Mr Pearson caused a hiatus in the show. To calm the restless audience over the delay, Pearson announced a member of the company would give a monologue, which was duly listened to. Meanwhile the altercation had taken a turn for the worse with both chorus and orchestra joining in. The only thing for Pearson to do was to refund the admission. After an announcement to that effect, he and Vincent – a member of the chorus – manned the pay box to return money as the audience filed out.
When Pearson realised he had paid out £2 more than he had taken in, he refused to refund any more, thus incensing a gang of roughs to attack the pay box, smashing it to bits. The mob then turned on to the two men, Vincent having the coat torn from his back. Miss Irving, a member of the company, trying to calm things was harshly handled. Pearson managed to bundle himself and Miss Irving back into the theatre and on to the stage, where they were pursued by the roughs. The pair made it to the flies, slamming an iron door behind them. The crowd now in the pit, started smashing up the seats and the glass lighting globes. Messengers went for the police who attended from two police stations, and with "the greatest difficulty" cleared the theatre. For some time after, Pearson and several theatre people were "obliged to remain in the building."

> "I'll come no more behind your scenes, David, for the silk stockings and white bosoms of your actresses excite my amorous propensities." Dr Johnson (1709-1784) to David Garrick.

1884_11_01 GLASGOW (Star).   FATAL NEEDLESS PANIC

[This venue was of the "cheap music hall class" but built as a conventional theatre with stalls, circle, pit and gallery. Access to the stalls and circle were by a wide lobby and doors on to the main street; the entrances to the pit and gallery were combined in one door down a side alley. On entering, a few steps led to the pay box with a gate, then a short corridor to the right led to the pit, while to the left six flights of steps went up to the gallery. These were 5ft wide – but spiral – so only about 3½ft were usable. This lay-out was, as we have often seen, typical and not unusual.]

It was a Saturday night and this 2500-seat hall had 2000 people in. After two hours of satisfactory entertainment, the Eugene Family – a trio of trapeze artistes – was announced. This entailed erecting a safety net over the stalls and pit, as the trapezes were suspended from the auditorium ceiling above, again a conventional arrangement of the time. However, people at the back were unable to see as they were under the dress circle so left their seats and pressed forward. In so doing they pushed against the barrier dividing stalls from pit breaking a section of it. This seems to have been the catalyst for some thoughtless person to shout "Fire!" causing the audience to panic and rush for the exits. In the case of the pit and gallery, the stream of people from each coalescing at the pay box, jammed into a struggling mass of bodies, with women and children screaming, and many suffocating. Some men and boys jumped from the gallery into the trapeze artistes' net.

A mere 15 minutes from the cry of "Fire!" the police were present and in control, the circle and stalls patrons quietly dispersing through their spacious lobby. But at the fatal pay box, over 30 insensible bodies had to be carried out, 14 of them dead, another 14 seriously injured.

Immediately the spectre of the previous horror fire at a Glasgow theatre arose when 64 were killed in February 1849. Questions were asked about the lack of emergency exits, and why the place had been given a licence when past experience obviously indicated that the layout of steps and passages was a total death trap. Of course, there being no fire, there was no need to panic but people in a crowd behave more rashly than in their own home. The search began for the culprit who gave the shout. He was believed to be a disaffected employee who, having been sacked, caused the panic through malice. A checktaker called Turner was accused of shouting the word, but he claimed he was warning one of the trapeze artistes that he was too near a gas jet. Apparently Turner had been laid off two weeks before this debacle, though not for any fault with the man himself. The lessee, seeking to reduce his expenses, had also dismissed some others at the same time. Before magistrates, Turner was released for lack of evidence.

Manager McKay paid for burial and other expenses from a fund he started. Another official fund was formed, and the distribution from that took place on 15 January 1885. It is salutary to note what pitiful recompense was made for the death of loved ones. The fund totalled £106 and was distributed between 32 people. The nearest relatives to the 14 fatalities received between £3 and £8 each; 18 people who were severely injured, or the nearest kin to them, were each given from £1 to £5.

1884_11_24 LONDON (Covent Garden).   STUDENTS BRAWL AT PROMENADE CONCERT

These annual concerts had been spoiled on several occasions by medical students shouting and brawling. Came this, the final night of the series, the student forces were at the maximum. Up to 10pm, apart from a few shouts, the concert had been listened to in reasonable comfort. At the juncture when a young lady vocalist came forward to sing, at a pre-arranged cue the malcontents got up and ran wildly round and round the promenade, hooting and yelling in such a manner not a note of the song could be heard.

The vocalist walked off, and Mr Crowe the conductor thought it advisable to play the National Anthem to end the concert. It was such a scene of disorder, rowdyism and confusion that the police entered to clear the building. The resistance was terrific, with the need for eight constables to eject one offender. Those taken into custody were liable to be rescued by vicious colleagues. Inside, the roughs invaded the stage after the orchestra had fled, while outside the mob was fighting the police, smashing windows and leaping on coaches drawn up to take concert-goers away. No motive was given for this outrageous display.

Only four persons were charged in court, none of whom was a medical student. The punishments were derisory fines of £3, 30/-, £1, with one offender having to find security for his good behaviour for a month. It was not always that punishments were much more severe in the olden days than today.

1884_12_18 PARIS, France (Folies Dramatiques).   FALL FROM GALLERY

A porter from the vegetable market fell head first from the gallery on to the tier below. He was taken to the Lariboisière Hospital.

1884_12_28c CHOLET, France.   COLLAPSE OF ROOF AND GALLERY

A temporary wooden theatre seating 1000 people had been erected on the Place Travot. A five-act play was in progress to a crowded house when the roof fell in on to the gallery, which in turn gave way so that the whole interior was a mass of broken timber, mixed up with the entire audience. "Shrieks and cries of terror mingled with the groans of the wounded who were powerless to extricate themselves."

To make things more difficult the manager shut off the gas to prevent fire starting, so everything was in the pitch black. The mayor and garrison, soon on the scene, dealt very efficiently in rescuing the wounded. Some 150 were seriously injured and taken to hospital. It was thought that recent storms had loosened the jointing of the fabric.

1885_02_03 HUDDERSFIELD (Harmston's Circus).   BOY HIT BY SWINGING BLOCK

The circus was that of W B Harmston of Warrington. A boy, Francis Nicholson, went to see the circus at Huddersfield on this day. A safety net was erected for the trapeze act, during which one of the supporting ropes broke, freeing a block which swung to hit the boy on the head causing injuries. The boy's father, a pub landlord, sued the circus for £10.10.0 on behalf of his son. Harmston was defended by Mr Jenkins, who started by saying he did not defend through a lack of feeling for the injured boy, but on the legal grounds that "no inconvenience, damage, or danger would be likely to be caused to persons attending his circus from any lack of the necessary precautions or from carelessness on his part." Then quoting case precedents, he brought several witnesses to show every reasonable and correct precaution had been taken to prevent accident and, as far as could be seen, the ropes were in proper order and condition. The judge agreed with this argument and found for the defendant.

FIRE PREVENTION

Many people and some editors were more exercised by fire prevention schemes than most MPs appeared to be, with numerous letters of advice and suggestions regularly pouring in after a fire. On March 1885, the *Pall Mall Gazette* printed a long letter from a Fire Brigade engineer containing various suggestions which I copy here. Canvas scenery can be made fireproof with tungstate of soda costing £4.5.0 a cwt. The writer claimed only one theatre in London did this. Costume materials should be made fireproof using the recipe of M Martin of Paris (recipe provided). Install carpet curtains in place of wooden doors. Do not have seats too close together. Gas connections should not be simple rubber tubing that can be easily pulled away but, as in the Alhambra Theatre, metal socket connections. Essential to have a proper fireman of sober character who is totally capable, and pay him £2 a week. Instead of theatres being individually insured, managers should combine their financial resources and insure themselves collectively, the premiums in total being sufficient to rebuild a destroyed theatre. This would ensure that greater care was taken in preventing hazardous defects remaining.

1886_01_23 BIRMINGHAM (Theatre Royal).   FALL FROM GALLERY

The victim was Alfred Manning (32) who should have been old enough to know better. He went into the gallery to see the pantomime, securing a place on the third row. Spying a chance to sit on the front row he stood and leapt forward, miscalculated, landing on the iron railings recently installed above the woodwork to prevent accidents of this nature. Trying to grasp the metal bars – but failing – he toppled forward into the pit below. He hit the front of the upper circle, and a chandelier protruding from the dress circle, and fell lengthways with "considerable force" on the benches of the pit, slightly hurting some seated people. He lay unconscious amid great consternation as he was thought to be dead. He was put in a cab to the Queen's Hospital where, astonishingly, he was found to be suffering from nothing more major than a few cuts around the face. He was kept in overnight but allowed to go home the next day.

1886_04_03 PARIS, France (Odeon).   FALL FROM GALLERY

A man, apparently the worse for drink, fell from the fourth gallery on to the balustrade of the dress circle. There he crushed a lady's hand which was resting on the velvet-covered top. Her injuries were attended to by a surgeon present – even in France there was always a handy doctor – and sent home in a carriage. The falling man appeared to have suffered no injury whatever.

1886_05_06 DERBY (Grand).   FIRE

Andrew Melville, an actor-manager, built a new theatre in Derby and called it The Grand, because it was very grand, or to be accurate, much grander than the inhabitants had been used to. Costing Melville £10,000, it had opened on 25 March. That's right – six weeks before. There were about 200 in the house half an hour before curtain up when fire broke out above the stage. The cause was not unusual, a border had wafted into a gas jet. At the request of Mr Melville, those people already seated left in good order. Things backstage were not as equable or organised. James Loxley – last seen just before the fire – had disappeared; his completely burnt body was found after the fire by

142

the stage door. John William Adams (24) a young comedian installed for the week with the touring company of Edward Terry was found partially suffocated with smoke in his dressing room and taken to the Infirmary where he died. With great difficulty other members of the company managed to escape.

Poor Edward Terry, off with a personal injury less than two years before, saw his entire livelihood go up in smoke, as all his touring repertory, scenery and costumes were destroyed. The interior was consumed in 20 minutes, the roof had gone before 8pm and, when finally subdued, all that remained were the fire-proof cloak-rooms, refreshment and store rooms at the front of the building. Though the fire brigade attended quickly, the hydrants, although sufficient in quantity, were linked causing the water pressure to diminish the more that were turned on. The brigade had to waste time moving hoses to different hydrants. Melville was fully insured, but still had losses of several thousand pounds. Astonishingly, a new theatre was immediately started and was ready to open on 13 November in the same year with a visit from the J W Turner Opera Co. The new theatre like the recently consumed one did not have electricity installed.

1886_07_14 PONTYPRIDD (Howard's Hall.)   COLLAPSE OF REAR GALLERY
The play was *Called Back*. The raised gallery at the rear of the hall suddenly gave way, and all seated there fell to the ground in a tangle of beams and planks. One woman was badly injured, but most escaped with nothing more than minor injuries.

143

1886_08_03 TINNEVELLEY (INDIA).   FATAL FIRE IN THATCHED VENUE
"A terrible and fatal accident occurred during a theatrical performance at Tinnevelley, India. It seems that the thatched building in which the performance was being held caught fire. There were 400 to 500 persons present, and as the doors opened inwards, the crush prevented their being opened. Seventy persons were killed and sixty more injured, many very seriously. It is reported that the fire was the result of a preconcerted design." *Shields Daily News* 1886_08_03.

FIRE PREVENTION

We return to the Ambigu Theatre in Paris. But the cause on 7 November 1886 was not an explosion but just the opposite. "M Edouard Philippe gave a series of experiments to prove the practical nature of his invention to replace gunpowder. The new explosive is a chemical compound, which makes all necessary noise without danger of any kind. Its use will avert the possibility of those accidents which so often occur when a gun or a pistol has to be fired close to an actor's face, and will moreover permit of the discharge of cannon on the stage. We shall see how it works to-morrow night in *Le Fils de Porthos*." *The Era* 1886_11_13.

1886_11_15 PARIS, France (Chateau d'Eau).   FALL FROM GALLERY
A man, falling from the second gallery into the orchestra stalls, escaped totally without injury. The man himself calmed the fears of all present, drank a glass of water, and insisted on staying where he was until the end of the show. A risky way to get a free upgrade, one feels.

1887_01_18 LONDON (Jews Hall). NEEDLESS PANIC

The venue was a hall in Spitalfields where 500 people were watching an amateur performance of *The Spanish Wanderer* given in Hebrew as a benefit performance. The hall, comprising a ground floor and a gallery on three sides, was full, and accessed via a doorway from an anteroom. The doorway was variously described as 5ft wide, and the width sufficient for two people to pass through at one time. There were other exits. Around 11pm there was a commotion in the gallery about escaping gas, seemingly arising because somebody had managed to break a gas bracket, possibly by hanging on to it. One man claimed he tried to stop the gas from leaking by tying his handkerchief around it. Of course some idiot then shouted "Fire!" and the panic and frenzy began. People in the downstairs got up to flee, simultaneously with an exodus down the stairs from the balcony. Then all the lights went out because somebody turned off the gas. Blame was heaped on this unknown person for adding to the confusion, but to be charitable it was standard procedure where there was a gas leak and fire together, and the person may have thought the cry of fire was genuine. Candles, lit upon the stage, revealed a struggling mass of people. As in the Sunderland disaster (*see* 1883_06_16) while the stronger fought their way out, the weakest were crushed and trampled underfoot. Police arrived and they, with the help of the amateur ushers, started pulling people from the doorway into the anteroom. When calm had been restored, it was found twelve women, one man, one girl, and three boys were dead.

1887_01_27 BRISTOL (Colston Hall). FATAL ACCIDENT TO BROTHERS

[The moving panorama was an innovation of the mid-nineteenth century. They were manufactured by making a long, continuous painted canvas scene and rolling each end around two large spool-type mechanisms that could be turned, enabling the canvas to scroll across the back of the stage, often behind a stationary scenic piece or object like a boat, horse, or vehicle, to create the illusion of movement and travelling. In the 1850s, several showmen such as Moses Gompertz – with his assistants the Poole brothers – toured the provinces. In the1880s, his business was taken over by the two Pooles who renamed the show as a myriorama to differentiate from others. By 1900 they had seven separate shows touring for 40 weeks of the year. They added elaborate effects to the scrolling paint-and-cloth panoramas: cut-out figures moving across the scene, accompanied by music, lighting and sound effects. Stories of travel and adventure, often military, were popular.]

WARNING: this accident is of a peculiar and terribly distressing nature. On Thursday afternoon, Poole's Myriorama was giving a matinee performance for a large number of schoolchildren. Among the first in the queue for admittance were the sons of Edward Austin Altree. A servant had been sent with Frederick (12) and Philemon (9) to the entertainment but, on the doors opening at 20 minutes prior to the start, the two boys raced upstairs to bag seats in the front row of the gallery. At the back of the gallery was a window with several shutters formed of a wooden framework covered with stretched canvas. The assistant caretaker, moving these, dropped one which clattered into the gallery. Startled by the sudden noise, Philemon, leaning over the balustrade, fell over the front and dropped around 20ft to land on the floor beneath. His elder brother, seeing him topple, fell back in a swoon. The servant, who had caught up with them by now, rushed to Frederick's aid and, finding him apparently dying, got assistance to take him down to the cloakroom. As the hall was now rapidly filling, efforts were put in hand to prevent a panic arising, and the two boys were removed as discreetly as possible. Philemon was also carried into the cloakroom, awaiting Dr Gloag who was hastening to the hall. Mr Poole's manager, acting under advice, wisely started the show. When Dr Gloag arrived he confirmed that Frederick's heart had stopped, presumably caused by the sudden shock, and that Philemon had fractured his skull and broken a leg. He was taken, still unconscious, to the Infirmary. The body of Frederick was held until the building was empty, and then taken to the house of his parents. What a shock those poor parents must have suffered.

1887_02_05 MANCHESTER (People's).   ACCIDENT TO DRUNK SPECTATOR

John Sullivan (23) went with a group of pals to the People's Concert Hall. In order to find a better view he moved away from them to sit on top of a partition. Being worse for drink at the time he overbalanced, falling backwards 9ft, injuring his back. He was taken to the Infirmary where he died from a fractured spine on 14 February.

1887_02_21 LONDON (National Standard).   FALL ON STAIRCASE

On this night, Mr Coulson, leaving the gallery in the interval, was descending a spiral staircase. A call came up from below saying the door was locked, and all must turn back. Coulson tried to do so but fell, breaking his thigh. He was in hospital for five months. In court on 27 October, Coulson sued John Douglass the lessee of the theatre on the grounds that the stairs were dark, and the gaslights had been turned off. The action was undefended, and damages of £20 awarded.

145

1887_05_25 PARIS, France (Opera Comique).   FATAL THEATRE FIRE

The opera was *Mignon* and, with reduced prices making it a popular night, the house was packed with 2000 people The fire broke out on the stage during Act I of the opera, most likely caused by a gas jet in an overhead batten catching a border, rapidly spreading to the scenery at large. One of the actors stepped forward to reassure the audience that all was under control when a great roar of flames appearing behind him with the entire cast fleeing for their lives visibly refuted his assertion.

Turning off the gas supply increased the panic and frenzy, giving the cue for the audience to evacuate without delay. By the time the fire brigade arrived the whole building was a mass of flames. At the time there were 150 singers and supers on the stage or in the wings. Many backstage people in upper floors sought escape via windows, others climbed on to the roof where they were rescued by firemen's ladders.

A total of 84 deaths were recorded, but it was thought that there may have been more, with bodies so badly burnt that nothing remained. The theatre recorded 17 fatalities among staff and performers.

69. *Opera Comique razed to the ground*

1887_06_09 MANCHESTER (Queen's).   SPECTATOR JUMPS FROM GALLERY ON TO STAGE

The play was a drama called *A Mother's Sin*. Towards the end of Act III, James Mandeville a warehouseman became so agitated at the treatment being meted out to the heroine he jumped from his gallery seat down on to the stage clearly injuring himself. Needless to say, both actors and audience were shocked, and the play halted while Mandeville was taken off to a dressing room and a doctor summoned. The medico had him taken to the Infirmary where it was confirmed that his leg was broken. The lessee went onstage to inform the audience that the man would survive, and the play continued.

FIRE PREVENTION

On 22 July 1887 in the Strand a new theatre being erected for Edward Terry was the location of a demonstration of the latest techniques. Each part of the theatre had two exits. The whole building was built from concrete and iron, the only wood used in the auditorium being for doors and windows. All woodwork backstage and front was coated with Sir Seymour Blane's fireproof paint. Fire hydrants placed at points throughout the building were controlled from the stage door. A system of water-sprinkling pipes over the entire stage fed directly from the mains at 90lbs pressure. A fire was lit in the middle of the stage with flames 25ft high. The fireman opened the sprinkler valves and the stage was deluged with water extinguishing the fire. "Capt Shaw and others interested in fire extinction" attended.

1887_09_05 EXETER (Theatre Royal).   **FIRE**

As a result of a fire destroying the Exeter Theatre in 1885, the owners, deciding that a replacement should be put underway without delay, turned to the current doyen of theatre architects – C J Phipps. The foundation stone was laid on 12 May 1886 and, only five months later, the new Theatre Royal opened on 13 October 1886. The principal approach was through a spacious foyer to the level of the dress circle. The pit and upper circle entrances were from Longbrook Street, and the gallery was entered from New North Road. A notable feature of the plan was that both the pit and upper floors of the theatre each had distinct separate exits on opposite sides of the building. The pit seating 650 had three exits. Total capacity was 1540. The site cost £3000, and the building £5,500.

On Monday evening about 10.15pm, during a performance of *The Romany Rye*, a fire was discovered in the flies. It was the usual case of a naked gas jet igniting a painted scenic border. The play was suddenly stopped, and the curtain lowered, to the bewilderment of the audience. Reason was soon satisfied as it became clear there was a rapidly spreading fire onstage resulting in a mass stampede for the exits. The house was about half capacity – around 800, and the people in the stalls and pit rapidly left by convenient doors. In the sparsely occupied dress circle and boxes, the patrons also left by a separate entrance without much difficulty while a group of people found their way on to the flat lead roof of the portico over the main entrance.

However, the rapidity of the spreading fire meant it soon reached the top level. This was divided into two sections, the front part – designated upper circle – held 150, behind that was a partition 3ft high, behind which was the gallery, seating 350. Each of these areas had its own entrance door and stairs. In the panic and haste some people went over the front of the upper circle, dropping down to the circle. Others made for windows, some climbing out, many others in desperation, throwing themselves out into the street 40ft below. Several managed to get on to the roof, even though they were trapped – the outside fire escape had not yet been invented. People naturally, but often foolishly, do presume the way they entered is the only way out, so inevitably most went for the stairs, thus the 200 people in the gallery were all trying to get down the stairs at the same time. There were 45 steps divided into four flights at angles to each other. These miniature landings between flights were bottlenecks, as was the inevitable pay box and gate positioned to permit entrance one at a time. There was also a pillar or post at this spot. When the firemen and police could get into the gallery entrance from below they found a wedged block of people on the first bend to the gallery. All had been suffocated and burnt. Removing them, progressing further up the stairs, more and more bodies were found. Half the gallery occupants had lost their lives. By 1.15am the fire was nearly out, but the theatre was a ruin and a lot of the dead were still inside, a continuing flow of corpses being brought forth and laid out.

70. *Theatre Royal, Exeter*

"Many of the bodies presented a frightful appearance. Some appeared to be crushed out of all semblance of shape, others were an unrecognisable charred mass of flesh, and all were cut and bruised and bleeding, pitiable heartrending objects. Unmistakably, the fight for life had been a terrible one and fought to the bitter end."

Deaths officially totalled 186, almost a quarter of the total audience present. This would have been a calamity in an old theatre, but in one only a year old designed by C J Phipps, the master theatre architect of the age, it was truly appalling. Following on from the recent major tragedies of The Ring (*see* 1881_12_08) and the Opera Comique (*see* 1887_05_25) it was finally decided that some major legislation was necessary regarding the building of theatres in the UK.

Theatres in London were under the jurisdiction of the Metropolitan Board of Works who laid down specifications, and inspected theatres, ordering alterations and improvements where conditions did not conform. There was no equivalent in the provinces, and theatre plans were, as at Exeter, agreed between the architect and the City Surveyor. The latter was told by Phipps that the plans conformed to London regulations. In the Exeter theatre, Phipps said it was constructed exactly as shown on the plans, but it had not been inspected before a licence was issued. At the inquest, Capt Shaw the founder and head of the Metropolitan Fire Brigade service, questioned the Surveyor using the London regulations as his guide. Most of the answers were woefully deficient. A major example of Phipps's errors was the proscenium wall. This is the party wall between the auditorium and the stage house and should be a minimum of 13in brick construction. The wall should be complete from the foundations to the roof with only one opening, the large one that gives the view of the stage ie the proscenium opening. One conventional doorway from under the stage into the orchestra pit was allowed, provided the door was fireproof. The Exeter wall was only 9" thick, and not of brick. Furthermore, it had two doorways with doors made of wood. The universal system of a paybox on the stairs, with a barrier placed across to funnel customers singly by, is invariably a death trap, even when the barrier is fastened back against the wall once the show starts. Here, in the middle of the stairs adding to the clutter, was a post or pillar. Other points raised included the construction of the walls, stairs and floors which were mainly of wood. Walls that should have been of fireproof material ie bricks, stone or concrete were of lath and plaster with matchboard.

But as Capt Shaw pointed out, there was no regulation in the land that said a provincial theatre had to conform to the same standards as a London theatre. He was careful not to fall into the trap of blaming the shortcomings on Phipps but said it was up to the jury to decide if any of these were material to causing the deaths. Phipps spoke out in support of his plan, claiming that if the gallery people had got over the low wall between them and the upper circle, they could have escaped that way and there would have been considerably fewer deaths. Phipps's reply was considered ludicrous and arrogant, as was his reply about his tortuous staircase:

"Is this correct (asked a juror) that from the top of the gallery there are seven steps down, then a turn at right angles fifteen steps further down, then a complete turn round, eight steps more, then another turn round, and then fourteen steps more on the 'skew'? – I think that is right (replied the great architect). Is it your opinion that there is a ready exit from the gallery in case of fire? – I think it was a very good staircase."

The jury said: "We deeply deplore that the architect, having been engaged by the Directors as a specialist, should have produced a building with so many structural defects." Phipps lost his credibility and much of his practice.

As a result of this fire – more than any other here or abroad – new UK regulations were seriously mooted. Manchester magistrates proposed that theatres should be licensed to accommodate a certain number, and if an accident occurred through exceeding that number the manager would be prosecuted. What a novel innovation! Sensible decisive methods were adopted by individual managers for their own theatre's protection – in the brand new Exeter theatre the wires supposed to prevent the borders wafting into the gas jets were 3in apart, and only joined together at 5ft intervals. As borders were often raised and lowered, the likelihood of the edge of a border entering a slot 5ft x 3in was forever imminent. When Isaac Tarry the young manager of the Northampton theatre heard the cause of the fire, he wrote to the press urging every theatre to do as he had done – put wire mesh all along. Today we would call this wire netting. So obvious, but only he seems to have thought of it!

1887_09_29c LONDON (Britannia).   NEEDLESS PANIC

Following on from the Exeter fire, theatre audiences were permanently keyed up, ready to flee on the slightest pretext. At Hoxton, the curtain had dropped at the end of Act IV of *Proof* and a disturbance arose in the pit. Some nitwit in the gallery shouted "Fire!" and a rush for the exits sprang up in all parts of the house. Attendants threw open wide all the exit doors and the audience streamed out. The orchestra, striking up, persuaded the non-fleeing patrons to stay put, and the false alarm was soon explained. A man, smoking in the saloon, on returning to his seat put his pipe in his pocket, thus setting fire to his coat. When order was restored the play continued to a much diminished audience.

1888_01_04 EDINBURGH (Theatre Royal).   BROKEN WATER PIPE CAUSES PANIC

This panic was caused by a man at the back of the gallery who, wanting a better view, climbed on to a water pipe installed as part of the anti-fire equipment. This broke under his weight and a great spout of water arose, naturally causing great agitation to all. Then, of course, some stupid person shouted "Fire!" and mayhem broke out in different parts of the theatre. The rich people in the dress circle and boxes, holding their ground, stood by their seats, the water was turned off, the stage manager came onstage and reassured the audience and, after a hiatus, the pantomime continued.

149

1888_03_20 OPORTO, Portugal (Baquet).   FIRE

The theatre was very full, the play was in its last act. The not unknown hazard of a scenic border flapping into a gas jet flame was the start of the fire that rapidly spread throughout the stage house. The Baquet Theatre was an old one catering for the lower classes, and the escaping audience had to struggle along narrow passages and down flights of steps from the upper levels of the auditorium. We have seen how in theatres – both in the UK and overseas – the struggle to escape, the inherent life force for survival, takes hold of every individual. The normal rules of society and morality are instantly discarded and only one law becomes paramount – "every man for himself". Previous theatre fires with large death tolls have told the depressing tale of men forcing their way out by trampling over women and children, individuals scrambling over increasing heaps of the dead and wounded, fighting for their own salvation. But this fire revealed previously unknown low levels of man's depravity. The "rougher class" of people included sailors, dock porters and the like who, not

71. *Baquet Theatre* **Oporto**

only pushed and shoved their way out, but with knives stabbed and slashed fellow human beings in the fight to be saved.

The body count was never officially confirmed as so few of the corpses were identified, many being nothing but separate parts, but 120 dead is the figure usually repeated, irrespective of the many hundreds injured. On the site today is the Theatro Hotel.

1888_04_22 BRUSSELS, Belgium (Alhambra).   FALL OF CHANDELIER

The time was a few minutes prior to opening the doors on Sunday. As the mighty central chandelier was being attached to the safety chain it fell to the ground with a thunderous crash. The only person present in the stalls – an attendant putting reserved tickets on the seats – escaped injury. The performance had to be cancelled and the theatre did not reopen until Tuesday. It appears that the chandelier was suspended on a wire cable, allowing it be lowered and raised via a pulley. Before each performance a safety chain was attached as an additional precaution, and it was while this was being put in place that the cable unwound due to the wheel feeding the cable breaking. Shades of *Phantom of the Opera*!

1888_09_03 SOUTH SHIELDS (Tyne).   SECTION OF FLOOR COLLAPSES

The venue, the Tyne Music Hall, built as Siddall's Grand Theatre and Cirque, having been closed for upwards of three years, was overhauled and reopened by Stuart Henry Bell a well-known scene painter of Sunderland. This was the opening night and everything went smoothly, with every turn well applauded by the large audience. Came the interval and everybody thronged the exits. The floor of the pit leading to one exit gave way, precipitating a score of people about 6ft into a void beneath. Several were injured, most seriously Isabella Aiken who suffered a spinal injury, and two more receiving undisclosed injuries. The show continued after the interval.

Unless somebody is actually killed and there is an inquest, rarely is anything further disclosed about these kinds of accidents, much less holding somebody to account. It seems that these collapsing galleries, falling tent poles, over-turning wagons, and all the rest of it, are just borne with a shrug and referred to as a 'pure accident'. In this particular case the building was probably a temporary one such as were erected by circuses prior to the widespread use of a canvas 'big top'. These were often dismantled when the season was over and the timber sold off, at other times they remained to be adapted for other uses or, as here, converted into a proper theatre or music hall. But they were only intended to have a short life. A good example of how easily a major accident could happen in these places is the case of Pablo Fanque's circus (*see* 1848_03_18).

1888_11_25c PARIS, France (Lyrique).   FALL OF CHANDELIER

This accident happened at the beginning of Act II. There were four matching chandeliers suspended over the stalls and one of them suddenly came crashing down on the folk sitting beneath. Fortunately only two people were injured, one a young man named Obrecht who, needing immediate hospital attention, was taken away. A woman in the back of the stalls was screaming as she was the youth's mother wanting to accompany the ambulance. It transpired they had initially been sitting together at the back but the son, wanting a better view, moved forward in the interval, his mother declining as she preferred the more distant view. She thus escaped the calamity that befell her son. She was pacified by an assurance that he was not badly hurt, while in fact he was very badly hurt indeed, expiring before reaching the hospital. After the hiatus caused by the accident, the manager stepping before the curtain, asked if the performance should continue; the audience replying in the affirmative.

EXPERT ON RECENT THEATRE FIRE STATISTICS

In its issue of 12 January 1889 the *Aberdeen Press and Journal* disclosed that Franz Gilardone, a German expert on theatre fires, had published a pamphlet on those of 1888. He declared that during that year 15 theatres had been totally destroyed by fire: England 4, USA 4, Belgium 2, Spain 2, and one in each of Portugal, Russia, and Romania. Since the notorious Ring Theatre fire of December 1881, and considering the vast amount of discussion and passing of laws, it is even more alarming to read that in eight years 96 great theatre fires had occurred, by far the largest number in the UK. These were listed as follows: UK 23, Russia 18, USA 17, France 12, Austria 6, Spain 5, Germany, Italy and Belgium each with 3, Holland, Sweden, Portugal, Romania, Japan and South America each with 1.

1889_04_27 JARROW (Albert Hall).   COLLAPSE OF GALLERY FRONT

The venue had for three months functioned as a music hall. On this night, a large net had been erected over the pit as a safety precaution for aerialists. However, after its function for that purpose, a number of lads were running along it in a race, causing great excitement, and the people in the gallery all rushed to the front to peer over so they could see the fun. Suddenly the gallery front gave way and 100 people were precipitated into the net, this fortunately breaking the fall of the victims and also protecting the people in the pit from falling debris. I cannot believe at that period a strong enough net could be made to stand the weight of 100 people and a lot of timber, when we read how often one is broken by a single falling trapeze artiste. In fact this one did eventually collapse but by then one assumes the pittites had removed themselves to safety. Remarkably, there were no fatalities and the three people – a pitman (19), a rivet boy (14) and a married woman – all found unconscious, were taken to the Memorial Hospital with concussion and were able to go home over the following few days.

1889_10_13 HANTING, China.   COLLAPSE OF THEATRE

Several entries back I remarked it was rare for an entire theatre to collapse. I spoke too soon as here is another. In the town of Hanting to the east of Shangtung there was a hill with a temple on the top. For reasons best known to the city fathers most of the hill was removed, leaving just the portion bearing the temple. It is not clear if the temple housed a theatre, or the temple itself was used as a theatre. Whichever, on this day, mid-performance the whole supporting wall of the temple-bearing portion gave way, and the entire theatre with audience of men, women and children was hurled into the street below, with immense blocks of stone and concrete showering down on them. Heads were broken open, bodies crushed, arms and legs smashed and often torn from the bodies. When the collapse had finally settled, 200 corpses were removed from the ruins, and many more were expected to be unearthed as work continued.

1889_11_04 SENICHIMA, Japan.   AND ANOTHER!

"On the 4th of November, a native theatre at Senichima collapsed during the performance. Twenty-five persons were killed, and one hundred injured." *Daily Gazette for Middlesbrough* 1889_12_02.

1889_11_16 LIVERPOOL (Shakespeare).   FALL FROM GALLERY

After Act III of *The Land of the Living*, a young man Richard Reynolds jumping down from the back part of the gallery to secure a seat in the front row toppled from the gallery into the stalls. He must have been very agile as the ornate front had rails which were breast high. Falling around 50ft, he landed on two unfortunate people who broke his fall, he coming out of it "practically scathe less" while one of the seated gentlemen was injured. Reynolds was taken to the Northern Hospital but discharged almost immediately, whereupon he went back to the theatre, demanded readmission and asked for a new hat. The most amazing part of this tale is that he did not have to wait 4+ hours for attention in A & E.

1889_12_11 JOHNSTOWN, USA (Opera House).   NEEDLESS PANIC

[The theatre, an old building condemned 12 years previously, had newly reopened to replace one swept away in a disastrous flood suffered throughout the area in June. The theatre had long been considered a death trap as there was only one entrance leading to a staircase.] The play was *Uncle Tom's Cabin* and the audience of 600 comprised mainly women and children. There were others outside still trying to gain admission, though I am not clear why as the show was coming to an end. It was one of those outside who shouted "Fire!" Immediately, the entire audience fled for the exit and soon the stairs were blocked with fallen people, with others trampling over them in the quest for safety. Those outside trying to get in caused a further blockage at the sole entry door itself. A fire engine arrived but, of course, there was no fire. The hose proved useful in turning it on the fit and active hampering the efforts of police to get to the dead and wounded piling up inside. At 3am the results were clear – 12 dead, 35 injured.

1890_03_13 LONDON (Deacon's).   INJURY CAUSED BY MAN FALLING INTO NET

The performance included the tightrope act of Menotti. Mr and Mrs Richardson were seated in the stalls, above them was a safety net. In his act Menotti walked the wire with a man on his back, then returned and reaching the centre, dropped his passenger into the net. The man fell into the net immediately above Richardson, crushing his hat and causing injury to his nose and eyes. In January 1891, Richardson sued for compensation for damage to his eyesight, shock to his nervous system, the consequent expenses, suffering, and loss of business. He alleged that the man had been

dropped without warning, and the net was not taut. In court, the defendant Captain Davis the owner of the hall countered with the following facts. The net was checked every night for tautness, it was 7ft

5in above the floor, and Richardson could not possibly have been struck unless he was standing up. This then seemed to be the case, as Richardson protested that nobody had given a warning to remain seated. Further wrangling came before the judge's summing up. He said that it was clear Richardson had been injured on the night in question, as Davis himself admitted his staff had seen the cuts and bruises to his face. The only question was the amount that should be awarded to compensate for those injuries and the losses consequent upon them. The jury found for the plaintiff with £45 damages.

1890_04_02 NEW YORK, USA (Thalia).   FALL FROM GALLERY

Israel Blumsohn, excited by the play at the theatre catering for the German population of the city, fell over the front of the gallery into the orchestra stalls 45ft below. He fractured a thigh and smashed his nose. The curtain was lowered as several ladies fainted with fright and the unfortunate chap was carried away.

1890_04_13 PHILADELPHIA, USA (New Park).   COLLAPSE OF ROOFTOP WATER TANK

The New Park Theatre was built with an in-house fire-fighting system. On its roof was an enormous water tank 20ft in diameter holding 5000 gallons of water weighing 25 tons. Shortly before noon on this day the whole thing collapsed, crashing through the roof and falling 110ft into the basement. The collapse reverberated round the area like an earthquake as the colossal tank wrecked all the stage house and parquet (stalls) area. The Wilson Barrett company was currently in residence and the entire scenery for *Claudian* was ruined. Amazingly, repairs were put in hand immediately, and the planned schedule for *Clito* was carried out without interruption.

1890_10_10 GLASGOW (Theatre Royal).   COLLAPSE OF LANDING

The venue was at Coatbridge. The play was *Belphegor* and the accident happened after the show as the audience was leaving. The gallery landing collapsed, seriously injuring four people. Others following were let out via a pass door to the backstage flies. An enquiry, held the next morning, found the landing was resting on joists riddled with dry rot, with further staircases similarly affected. The gallery was ordered to be closed until all the supports were replaced by iron ones. The four injured sued Mr Tully the manager for damages, but the claim was dismissed on the grounds that Tully had fulfilled his duty of care, and the correct person to sue was the owner. Eventually, after a lot of legal to-ing and fro-ing, in March 1891 the four were awarded compensation of £45, £18, £12 and £5.

1890_12_27 CANTERBURY (Theatre Royal).   SPECTATOR FALLS DOWN STEPS

During an interval of a performance of *The Shaugraun*, a popular play by the Irish playwright Dion Boucicault, a seaman – with the splendid name of Cornelius Grandfield (21) – was leaving the gallery and, on missing his hold on the handrail, fell headfirst down the steep flight of steps for some 30ft. He was taken to the hospital unconscious where his injuries were found to be a fracture of the skull and concussion of the brain. He was home on leave for Christmas. I can find no further report or an inquest, so I assume he survived to fight on for Queen and Country.

153

"I will never never do another play where a guy writes with a feather." Max Gordon (1892-1978)

1891_01_08 PARIS, France (Opera Comique).   FALL FROM GALLERY

Out of all the reports regarding people falling from the gallery only one newspaper deemed it worthy enough to provide an illustration!

In the middle of the performance, M Robin at the end of the second gallery, having leaned a little too far forward, lost his balance and fell into the stalls. On his descent, he firstly managed to hang on to the lower gallery, then dropped on the stalls chair of someone who was briefly absent. Robin being taken up unconscious, an ambulance was called which returned him home. He had received only minor bruises, and the manager offered a box for his use later in the week.

The accident was illustrated and this can be taken to represent all the many other similar ones detailed herein.

72. *Man falling from the Gallery at the Opera Comique*

1891_05_04 NANTES, France.   "A tier of seats at the Theatre of Chantonay, near Nantes, gave way last night under the weight of the occupants. Although 50 persons sustained contusions, nobody was seriously injured." *Western Morning News* 1891_05_06.

1891_06_11 OLDHAM (Theatre Royal).   MEMBER OF THE AUDIENCE SHOT

Often actors have been shot onstage, this is the first example of it happening to the audience. Dr Briggs and his friend Mr Cash were watching the play *Enlisted* from the side circle. During the dramatic action of one scene where an escaped convict is fired at, Dr Briggs suddenly exclaimed "I am shot!" – a statement which turned out to be correct. A small wound on the temple showed the tip of a brass pin which Mr Cash, with some difficulty, was able to remove. It was around half an inch in length and looked like a brass rivet used in boot making. Fortunately the wound was slight but only slightly lower could have left Dr Briggs blind.

1891_12_26 GATESHEAD (Theatre Royal). FATAL NEEDLESS PANIC

The pantomime *Aladdin* had opened on Christmas Eve, and this was its second performance. Being a popular attraction, the theatre was well filled, though not to its legal capacity. All proceeded well until 11pm when, in the gallery, a boy dropped a penny, and some helpful person struck a match to search for it. Whether the coin was found I know not, but the lighted match fell into a crevice under the benches where accumulated dirt, dust and rubbish immediately caught fire. Staff produced buckets of water to throw on the blaze, while a policeman with a hose attached to a hydrant squirted more water. The small fire, easily contained and swiftly extinguished, had only created damage taking no more than £5 to rectify.

However, a nervous woman seeing the flame had shouted "Fire!" and immediately panic seized the entire audience. Turner the lessee, playing in the panto, immediately went on to calm and pacify the audience, his performers too went forward to converse with the public and assure them of their safety. They would not listen, a few in the better seats sat on, but the pit soon emptied, as did the boxes and balcony tier (this taking the place of the customary dress circle). As usual it was the gallery which suffered the most, where about 500 people, many women and children, all made a rush for the door that they came in by. Some wise ones, finding an exit door leading to the paint shop, went that way.   Others tried to get out of windows, or lowered themselves down to the balcony, then out. But most fled down the stairs. As has been explained countless times earlier, at some point on the gallery steps is a barrier which is pulled across to permit only a single body to pass the pay box. This barrier should always be thrown aside at the start of the show.

Checktaker Thomas Forster (29) seeing the people rushing down the stairs tried to stop them. He had opened the barrier but was aware that children had fallen at a bend in the staircase; and they kept falling because they could only get past the fallen by trampling over them. The blockage grew greater as the police arrived trying to clear the way. Pc Waddington, one of the first on the scene, started lifting out the children. One of the first bodies was his own 13-year-old son. Eventually there were nine child corpses aged between 13 and 16. The only adult killed was Thomas Forster who left a widow and four children. The panic was totally unnecessary, the fire had been extinguished and all was safe. Again it was the dread shout of "Fire!" alone that was responsible. It was said a man near the woman clapped his hand over her mouth. Magnificent but too late!

1892_02_06 BLACKBURN (Prince's). NEEDLESS PANIC

Pantomime time and this house, holding 3000, was packed. Two men at the back of the pit started a fight, greatly disturbing the surrounding audience. In an effort to get a person in authority to deal with the fracas, a voice shouted "A fight!" which was instantly mistaken for a warning of fire. Masses of people rose and fled to the exits with the result that benches were smashed and clothes torn but, fortunately, nothing worse. The pantomime performers had carried on and the orchestra kept playing, preventing a wild panic, so the hundreds that had fled crept back somewhat shamefaced. There was no statement concerning the fisticuffs pair who caused the chaos

1892_04_27 PHILADELPHIA, USA (Grand Central). THEATRE DESTROYED BY FATAL FIRE

The theatre was normally used for variety performances but for this week a spectacular production called *The Devil's Auction* was to be staged. The audience was assembling for an 8pm start, and on the stage scenery was being lowered into position from the flies. It was during this operation that the scenery became entangled with the lights, the flimsy borders and canvas cloths then bursting into flames. There were some 70 people on the stage with a large cast fully costumed ready to open the show who immediately panicked. With flames suddenly roaring through the front curtain, the audience too knew the place was on fire. Everybody fled for the exits and soon the entire audience was outside. Two hospitals received casualties of which there were 60 detained with severe injuries of broken limbs and burns as well as some 50 others who were swiftly treated and allowed home. Five of the worst injured died the following day.

Meanwhile, on the stage, panic ensued with flimsily- clad ballet girls running aimlessly around, or making a mad rush for the stage door and other exits. The dressing rooms were under the stage with stairs leading up to street level on either side. There were exits at the top of each flight, and those who ran up the left side got out uninjured whereas the personnel attempting the stairs at the right side were thwarted by the fire, and in trying to cross to the opposite side succumbed to smoke suffocation. The following members of the company were found dead in the ruins: Thomas Lorella, and his wife Flora, Vincentina Chitten, Fannie Conners, Sarah Golden, and William L. Brooks. It was rare for performers to perish in theatre fires as usually there were easier exit routes backstage, and as fires nearly always started backstage they had the first chance of fleeing. It seems that Thomas Lorella was one of the first out but finding his wife was not, as he thought, ahead of him, went back to find her.

This was a major disaster not only for the theatre but also for much adjacent business property which was consumed by the conflagration.

156

1893_06_09 WASHINGTON, USA (Ford's).   COLLAPSE OF FORD'S THEATRE

73. Ford's Theatre in 1865

[Ford's Theatre was the site of the infamous assassination of President Lincoln in 1865 when he was shot by actor John Wilkes Booth while he was watching a play.

Following the assassination, the United States Government, decreeing the venue should no longer be a place of public amusement, paid Ford $88,000 in compensation. Between 1866 and 1887, the theatre, taken over by the USA military, served as clerks' offices for the USA War Department.]

On this day, the front part of the building collapsed, killing 22 clerks and injuring another 68. After major repairs it was used as a government warehouse until 1911, and thereafter fully restored by degrees until now it is a replica of how it was in Lincoln's day, flourishing once more as a theatre and museum.

1893_06_20 MADRID, Spain (Circus).   FATAL COLLAPSE OF CEILING SECTION

On this night, during the performance before a crowded house in the huge auditorium, a large chunk of the ceiling collapsed. It fell mostly on to the expensive seats occupied with the younger members of various noble families. People nearby who had not been struck fearing further portions may detach themselves fled for the doors. The weaker were trampled on in the zest to evacuate the building. Once the greater part of the audience had gained the outdoors and no further falls had occurred, common sense was restored, and the rescue of the unfortunate people under the wreckage took place. The grandson of the Marquis of Havana was pulled out suffering multiple shocking injuries. He had been struck down by the initial collapse and then trampled upon by the panicking crowd. He was removed as quickly as possible but expired in agony within the hour. The son of the Marquis of Guadelcat lost his life in a similar way.

1893_09_04 OSTEND, Belgium (Eden).   FIRE

Shortly before the rise of the curtain, part of the proscenium was set alight by a gas jet. The flames rapidly spread to other parts of the stage and the audience fled for the exits. The panic stricken people fighting to escape caused many injuries. The whole of the contents of the stage house were destroyed before the fire was extinguished at 9pm.

1893_09_13 PARIS, France (Opera House).   NEEDLESS PANIC

The opera in progress was *La Valkyrie*, the scene where the sleeping Brunehilde is enveloped in fire and smoke. Some accident caused a jet of flame-coloured steam to be projected from the wings, across the footlights, to the auditorium. This was accompanied by a bang followed by a loud hissing noise. The two performers onstage, Mdlle Bréval and M Fournets, "quite lost their presence of mind" the former running screaming into the wings, the latter jumping into the orchestra pit. The musicians also began fleeing. As a result, hundreds in the audience made for the lobbies with a great deal of pushing and shoving but causing only slight injuries. The theatre director came onstage to explain there was no danger, and the absent audience returned to their seats. The two fleeing artistes duly reappeared "none the worse for their poltroonery". The panic was all over in under five minutes but was further proof that "a theatrical audience never retains any presence of mind. Such arrant funk on the part of the artistes, is, however, an occurrence of greater rarity."

1893_09_19 CANTON, USA (Opera House).   THEATRE DESTROYED BY FIRE

The play was *Michael Scrogan* and around 9.30pm the scenery caught fire. The audience was asked to remain and not panic. However, it is fortunate they did not obey this advice as the fire spread to the entire building. One fatality, around 20 people burned, four severely so.

1893_10_31 MORECAMBE (Lyric).   PARTIAL COLLAPSE OF ROOF

The play was the popular *Uncle Tom's Cabin* with the Charles Hermann Company. The place was crowded and some young men and youths clambered on to the wooden roof covering the staircase to the gallery at the rear of the hall. Part of this gave way and two dozen people were plummeted on to the staircase some as far as 20ft below. There was no panic and assistance was prompt. Ten people were injured to a greater or lesser extent. After some delay the performance proceeded.

1893_11_07 BARCELONA, Spain (del Liceu). ANARCHIST BOMB EXPLOSION

On the opening night of the season, Santiago Salvador bought himself a seat in the gallery for Rossini's *William Tell*. He let Act I finish, and at 11pm during Act II, he threw two bombs into the audience in the stalls. The first bomb, landing in Row 13, exploded immediately, whilst the second landed in the lap of a woman, who was already dead, and failing to explode fell to the floor, rolling under a seat. Seven people were killed instantly, thirteen more died over the next few hours and twenty-seven were injured. During the aftermath two further unexploded bombs were found in the gallery.

Santiago Salvador was an anarchist who targeted the theatre in revenge for the execution of fellow anarchist Paulino Pallás. In the confusion, Salvador managed to get out of the theatre and fled to his home town of Teruel. The police finally caught up with him in Zaragoza where he tried, but failed, to commit suicide by shooting himself in the stomach. He was imprisoned in solitary confinement on 1 February 1894 and executed by garrotting. Just prior to Christmas, a fellow anarchist confessed that he also took part in this outrage.

74. *Theatre del Liceu anarchist bomb outrage*

1894_10_06 DUBLIN (Star). ACCIDENTAL FALL THROUGH EXIT DOOR

Dan Lowrey's Star of Erin Music Hall was an extremely popular venue and on this Saturday night there was standing room only in an area behind the back row of seats in the stalls. Thomas Cox (40) went with friends and they paid to stand but were separated from one another as they each found a sufficient space.

Cox discovered a perch that nobody had deemed suitable before – an iron bar in front of an emergency exit. He stood on this bar, which was 2ft 4in above floor level, supporting his balance by placing his hands on railings at the side of the door. Suddenly losing his balance he fell backwards, hitting the door of the emergency exit which flew open on contact, depositing Cox on the street outside. The bottom of the doorway was 2ft above street level.

Cox fell on his head and was rushed to Mercer's Hospital where Dr Elliott saw he had a fracture at the base of his skull. Realising the situation was perilous he sent for Dr Nixon, but before he arrived Cox had died. He left a widow and eight children.

"Some of my plays peter out, and some pan out." J M Barrie (1860-1937) *attributed*

1895_01_14 DARWEN (Theatre Royal).   FLAMES ONSTAGE CAUSE STAMPEDE

The pantomime *Aladdin* was just about to start when a steam pipe near the orchestra burst sending out a jet of steam. Nevertheless, the show started but in the second scene flames were observed to break out causing a woman in the front row to scream and make for the exit with a child in her arms. This caused chaos with yelling and a noisy stampede to all the exits. The company took to the stage urging people not to panic, and there was a lull as people began to heed the words of some respectable gentlemen in the audience to keep their seats. Then a further burst of sparks, blowing upwards with great force, regenerated the panic. Men started climbing over the backs of seats irrespective of their occupants and there was a danger of people getting trampled underfoot. Fortunately, with all exit doors flung wide open, there were few accidents, and those of a very minor nature. While all this was going on in the auditorium, onstage actors had dragged out a hosepipe and were playing water on the stage where there was burning timber.

1895_12_28 BALTIMORE, USA (Front Street).   FATAL FLEEING FROM GALLERY

There was a Jewish opera taking place when a gas pipe broke backstage, sending a flash of flame visible to the audience. On the immediate cry of "Fire!" people rushed to get out of the building. The stage manager turned off the gas supply at the main, plunging the place into complete darkness. This intensified the panic, with people climbing over seats and each other. A sharp angle in the gallery stairs caused a blockage, and it was here that bodies were compacted in layers. The lights returned after a few minutes, but the devastation had already taken place. In the melee 24 people were killed – eight men, five boys, three women and eight girls – and 40 seriously injured.

159

1895_12_31 VISTER, USA (Union).   GUN FIGHT AT THE UNION THEATRE

This despatch is too incredible to believe, but as I have not been able to find any further verification I précis the facts as told. The venue was called the Union Theatre of Varieties, the town described as a "thriving little mining town" was stated to be Vister near Denver, Colorado. Mr Smith the manager had got word that a gang of local roughs proposed causing trouble at a certain performance. Halfway through the show Smith accosted Tom Pascoe. Harsh words were said on both sides and Pascoe, drawing his gun, shot five bullets into the head and chest of Mr Smith. Falling to the floor, the manager succeeded in firing four retaliatory shots, one of which pierced Pascoe's heart, ending with both men lying dead on top of one another. Four of the performers drew guns and fired from the stage into the roughs, who retaliated. Thus with bullets flying around in profusion, and women screaming, somebody turned the lights out, the gun fight continuing in the dark. When it eventually ceased, the lights were relit, revealing 20 wounded men sprawled out over the floor, three "in the agonies of death." The wounded were taken home by friends, thus casualties remain unknown.

1896_01_20 EKATERINOSLAV, Russia (Kopyloff).   THEATRE FIRE

During an afternoon performance for children, an actress rushed on to the stage shouting "Fire! Fire!" followed by clouds of smoke. Immediately the audience rushed for the exit doors. People in the gallery were jumping down into the pit, and as others gained the exits it was found that six out of eight doors had been closed because of the cold. Then the roof fell in. The building, being made entirely of wood, was totally destroyed. The dead numbered 49, mainly children, and three firemen.

1896_05_20 PARIS, France (Opera House).   FALL OF CHANDELIER

In many continental opera houses the tiers of boxes rise up virtually to the roof; this accident happened in the top tier. The large grand chandelier, hanging from the ceiling and dominating the space above the stalls, was balanced by eight counterweights on wire cables, inspected daily for any signs of wear and tear. Notwithstanding these precautions, the chandelier also had a reflector above weighing 19cwt and its own counterpoise comprising 25 weights of 50lbs strung upon a long iron bar. This bar gave way, shedding half the weights but, with 12 still attached, fell through the ceiling into a top tier box instantly killing a lady occupant and injuring her daughter and another woman.

The theatre management was responsible for everything in the building except the lighting system which was government controlled, with maintenance and safety being the responsibility of government inspectors. There were now suggestions that the "imposing central lustre" was an anachronism in the age of electricity and should be dispensed with.

1896_07_10c SYDNEY, Australia (Rickard's).   FALL FROM GALLERY

Alfred Neander, a baker, and his wife went to see the play and were seated in the stalls prior to the performance with Neander leaning forward, bent over a newspaper, filling the time to curtain up. Up in the gallery the usual crowd, pushing and shoving to find a good seat, resulted in a young man falling over the front down into the stalls, a distance of 30ft. He landed sideways on Neander's shoulders but was not harmed much as he leapt off and made a hasty retreat. Neander, however, was seriously injured and unconscious when taken to the hospital. There he was found to have fractured his spine at the base of the neck, with death a foregone conclusion within days or even hours. So ended the blameless Mr & Mrs Neander's night out at the theatre before the play had even started.

160

1896_09_30 ABERDEEN (Palace of Varieties).   BORDER FIRE DEVASTATES THEATRE

This venue had for many years functioned as a music hall. The show had not been under way for very long when flames were seen at the back of the stage. Gas jets in the flies had caught a scenic border and, as the reader will by now know, the inevitable result was the fire spreading to the rest of the scenery thence to the building itself. The performers fled for their lives, as did the audience. In the panic, as people rushed to preserve themselves rather than their fellows, many were hurt, some 30 people in hospital suffering burns and other injuries. When the fire was extinguished and the debris searched, four dead bodies came to light, a further person died at the Infirmary.

One performer who lost everything was the ventriloquist Neiman, but when the news spread he was offered dolls from fellow ventriloquists Vento, Millis, Horace White and Capt Slingsby so he could fulfil his outstanding contracts.   75. *Palace of Varieties*

image© The British Library Board

1897_04_17 EDINBURGH (Empire Palace).   FALL FROM GALLERY

Shortly after 8pm with the normal performance under way, Charles McCanny (13) trying to improve his seat in the gallery by clambering over a railing, fell over the front of the gallery. With great good fortune he did not, as most of the similar previous recorded incidents, fall into the pit, but caught the padded front of the dress circle and fell among the well upholstered seating. He suffered a cut head and a fractured shoulder blade.

1897_06_11 BURY (Theatre).   POINTLESS MINOR PANIC

Nearing the end of the performance of *Woman's Honour* on this night, a startling bang was heard followed by a hissing noise. A woman screamed, somebody shouted "Fire!" causing an immediate rush for the exits. Several women fainted, and with men scrambling over the backs of seats knocking each other down, general mayhem was imminent. The theatre management – aided by the arrival of the police – eventually quelled the likelihood of a major disastrous panic. The frenzy was even more pointless than usual as there was absolutely nothing amiss within the theatre. "The noise was caused by the bursting of a pipe in a passing tram engine."

1897_10_15 CINCINNATI, USA (Robinson's OH).   COLLAPSE OF THEATRE'S DOME

76. *The fallen dome at Robinson's Opera House*

The reader may recall a previous disaster at this venue when an overcrowded house at a charity matinee was stampeded by a false cry of fire (*See* 1876_02_05). On that occasion there were 11 fatalities and 30 injured, and the event in the city's history became known as "The Horror".

Alas, fate had not finished with the venue as on this day a further calamity fell on the audience. Alice Opie, a child impersonator, was taking her bow to thunderous applause when "there was a cracking sound. A stream of dry mortar and plaster poured from the ceiling. Then there was another, more terrible crash" as the entire dome of the theatre above the stalls fell to earth. The audience scrambled in the dark to get out as the rest of the ceiling fell in following the dome.

Amazingly only five people were killed, with around 25 further suffering broken limbs.

1897_11_12 LONDON (Surrey).   DISORDERLY CONDUCT BY DRUNK STUDENTS

The play was *Sporting Life* and on this night medical students caused riotous mayhem during the performance. They shouted loudly, threw things on to the stage, kissed their hands to ladies throughout the building, and caused a shocking and disgusting disturbance that prevented the show continuing. They tried to force their way into a box containing manager Mr Conquest's daughter and niece, and refused to leave when asked to do so by Mr Leonard the acting manager. There was a scuffle with the students brandishing their walking sticks, during which an attendant named Salter was accused of striking student Edward Rowlands, injuring him in the eye. Rowlands charging Salter with assault, was unable to be in court in person as he was suffering from concussion of the brain, bleeding from the mouth, a black eye and was, according to his doctor, "in a very serious condition".

In response, Conquest sought summonses against six medical students for disorderly conduct. This was granted and Salter was remanded on bail of £60. This trial continued on five occasions with claims and counter-claims arising each time until on the fifth occasion the case against the students was dismissed, Rowlands now having fully recovered. The judge decided it was not a serious case, merely students egging each other on resulting in anti-social behaviour so he would not grant them the damages requested. However, the charge against Salter was sent to Sessions. There the jury found the unfortunate Salter (50) guilty of assaulting Edward Rowlands and sentenced him to prison for a month with hard labour. Outrageous – the man was only trying to do his duty, but in those days students were classed as 'gentlemen' rather than hooligans.

1898_01_17c CHESTER (Royalty).   FIRE AT THE REAR OF THE CIRCLE

In the middle of his act, Tom Wood noticed a door curtain at the back of the circle was on fire. Pointing to a chap in the circle, he quietly asked him "to put out the small light behind him." The audience thought the performer was joking, as did the individual indicated, but Wood repeated his request and, with the curtains now well ablaze, the chap on turning saw what was meant and quickly pulled down the curtains. Presumably he stamped out the flames, or somebody came with a bucket of water. All this seems to have gone unnoticed by the audience so perhaps it was a thin house and few were in the dress circle.

162

1898_02_02 LONDON (Gaiety).   MAN FIRES GUN IN GALLERY

This is a weird one! The show was the highly popular musical comedy *The Circus Girl*. Alfred John Hickey (23) sitting in the gallery took out a gun and started firing it indiscriminately. Seized and held by people sitting near, the constable in attendance at the theatre arrested him. In court the next day Hickey was charged with "discharging firearms in a public place to the public danger". When searched he was found to have a few loose cartridges in his pockets, and a letter from persons trying to place him in a lunatic asylum. Taken to an asylum to be examined, it was decided he should be temporarily detained, pending further legal action. Hickey claimed he had escaped from prison in Australia, and had bought the revolver to protect himself from a man who was following him.

On 24 February, Hickey was formally charged and further details emerged. Police had ascertained that only one bullet was fired, and hit the ceiling of the gallery approximately above the suspect's seated place. The gun had thus been fired almost vertically, and certainly not at anybody onstage as had been rumoured, nor at any member of the audience. The prisoner claimed the letter which said he was "influenced by electric batteries worked by mind readers" was written by a man named Thomas Ryan. Hickey further claimed he had never been in a lunatic asylum but had been imprisoned in Australia for horse stealing and had escaped, arriving in England several months previously. The firing of the revolver was an accident, the pistol being in his pocket. He then showed a hole in the material of his coat which appeared singed. The magistrate remanded him to see "what could be done with him". On 2 March, the case was heard again. The magistrate declared Hickey was no longer thought to be insane, his explanation would be accepted, and he would be bound over to keep the peace for three months on two sureties of £25 each and discharged. All very odd!

1898_02_28 CROYDON (Grand).   FAULTY SAFETY CURTAIN

Partway through the evening performance of *Human Nature* the iron safety curtain started to descend. Fearing fire was the reason, the packed audience started fleeing for the exits leaving hats and sticks behind them. This belief was fostered by the offstage shouting of stage crew and the exit of the actors from the stage. The musical director promptly addressed the crowd, explaining there was no fire, no danger at all, it was merely a fault in the motor that raised and lowered the mighty iron. As they could see, the problem had been found and solved as the iron curtain slowly began to rise out of sight and the performance continued.

1898_04_11 MAIDENHEAD (Theatre Royal).   COLLAPSE OF GALLERY FLOOR

During a performance of the pantomime *Aladdin* with the hero in full song, a person in the gallery shouted "Stop the play! Fire!" Panic immediately ensued, with the gallery occupants fleeing for the exit. This mass rush caused the floor to collapse, and 320 people tumbled down a distance of 10ft. As a result there were many cuts and bruises, a profusion of twisted ankles, and fainting ladies. Mr Rider the manager taking to the stage and shouting appeals for calm, eventually subdued the confusion and explained there was no fire, no danger, and the cry had been given by a malicious person. The gallery and its seating suffered "considerable damage".

1898_11_10 DETROIT, USA (Wonderland).   COLLAPSE DURING NEW BUILD

[My self-imposed remit decreed that I would not include accidents that happened during building work on theatres, as such accidents would happen with any kind of edifice. However, a few excessively horrible accidents happened during the construction of some theatres so have been included. This is one of them.]

Detroit was just starting its reputation as Motor City, and the city was booming. The building of a new five storey theatre was in progress. The shell and the steel skeleton of the new theatre had been completed when the roof suddenly collapsed, dragging down the completed work underneath. Two galleries in the auditorium were crushed by the weight of falling debris. Within minutes the building had been transformed into a collection of twisted beams, broken timbers and great chunks of brickwork and cement. When the accident happened, 35 labourers were all swept down in the deluge of wreckage. The walls survived the initial impact but one side-wall collapsed a short time later. It was argued that the roof was too heavy for the structure, having been topped with an 8in thick layer of concrete. Others questioned whether the steel girders had sufficient toughness and durability, or had been made of inferior metals. Whatever the reason for the calamity, 15 men lost their lives and many more were seriously injured.

1899_03_12 LIEGE, Belgium (Gymnase).   NEEDLESS PANIC

The play *La Tosca* featured shooting which caused some "over-excited women" in the gallery to raise a pointless cry of "Fire!" Immediately there was a mad scramble for the exits, and though the manager tried to calm the audience he was ignored. Seats were torn up, windows smashed, and among the fearful din were the shrieks of women, some crushed as they were trampled over. As usually occurs, the gallery suffered the most as people poured out on to a flight of stone steps, several of those at the head of the stampede were knocked down by the crowd following. Many wounded but no fatalities.

1899_07_01 NEW YORK, USA (Coney Island)

image© The British Library Board

164

MURDER ON THE MUSIC HALL STAGE

This was no accident but a determined assault at a place of entertainment in Coney Island. "An Asiatic performer, for a reason unknown, became violently enraged with a young lady attendant. He finally lost all control of himself and, armed with a sword, rushed upon the unfortunate girl; and before anybody could interfere, hacked the girl repeatedly in a most frightful manner." The police eventually arrived to overpower the villain. However, the girl was so shockingly injured that she was dead when rescued. The sickening assault was viewed by 200 helpless spectators.

The artist at the *Illustrated Police News* allowed his imagination to run very freely when depicting this outrage.

77. *An Asiatic performer commits public murder*

1900_03_08 PARIS, France (Français).

Shortly before noon, while the audience was gathering for a matinee of *Bajazet*, fire broke out within the interior of the building. Flames were soon shooting from every window and then the roof caught light. Fire engines arrived, but the water supply faltered. The artistes, already in the dressing rooms preparing for the show, were mostly soon evacuated, but M Lambert emerged, hands severely burnt, with news that Mdlle Henriot (19) had succumbed by asphyxiation. Mdlle Dudlay, dressed ready to play the leading role, managed to make it to an exterior balcony where a fireman climbed a ladder, tied a rope round her waist, and she was thus lowered to the ground. The theatre was 100 years old and a repository of many historical and cultural artefacts. A lot of these were actually saved but plundered as nobody seemed to know who was authorised to search in the ruins.

78. *Mdlle Dudlay in costume lowered on a rope*

FIRE

1900_05_14 LIVERPOOL (Haymarket).   FATAL FALL FROM GALLERY

JohnWalker (17) one of the first arrivals for the Second House, quickly made his way to the front of the gallery. "In his haste and excitement he must have overbalanced himself" as he plunged over the front of the balcony falling down to land in the pit which was fortunately empty. Obviously desperately injured, he was taken to the East Dispensary but died before arrival. I was beginning to think falls from the gallery were a thing of the past as I have recorded only eight instances throughout the last decade, though three of them were fatalities.

1900_09_17 WIDNES (Alexandra).   FIRE ONSTAGE

The Leonard & Conquest Company was playing the drama *Serving the Queen* to a rapt audience of 1200 when sparks descended from the flies, followed by blazing scenery dropping on to the stage. Immediately alarm and panic set in, with players jumping from the stage into the orchestra pit, women fleeing then, realising they had left their children behind, rushing back to grab them, and men clambering over the seats to reach the nearest exit. The manager and several actors tried to stop the panic but their voices went unheeded or were drowned in the uproar.

The audience all reached the outside without any major mishap, and the fire brigade, attending promptly, extinguished the blaze by midnight. The stage house fittings were badly damaged, but thanks to the lowering of the safety curtain the fire was contained and the rest of the theatre building was untouched. This seems to be a rare occasion when the iron safety curtain properly did the job it was installed for. The fire had started by a border coming into contact with a gas jet above the stage. Of course it had! Nearly all occupied theatre fires in the 19th century started that way. The damage was estimated at up to £3000.

165

The last entry was one of the rarer ones where an actual fire was a real reason to flee in panic. Most frenzies and panics in this section have been caused by the mere cry of "Fire!" and therefore totally unnecessary.

Major outbreaks of fire were most likely on Saturday/Sunday. One can see the logical reason for this – fires most often break out when the theatre is empty, usually in the early hours. Saturday night was when the theatre was at its most full and when touring companies on their last night, packed up their props and departed. Theatres in those days never opened on Sundays so it was inevitable that, unless there was a night watchman, a fire that might have smouldered for some hours before breaking out, would have got a firm hold before it was spotted. Most fires were caused by one of two things – a stray spark from fireworks or gun effects used in the play lying dormant for some hours, before bursting into life in the empty theatre, or a gas jet catching a drape or piece of scenery. In the latter case this usually happened in a performance with the stage crew present to deal with it. Unfortunately, the lack of fireproofing to the scenery often meant the fire taking an immediate spreading hold that overwhelmed anything stage hands could achieve. As apparent from the occasional entries, there was ongoing concern about methods of fireproofing scenery but progress was intermittent and slow.

However, in the Victorian period actual theatre fires were commonplace and I have located some 283 fires in which 212 theatres were totally destroyed

AFTERWORD

In the 21st century things are very different. Because of building regulations, modern materials and new techniques, theatres seldom catch fire. Through the universal use of electricity for lighting, plus laws governing the fireproofing of scenery and props, theatre fires are now very rare events.

Parts of theatre buildings collapsing are no longer commonplace, though in 1974 at the Olympia Theatre, Dublin part of the proscenium arch and ceiling above did so, in 1997 part of the ceiling at Edinburgh's Usher Hall collapsed, and in 2002 part of Matcham's Royal Hall ceiling at Harrogate fell in. In 2004 a chandelier fell mid-performance at the Haymarket Theatre but was restrained from plummeting to the stalls by a safety cable. The theatre was evacuated and four people injured by falling plaster were taken to hospital.

The most notorious ceiling collapse of recent years was at the Grade II listed Apollo Theatre, London, in December 2013 with an audience of 700 watching the play. It was a major incident in the West End involving fire engines, hundreds of police, and nine ambulances. Forty walking wounded were treated at the nearby Gielgud theatre, and three bus loads of people taken to hospital, most suffering cuts and bruises, but several with broken limbs.

On 6 November 2019, part of the ceiling at the Piccadilly Theatre in London's West End collapsed. Twenty minutes into the show water started pouring through part of the ceiling followed by a collapse of plaster. A thousand people had to be evacuated. Fortunately, on a lesser scale than the Apollo, three men and two women were treated at the scene by paramedics and another four taken to hospital. Performances were cancelled for four days before the theatre reopened.

The Apollo was built in 1901, the Piccadilly in 1928. Many West End theatres have been in nightly use for over a hundred years so wear and tear may be anticipated. Readers will now know that the famous London theatre the Old Vic opened in 1818. The walls and roof timbers are mainly original, the interior was remodelled in 1871. There have been many alterations since.

Accidents to audience members are also fortunately rare. Nobody falls over the front of the balcony to land in the stalls any more. I know people still sometimes stumble on stairs – I have done it myself. But stairs today being wide with shallow risers and comforting carpeting are rarely harmful, and people are civilised enough to ascend and descend decorously rather than in a horrendous scrimmage, often trampling over fallen bodies

79.

For many years separate theatre seats in all parts have been bookable in advance though it is astonishing how recently it was still necessary to queue for seats in pit and gallery. Edwardian ladies paid messenger boys to keep their places – over 100 boys a day gained money this way. Queuing actually persisted into the 1960s, somewhat improved with folding stools available and buskers to entertain, and often a numbered ticket system similar to the deli counter at the supermarket.

I remember such queues just as I can

easily recall the wooden tea trays served to elderly ladies in their seats during the intervals of matinees. But now no more frenzies and stampedes on opening nights – just think how many lives could have been saved and injuries avoided simply by introducing individual seats and advance booking for every seat in the theatre 200 years ago.

I thought fights in the auditorium, too, had long disappeared, but in January 2019 two men quarrelling over an empty seat in the front row of the august Royal Opera House resorted to fisticuffs, ending up before the magistrate! *Plus ça change, plus c'est la même chose.*

Backstage flymen no longer fall from the fly gallery to the stage. Do fly galleries still exist? Scenery is raised and lowered by a counterweight system operated by one man usually at stage level. In fact, the whole business of scene changing and lighting is largely automated. In my day, setting and focussing the above-stage lighting was done by the use of a 'tallescope' – a tall ladder on a trolley wheeled about the stage and still essential equipment. However, in some theatres without flies, focussing is made safe and easy by having what is basically a strong wire netting floor below the lighting grid that the electrician can walk about on, adjusting the lights conveniently at waist height.

Finally, have audiences changed? Very much so, although there are signs of regressive changes creeping back. Victorian audiences were very class conscious and theatres were deliberately designed to pander to that with 7/- dress circle seats and 6d galleries. In the 20th century democracy took over and, while seating divisions remained, galleries were improved with hard benches being replaced by separate tip-up seats and renamed the balcony. The area seated far fewer with greater comfort and improved sight lines which warranted 1/- admission charge. Similarly, the class of people who dressed in white tie to sit in the dress circle began disappearing after the Great War and that area was occupied by a more affluent aspiring middle class who did not need to swank but were only prepared or able to pay 4/6 for their seat. The typical audience was now melded as one, the price of a seat was no longer a sign of class but differentiated only by the ability of its position to see and hear the play.

In 1879, *Dickens's Dictionary of London* gave seat prices for the Lyceum Theatre as Stalls 10/-, Dress Circle 6/-, Upper Circle 3/-, Pit 2/-, Gallery 1/-. Today that theatre's prices range from £128 to £48

We have far more entertainment than the Victorians enjoyed. We no longer have music hall and variety but we still have live theatre and circus. We have gained films, television, radio, comedy clubs, pop music concerts, and the internet.

So things have improved enormously from Victorian times but accidents in the audience do still happen occasionally. From time to time I have intruded the text with a few random personal notes from our 40+ years in the profession as international speciality act Pavlov's Puppets. Definition of an "international speciality act" – one that's out of work all over the world! Since we have retired from showbusiness, as members of the audience we attend theatres to see plays for enjoyment, usually numbering forty or so productions a year. We both like Shakespeare and the so-called well-made play such as those of Terence Rattigan and the comedies of Alan Ayckbourn. Brenda is more open to directorial gimmickry than I am but we both enjoy live theatre. The Audience Section is finished so I will close with a last *Personal Note* as a member of the modern audience . . . .

In 2016 we went to Bristol especially to see A Long Day's Journey Into Night *with Jeremy Irons and Lesley Manville, both actors we admire. The Bristol Theatre Royal, dating from 1766, is the oldest continuously working theatre in the world so as a theatre historian there was an added interest for me. On this jaunt we went from our home in the Weald of Kent by train and stayed overnight in a Travelodge. Prior to the show we ate in a nearby restaurant where I took the opportunity to take my warfarin which I am obliged to do at 6pm each day. When I booked for the show it was not possible to get two seats together so we were at each end seat of the front row of the dress circle. We often sit separately because you don't talk when the play is on do you? It's a pity we did not on this occasion because I was taken ill and Brenda from her far seat could see me slumped comatose in my seat. At the interval she hared round and roused me and we went into the foyer. Then back for the second half. It is a very long play and it was very warm and I found it difficult to focus and kept wiping my glasses to no avail. But it seemed soon over and we walked back to the Travelodge with Brenda holding me up because I had lost my balance and couldn't walk straight. She was worried out of her mind and thought I'd had a stroke. We debated whether we should go to A&E but decided not. At the Travelodge we always have a coffee and biscuit, and not being in my usual bed I take a Zopiclone sleeping tablet. That was when Brenda found my warfarin tablet.*

DENIZENS OF THE STAGE OUT OF THEIR ELEMENT

When Victoria came to the throne people travelled in stage coaches but the 1840s brought the steam railway which developed exponentially enabling theatres that housed stock companies to change into receiving houses which welcomed a new company each week.

Unless an actor or entertainer was engaged for a static season such as a long running play in the West End, he was forced to spend his working life travelling from venue to venue. In the Victorian era, music hall and variety artistes usually worked on the system of obtaining separate weeks in venues throughout the country. The weekly professional press carried column after column of small ads on the lines of

> THE MERRY MACS Eccentric Comics
> This: Empire, Goole, Next: TR, Margate
> At liberty: 28th April

Apart from actors who were lucky enough to never leave London, and those who obtained a season in a resident stock company, most players were engaged in long tours in the provinces. A successful play in London would invariably be sent on an extensive round of provincial theatres with a less starry cast, playing a week at a venue, then moving on Sunday to open in a different town on Monday. Often several units would be out playing the same show, thus known as Mr Blank's No 2 *After the Ball* Company, Miss Blogg's No 1 *Finding Fifi* Company and so on. Theatres were classed as No 1, No 2 and No 3 circuits so a management could get several years out of one production which worked its way down through them. Often a successful play like *Humanity* could go out year after year with the same star and many of the same cast. All this activity had been impossible before the land was blessed with the railway system.

Sundays were travelling days with the entire theatre industry on the move from town to town. The rail network was full of trains of players and variety artistes criss-crossing the country enduring tiresome waits for connections on complicated routes. Railways gave special terms for shifting productions and performers in carriages which were taken from station A and left unhitched at station B awaiting another train going from station C to station D which will stop at B and hitch the carriages on. Major junctions offered actors from different companies opportunity to meet up, gossip and exchange news with old acquaintances. Hence the well known story of the two railway men overheard by an actor – First Man: 'What's on this train, Fred?' Second Man: 'Fish and actors.' Outraged actor: 'I can live with being billed below Sir Henry Irving, but it's a bit much playing second fiddle to fish!'

However, the development of the railways was, like the internet, piecemeal fashion with different companies building lines and linking together. As a result the system was open to more accidents than would be tolerated today. As performers travelled for their work they used the railways far more than the average person, and it is not surprising that accidents on trains were an additional hazard to the profession. With the rapidly spreading railway system a new menace arose – death and injury by steam engine. In the following pages there will be noted several railway accidents involving performers. These are a mere handful out of lots with a theatrical connection. Railway accidents happened daily and newspapers ran regular columns listing them.

169

Neither were artistes and actors immune from the same risks as everybody else in everyday life. They slipped on ice, they crashed horse-drawn transport and got knocked down. So this chapter includes all kinds of accidents to thespians and entertainers that occurred away from their place of work. Fatal accidents have the date in **BOLD** type.

1839_04_25c PARIS, France.

ROAD ACCIDENT TO ANDREW DUCROW

Andrew Ducrow (1793–1842) was the leading equestrian of the day, star and proprietor of Astley's Amphitheatre. He performed throughout Britain and Europe. On his way by coach to Paris, leaning with his arm out of the window, a coach coming the opposite way passing extremely closely, injured his arm. It was set by a skilful surgeon and the prognostications were highly favourable. Ironic he should be injured in that way when in his profession he risked his life daily without mishap.

80. Andrew Ducrow

1840_06_03 LONDON.

ACTOR THROWN OUT OF GIG IN ROAD ACCIDENT

Frank Matthews of Covent Garden was on his way back from Epsom races in his gig – a two wheeled cart pulled by one horse – when on reaching Clapham, the horse became restive and Matthews, losing all control, was thrown out of the gig into the roadway. The road was busy and he was run over immediately, both legs suffering serious injuries, one being almost "torn to pieces". He was placed in the care of Dr Carpue, who intended to operate rather than amputate, though the man was in a "very precarious state". He survived two-legged and was back in action by 31 August when he appeared at his benefit which raised £200.

1841_10_27 HARTFORD.

RAILWAY ACCIDENT KILLS RETIRED SINGING STAR

Stage coaches, private gigs and horse-drawn vehicles of all kinds had been overturning and bumping into each other for decades as the roads got busier with increasing traffic. Annually, many people were killed or injured in this way. Thomas Phillips, a well-known singer and a favourite at all the principal theatres, now in retirement and occupying his time giving lectures on vocal music, was travelling by train. He alighted for a pause at Hartford station, and, attempting to regain his seat as the train began moving, he was thrown under the wheels of the train, breaking both legs and suffering instant death.

1842_08_26c BADEN-BADEN, Germany.

SIGHT-SEEING MUSICIANS IMPRISONED

This is a very unusual accident and is not really theatrical at all, but as it involves Laura Cinti-Damoreau, a leading soprano in Rossini operas, and Artot a violinist who had recently toured with her, I think it has a place here. Having some leisure time in Baden-Baden the two colleagues took a sightseeing trip around the ancient castle. While exploring the underground passages and cells, one of the party inadvertently closed a massive door consisting of a huge block of stone. The

81.

guide, terrified and in despair, informed the party that the door could only be opened from the other side. The man was helpless and the stupefied party was at a loss what to do. There was no daylight and the torches were rapidly burning low. After waiting four long hours, they were rescued quite by chance by another guide taking an English family on a subterranean tour. One hopes that after this gruesome incident the guides instituted a system whereby they kept tabs on visitors!

1843_07_19   AT SEA.

82. *Ship* Pegasus *going down*

ACTOR LOST IN MAJOR SHIPWRECK

[Edward William Elton (1794–1843) was born in Lambeth. As a youth he appeared at a private theatre in plays produced by his schoolmaster father for his scholars. Starting out in provincial touring companies, he made his London debut in 1823 at the Olympic, and thereafter made a good but unadventurous provincial career. In 1836, he returned to the London theatres gaining recognition for various parts, especially as Walter Tyrrell in a play of that name at Covent Garden.]

In July 1843, Elton had been playing a month's engagement in Edinburgh and was travelling from Leith to Hull in the steamship *Pegasus* which struck a hidden rock in the same area that Grace Darling had carried out her famous rescue some years previously. Only six people were saved from the 60 thought to be on board. Elton left a widow (his second wife) who went mad, and seven children. He was well respected in the profession and several benefit performances were held and a fund established for his family.

1843_12_18   GREENWICH (Powell's Circus).   ACCIDENT TO THEATRICAL HOSIER

Mr Powell's circus had set up in Greenwich for the season in an elegant newly built temporary pavilion. Mr Abraham Haig, a theatrical costumier was delivering costumes and seeing the opening of the show. Mr Haig, on leaving the building, accidentally trod in a hole that had been made by a support pole but not filled in when the pole was removed. The damage to the man's ankle was the breaking of two bones. Mr Powell accepted responsibility for the hole and paid £50 into court. There the matter remained until 2 March 1845 when Haig took Powell to court on the grounds that the cost of his treatment was in the nature of £150. During the case it came to light that Mr Haig was the only man who made 'fleshings'. According to Haig's lawyer these were built up shapely calves to make up deficiencies not only in actors, but lords and ladies in society. Fleshings will certainly encompass that work, but the term was used more widely as the naked body was not permitted in the Victorian era. When characters such as Mazeppa (who was strapped naked on to the back of a horse) were portrayed, the actor's entire body was covered in fleshings – a forerunner of the modern 'body stocking'.

In court the doctor claimed his bill was £63.7.6d. The court awarded damages of £70.

1845_02_13 BOULOGNE (France).   ROAD ACCIDENT TO LEMAITRE

    The eminent French actor Frederic Lemaitre was in a coach bound for Boulogne to board a ship for England where he was to perform at the St James's Theatre. A league from Boulogne the coach had to descend a precipitous hill. The postilion ignored the use of the sabot (a brake shoe) with the result that the coach veered violently, the horses took fright and the coach overturned, killing one of the horses on the spot. Lemaitre, cut and bruised, escaped without any serious injury. "His escape with life was most miraculous and providential." Tended by Dr Billing on arrival in London the actor was expected to appear as announced.

83

1845_05_02 GT YARMOUTH.   FATAL DISASTER AT CLOWN'S PUBLICITY STUNT

    Among all the dreadful accidents, fires and other calamities, there are a handful of disasters that resound throughout history to the present day. Such is this one, although perhaps out of place in this collection as it happened in the open air, and was not really a performance. However, the gathering was for a clown appearing at Cooke's Circus, so where other is more appropriate than herein?

84.   Cooke's Circus was appearing at Gt Yarmouth. It was announced via handbills that as a publicity stunt, Arthur Nelson the clown would travel in a washtub drawn by four geese up a certain stretch of the River Bure. This stunt had been performed by the late Dickie Usher, and copied by several performers since. Nelson was to start at the drawbridge and travel to the suspension bridge which had been built in 1829 and recently widened. Thousands lined the banks to see this spectacle, progressing as planned almost to the end when, to gain a better view, hordes of people flocked on to the suspension bridge. As the clown appeared, all the people on the bridge flocked to the south side. This had the effect of distorting the bridge causing rails and chains to break until the footway was hanging perpendicularly, thus shooting the whole mass of spectators into the water.

    Among the subsequent chaos, messengers were sent to every doctor in town to come immediately, every able bodied local man was performing feats of untold bravery assisting with the rescue, and the adjacent inns were used to house the increasing number of dead bodies as they were pulled from the water. When all was over, out of a total of 79 people found dead, the eldest was a woman of 64 years, and 58 were under the age of 16.

    Mr Cooke announced he was withdrawing his circus from the town. Mr Nelson had already left, suffering great mental and bodily anguish, having been deeply affected by "the consequences of the foolish exhibition". One wonders how Nelson fared after this catastrophe. The following year he spent some time in America where he developed his 'musical novelty' act to much applause, a unique theatrical experience that ensured that he was rarely out of work, whether performing as the star attraction, or as an accompaniment to others. He appeared in a number of London pantomimes in the period 1849-51. At the age of 44, Nelson was to unexpectedly die from gangrene of the leg while touring with Pablo Fanque's tented circus.

1847_06_23 CARLISLE.   FATAL ROAD ACCIDENT

Mr J H Andrews was returning with Mr and Mrs Coleman, Mr Edwards and Miss Fife from Wigton where they had all been appearing. The phaeton in which they were all travelling was driven by Mr Andrews. The horse becoming restive set off at a furious pace, and Andrews, too fatigued to pull it back, gave the reins to Mr Coleman. He had barely taken them when they broke and the horse galloped on without restraint. Andrews then stood up with the intention of leaping out, but the others tried to persuade him otherwise. Ignoring them, he duly leapt from the careering carriage and fell to the ground. The horse galloped wildly on until it reached the next tollgate where it crashed into it, smashing the shafts of the vehicle, and throwing the passengers to the ground. Fortunately all escaped serious injury, and as soon as practicable Mr Coleman retraced his steps whence they had travelled. He found Mr Andrews unconscious but got him to the nearest inn where a surgeon was sent for. This medic said the case was hopeless, and Andrews was taken home but was dead on arrival.

1849_11_10c BATH (Theatre Royal).   RAIL ACCIDENT TO MADAME WARTON

Madame Warton had for some time been presenting a show of *Poses Plastiques* at a venue in Leicester Square known as Walhalla. She then took the show on the road where it proved very popular. While playing in Bristol the troupe made a flying visit to Bath. Just as Madame Warton was entering her carriage, one of her attendants slammed the door prematurely catching two of her fingers between door and post. "Her screams were truly distressing and the train was delayed for a quarter of an hour." On arriving back at Bristol she was attended by Mr Lang who found it necessary to remove one of her nails, an operation delicate and painful. Madame Warton was back on stage after a weekend's rest but it was thought more than likely she would lose the use of that finger.

1850_01_11 LONDON.   ROAD ACCIDENT SUFFERED BY MR VANDENHOFF

[John Vandenhoff (1790–1861) was of Dutch extraction, born in Salisbury and made his stage debut there in 1808. Slowly but surely learning his business in the provinces, he graduated to major tragic roles. He was leading man in companies at Liverpool, Manchester and Bath, making occasional visits to London. In 1838 he was in the company when Macready took the management of Covent Garden. When that ceased he relied on the provinces for most of his work, making regular visits with his daughter to the principal cities. At this time he was on one of his spells at Drury Lane.]

After rehearsing in the afternoon, Mr Vandenhoff returned home in his carriage for a rest before the strenuous evening ahead. Descending from the carriage, he slipped on the icy pavement, falling to the ground. On being raised it was discovered he had dislocated his shoulder, rendering him unable to perform. A message was hastily sent to the theatre as Vandenhoff was due to play Jacques in *As You Like It* that evening.

85. *John Vandenhoff*

He was out of action for some days, returning on 17 January with his shoulder bandaged and his arm in a sling.

1852_03_19 BOSTON, USA (Howard Athenaeum).   MRS MOWATT IN RIDING ACCIDENT

[Anna Cora Mowatt (1819–1870) American playwright, actress and poet was born in Bordeaux, France, the ninth of fourteen children. She emigrated to the USA when very young. In 1834, at the age of 15, she eloped with and married James Mowatt, a New York lawyer who died in 1851.]

On the conclusion of her visit to Boston, actress Mrs Mowatt had a very successful farewell benefit. Unfortunately, on this day she met with a severe riding accident. While out on her horse, it reared up throwing her to the ground, breaking a rib and causing other injuries. This made her unable to resume work for some time.

1852_08_16 LONDON.   FATAL ACCIDENT TO OLD STAGE FAVOURITE

The pantomimist Frank Hartland (70) who worked with Grimaldi and Dubois was now retired. When walking along near Cox's livery stables, a four-in-hand driven by a nobleman drew up at the stables, so Hartland stopped out of interest. Opposite the livery stables some building work was taking place, and at that moment a plank from the scaffolding fell with great force exactly on to Hartland's head crushing his skull. He died on the way to the hospital, leaving a large family that was entirely dependent upon him.

1852_10_22 LONDON (Victoria).   ROAD ACCIDENT TO THEATRE PROMPTER

Mr Cowan the prompter, together with Mr Johnston the manager at the Victoria Theatre, were driving over Blackfriars Bridge around 10pm when two heavily laden wagons obstructed the way. Cowan attempted to drive between them but became hemmed in, the wheels of his chaise broken, and the vehicle overturned. Both men were thrown on to the ground and trampled on by horses. Several people went to their assistance and Mr Cowan was taken to Guy's Hospital. Johnston escaped with a few bruises of a not very serious nature, but Cowan had a badly fractured leg that confined him to bed for several months.

1858_06_29 CARLTON.   RAILWAY ACCIDENT TO CHARLES DILLON

[Charles J. Dillon (1819–1881) was an English actor-manager who gained a reputation through extensive touring. He became manager of Drury Lane in 1857. From 1860 to 1866 he toured with his wife in America and Australia, thereafter returning to Britain to continue his domestic peregrinations.]

The actor Charles Dillon was travelling from London to Manchester by train when one of the wheels of the tender broke and at a speed of 40 to 50 mph the train left the line. Only one man received a serious injury, Dillon and the rest of the passengers escaped with some severe bruises.

86. *Charles Dillon*

Acting is merely the art of keeping a large group of people from coughing.
Ralph Richardson (1902-1983)

1859_07_21c VILLERS-SUR-MARNE, France.   SHOOTING ACCIDENT TO M ROGER

[Gustave-Hippolyte Roger (1815–1879) was a leading French tenor who created many major roles. He made his debut in 1838 at the Opera Comique and starred there until 1848. He toured England with Jenny Lind and on his return to Paris joined the Grand Opera. He was the star tenor for many years, and apart from playing leads there he undertook concert tours in Germany on almost an annual basis].

"M Roger, the celebrated tenor of the Grand Opera met with a terrible accident the other day while walking out with his gun in his park at Villers-sur-Marne. While getting over a hedge the gun went off and lodged the contents in his arm. Amputation was found to be necessary. The operation was successfully performed and no danger to his life was anticipated."

87.

It seems the great man walked home after the accident and summoned the surgeon. When told it must be amputated, he simply said "Do it." It was amputated below the elbow and a celebrated surgical-instrument maker promised to make him an artificial hand with wrist capable of movements. Although the popular tenor had for years made between £4000 and £5000 annually, it was thought that he had saved no money. But at 44 he was expected to continue with his ebullient career which he did, singing in concerts, and teaching.

175

1859_12_27 BRIGHTON.   ROAD ACCIDENT TO ACTOR

[Robert Soutar (1830–1908) was an actor, comedian, stage manager, writer and director. He began his career as an amateur actor in 1852, starting his professional career in Brighton where the accident detailed underneath occurred. He went on to greater things, marrying Nellie Farren in 1867, and becoming a staple figure in the London theatre utilising his several talents.]

Robert Soutar, an actor with the Brighton theatre company, was appearing at Lewes in the short break before the pantomime opened at Brighton. Returning in an omnibus he was standing near the exit enjoying a cigar, when the sudden jerking of the horses made him slip from the step, breaking his leg just above the ankle. Soutar was thus rendered incapable of taking part in the pantomime in which he was to play a principal role.

1861_03_24 LEEDS (Theatre Royal).   FATAL ROAD ACCIDENT TO ACTOR

On his day off, actor Augustus Fortescue (32) went for a jaunt in a dog cart with Charles Thompson an architect, and two females. They had lunched together then went on a trip to Bardsey where they had tea before returning via Harewood to Leeds. They were going through Chapeltown around 8pm when Fortescue, suddenly standing up, shook Mrs Wilson who was driving. She lost control and the dogcart hit another vehicle, with the result that Fortescue was thrown on to the road receiving such injuries that he died within an hour.

1861_09_18 HULL (Queen's).   FATAL ROAD ACCIDENT TO THEATRE MANAGER

Four friends Messrs Walker, Fisher, Wallett, and Wolfenden the lessee of the Queen's Theatre set out to go to Cottingham. Three travelled in a dog cart, while Wallett travelled on horseback. On arriving at a toll bar Wallett and Wolfenden changed places, whereupon the spirited horse galloped off leaving the dog cart far behind. When this caught up with Wolfenden he was lying unconscious on his back in the middle of the road. Wallett attended to his friend while Walker posted off to Cottingham for assistance. Dr Watson was swiftly brought, a light cart found, and Wolfenden conveyed to Hull Infirmary where he died five days later never having recovered consciousness.

1862_09_30c NEWTOWN.   ROAD ACCIDENT TO SAM COWELL

[Sam Cowell (1820–1864) started life as an actor but gained popularity on the music halls as a comic singer. He was known especially for *The Ratcatcher's Daughter*, and *Villikins and his Dinah*. It was the immense popularity of individual performers like Cowell that helped boost the development of music halls.]

Sam Cowell was touring Welsh halls and on his way by coach between Newtown and Aberystwith a wheel on the coach broke and he was thrown out into the road. He was unable to work for three weeks as a result, next appearing at Manchester on 18 October.

1867_06_29 WARRINGTON.   RAILWAY ACCIDENT TO MR WORBOYS

Worboys was an established low comedian who had an engagement with Mr Sothern at the Paris Exhibition. He was travelling from Liverpool to London in a third class carriage when, because of an error at the points, the train ploughed into a standing coal train. Worboys was thrown on to his knees then violently backwards. When he was rescued he found his legs would not function properly. He went to see Sothern when he arrived in London, and Sothern suggested he saw Mr Adams the eminent surgeon.

The railway company accepted responsibility and paid £300 into court. In February 1868, Worboys went to court to claim that the amount should be increased to compensate for his inability to work, plus the extra expenses caused by his handicap, including £40 to medical men. Several fellow performers came forward and said that his wage would be £4 or £5 a week in London (Sothern's secretary), £4, £5, or £6 (E L Blanchard), Charles Mathews the comedian said he had worked with Worboys and he was a very active performer, worth £4 to £5 a week for a run, £7 to £8 for a special part. One of the lawyers asked: 'Would you be surprised to hear from October to January he was only earning £2.10.0d?' To which Mathews replied 'I would not be surprised at anything in the theatrical profession,' (laughter in court). There was then a long wrangle about how long it would be before Worboys could work properly again, the upshot being he was awarded another £200 from the railway company.

1868_01_24 LONDON (Lyceum).   ASSAULT ON DANCER BY LANDLORD

Lydia Myfton, a dancer at the Lyceum Theatre, had a room at 49 Whitcomb Street. Mrs Trigg, the wife of the landlord's deputy, had a screaming do complaining that Lydia came in at 4am accompanied by a gentleman. This Lydia denied, saying she was always back by 12.30am and her work at the theatre prohibited her getting home any earlier. Mr Trigg, the landlord's deputy, attacked her verbally calling her offensive names. (At a guess these will have been on the lines of whore, trollop, etc). He then physically attacked her, knocking her down. She said if he struck her again she would take out a summons against him, so he knocked her down the stairs, banging her head on the wall

176

rendering her deaf in that ear.

Lydia brought a charge of assault, and another lodger swore that she had seen Trigg hit her three times and knock her down the stairs. In response Trigg said Lydia had been given notice by his boss, which Lydia refuted. The magistrate found for Lydia and fined Trigg £3 plus costs, and said the sooner landlords got rid of deputies like Trigg the better. It was not stated if Lydia subsequently changed lodgings, but I presume she did.

1868_08_01 LIVERPOOL.　　　　RAILWAY ACCIDENT TO THE SWANBOROUGHS

Arthur Swanborough was the acting manager of the Strand Theatre, and lessee of the New Greenwich Theatre, his wife was Eleanor Bufton an actress well-known at the St James's Theatre. They left on an express train from Euston at 2.45pm, due at Liverpool at 8.15pm. Approaching Lime Street Station in Liverpool was a descent, and a brake van was coupled to the train to check its downward speed. This was done, but nobody was in the van to work the brakes, and the train entered the station at 30mph. By good fortune in the station were a luggage van, a mail van, and two empty trucks, not linked but with short distances between. When the train hit them they, absorbing the impact, were smashed to bits. Several passengers, being thrown about, suffered badly bruised limbs but no broken bones. Mrs Swanborough escaped all injury, but Mr Swanborough was left unable to walk without assistance.

1868_09_18 SITTINGBOURNE (Sanger's Circus)　　　FATAL ACCIDENT AT CIRCUS PARADE

Although steam powered traction engines were used by showmen from the mid-1850s, circuses mainly relied on horse-drawn transport. The arrival of Sanger's Circus at Sittingbourne was attended by a fatal accident. A boy named Alfred Saywell was watching the parade when the fore wheel of one of the carriages slipped into a rut on the road. The horses became restive, turning round. This resulted in the wagon pole knocking Alfred down and the rear wheel ran over him. He was instantly killed with his lungs punctured by broken ribs. At the inquest the driver was fully exonerated from blame and a verdict of Accidental Death returned. "The proprietors of the Circus expressed their regret at the accident, and gave £10 to the lad's father".

In the mid-19th century 40% of children died before the age of twelve, mainly through disease though accidents contributed to the total. It was a veritable triumph for one's sons and daughters to attain adulthood, but even then many young adults were slain by tuberculosis. So 'Life was Cheap' – but £10? I know £10 then was worth more than now – around £880 – but such a derisory offer of that amount today would be no more than an insult.

1869_03_07 TODMORDEN.　　　　RAILWAY ACCIDENT TO OPERA COMPANY

The Edmund Rosenthal Opera Company was travelling by train from Rochdale to Leeds on the way to Newcastle to fulfil an engagement at the Tyne Theatre. Just prior to Todmorden, the train came to a concussive stop, with lurching carriages throwing the passengers around like dolls. One carriage was completely destroyed, others damaged to a greater or lesser extent. The reason for the crash was put down to "imperfectly laid" rails, as no other train was involved. The passengers arrived at Leeds, late, shocked, but all uninjured. The opera company continued to Newcastle .

1869_09_10 PERPIGNAN, France.   ROAD ACCIDENT TO ADVANCE AGENT

It is the advance man's job to go some time ahead of a travelling show and make all the practical arrangements and get out the advertising material. Signor D'Allessandri, the advance agent for Myers's Circus, was travelling from St Paul to Perpignan in the Pyrenees. The horse pulling his trap fell, dragging the poor chap to the ground and breaking his arm. He was obliged to travel another 33 miles before he could get any medical attention. At Perpignan he was forced to telegraph his employer that they would need somebody to take his place.

He then languished in that town's Hotel des Ambassadeurs under the care of Dr Mossat who dithered whether he should amputate or not. It was eventually carried out on 21 September under chloroform. The circus arrived the same day, all bewailing the unfortunate agent's plight. The show was there for three days during which Mrs Myers and every performer visited D'Allessandri. They then moved on to the next town leaving the agent still at the Hotel des Ambassadeurs, recuperating as best he could. I do not know how long the poor chap was out of action, but by January 1870 he was back at work at the Royal Amphitheatre in Manchester.

1870_12_06 SOUTH SHIELDS.   FATAL RAILWAY ACCIDENT TO THEATRE MANAGER

This was another major railway disaster. It occurred on the Sunderland to Newcastle line due to the pointsman diverting trains so that they crashed into one another. Some 39 people were injured, and five people killed, including Frederick Younge manager of the London Comedy Company currently playing at Sunderland. The pointsman, Robert Hedley, absconded after the accident.

1871_04_25 CRANFORD, USA.   FATAL RAILWAY ACCIDENT TO BARNUM'S CIRCUS

Barnum's travelling show was on its way from one stand to the next. The road at a certain place crossed the Central New Jersey Railway line, the railway track on the approach to the road descending a steep gradient where the train perforce increases speed. At the very moment when the circus provision wagon was crossing the line, a train came rushing down the incline and smashed into the side of it, splintering it into smithereens, killing two of the four mules pulling the wagon, and three men – Theodore Conklin (27) the driver, Edward Dyer (30) a cook, and George Sickles a cook, who all died instantly. Three more men were very badly injured and in danger, but with a possibility of their recovery. At the inquest the men "accidentally and by misfortune, were run over and killed" and "no blame is attached to the employees of the New Jersey Central Railway Company."

1871_08_02 LONDON.   POPULAR ACTRESS IN RAILWAY ACCIDENT

On Wednesday evening in a railway collision at South Kensington Station, one of the injured was Mrs Swanborough better known as Eleanor Bufton of the Strand and Court Theatres. She was violently thrown to the end of the carriage, receiving many bruises to her body, but worst of all a scalp wound several inches long. She was attended by Mr Haffenden a neighbouring surgeon who staunched and stitched her wound although she was in great pain thereafter, and reliant on soporifics. Three years previously Miss Bufton had been in a railway accident at Liverpool Station but escaped unharmed (*see* 1868_08_01).   On 15 June 1872, Miss Bufton took to the courts for compensation from the railway company as she had been unable to work since, and could not see that she would be able to do so in the immediate future. The company had accepted responsibility, and the court hearing was to agree the amount of compensation.

Miss Bufton had been on the stage for a dozen years, reaching a certain eminence which commanded £8 to £10 a week with every likelihood of progressing to £15, but having a full year out of her profession had halted her progress. After much discussion the jury awarded her £1600 which was challenged by the railway company. It was settled that she would receive £1200 within 14 days as her expenses etc had been agreed at that, the other £400 would go to a bench of judges to decide. The judges decided in November, saying the damages were fair and not excessive, the £1600 (£150,000 today) would stay. Eleanor Bufton, finally made a return to the stage at a benefit at Drury Lane on 14 December 1872.

88. *Eleanor Bufton*

1871_09_01 AT SEA.   **FATAL ACCIDENT TO MR EDWARD ROBERTSON**

Edward Shafto Robertson was an actor and younger brother of the popular dramatist T W Robertson creator of the 'cup and saucer' plays that discussed contemporary problems in realistic modern sets. Edward, having made his debut in London in 1870, went to work in Australia, and from there joined a company that was to travel to India. Accompanied by J B Howe the tragedian of the company, he travelled in the steamship *Avoca*. One day, chatting on deck, a sudden lurch of the ship unbalanced Robertson and he fell through an open hatch into the engine room 14ft below. He suffered from concussion of the brain and died three days later, "his body being committed to the deep in the most impressive manner by a clergyman on board".

179

1872_05_24 MANCHESTER (New Queen's).   **DOMESTIC CELLAR STEPS FALL**

After the performance Mdlle Nita de Castro a principal known for "her tasteful acting and superb singing" went home and accidentally leaned on the door that led to the cellar. The door, not fastened in any way, opened allowing the unfortunate young lady to tumble down the stone steps fracturing her leg in two places, injuring her ribs, and sustaining internal injuries.

1872_09_13 LONDON.   **RAILWAY ACCIDENT TO SEVERAL EMINENT SINGERS**

The accident happened near Westbourne Park Station when a goods train ran into the express train from North Wales. On the train were several eminent singers who had been taking part in the Worcester Music Festival. A van containing a large number of valuable musical instruments was smashed into and overturned, but fortunately passengers' injuries were confined to shock and bruises.

1873_01_08 WORKINGTON (Lyceum).   **FATAL PLUM PUDDING**

Lyceum actress Ellen Parker, the wife of actor William Parker, died under very singular circumstances. It seems that some time before this day Mrs Parker broke a blood vessel in her head, and her doctor advised her to refrain from taking an active part on the stage in case she injured her brain. On 2 January she performed in the pantomime at the theatre, and returned home with her husband. While enjoying plum pudding, Ellen crushed a stone on a nerve of one of her teeth and immediately fell back insensible. Until 8 January she remained totally unconscious, though her pulse continued to beat and her breathing was discernible. Then "Death claimed her as his own."

1873_02_11 TEIGNMOUTH.   MUSICIAN FALLS FROM TRAIN

Charles Allen Windeatt was a musician at the Exeter Theatre. A married man with seven children, he earned £100 a year with his 15/- a week from the theatre, plus other income from music lessons and playing at occasional functions. On this day, he was travelling by train to Teignmouth where he had two lessons to give and then play at a ball in the evening.

He was travelling in a third-class carriage and had it to himself. As the train slowed nearing its destination, Windeatt saw a person he knew and "leaned against the door" which flew open and he fell out on to the lines. He was severely injured with both legs paralysed and pains in his back and head.

As he was unable to play his violin and function normally to earn his living, he took the railway company to court in July. His medico Dr Lake said his legs would still not function and it could be a year or longer before he regained the use of them; Windeatt complained of a permanent loud noise in his head which prevented him hearing his pupils playing. Dr Lake could not say whether he would ever properly recover or even be able to resume his occupation. He also said his fees to date amounted to ten guineas. Another medical man Dr Whidbourne had known Windeatt for seven years, and he agreed with his colleague, but hoped there would be a "useful recovery" in two or three years. His charges so far were about £25. He said that if Windeatt continued needing attention as at present it would cost about £30 a year, plus the extra comforts he would require but could not afford.

It was a long case with many witnesses called. The plaintiff claimed the door was slammed closed by a railway employee at Exeter and he had not touched the door or window, it flying open as he leaned on it. The defence was that Windeatt had himself turned the door handle when he saw his friend the pointsman Green, and that at several stages on the journey different employees had noted the handles were all turned correctly. Passengers in adjoining carriages had given evidence in favour of the railway company too. The jury found in favour of the defendants.

How would a man with a wife and seven children who can no longer earn a respectable £2 a week possibly manage? I do not know.

1873_10_11 LONDON.   MRS SWANBOROUGH IN CARRIAGE ACCIDENT

Poor Eleanor Bufton (Mrs Swanborough)! After the railway accident that kept her off the stage for half the year in 1871 (see 1871_08_02), here she is injured again in a road accident only two years later. This time in her own brougham, which was crashed into and overturned. She received a scalp wound and other injuries, her daughter Ada was bruised and shaken. Ada returned to the boards for her benefit on 29 November essaying the role of Letitia Hardy in *The Belle's Stratagem*.

1873_11_29 SYSTON.   RAILWAY ACCIDENT INVOLVING OPERA COMPANY

The Carl Rosa Opera Company travelling by train to Nottingham was scheduled to open this night with *The Bohemian Girl*. The train was involved in a serious accident and many of the personnel were thrown about. At the theatre the curtain was due to rise at 7.30pm and the audience groaned when the manager walked on. However, he announced that the performers had "miraculously and providentially escaped with very slight injuries" (Applause) Rose Hersee – who was to take the leading role – had sustained a shock to her nervous system from which she had not recovered. But "with the indomitable pluck of an English lady, she had determined to fulfil her engagement that night." (Loud cheers). So that was all right then.

180

1874_03_05 LONDON.   "ETHIOPIAN DUETIST" IN CARRIAGE ACCIDENT

Mr W Harman, partner of Mr H Elston in a black face act, travelling from the Raglan Music Hall to the New Star at Bermondsey, was thrown from his vehicle breaking his arm in two places. Performers often played more than one hall a night, dashing from one to another, and perhaps a third after that. *Personal Note: A similar situation arose in the 1960s in cities like Manchester and Birmingham when pubs and clubs all had entertainment every night, and artistes would be zipping here and there criss-crossing all over the district. Easy for a comedian or vocalist, but hard graft for a puppet act with props and a baby in a carry cot as your authors can vouch.*

1874_08_17 NEW YORK, USA (Wallack's).   J L TOOLE IN NEW YORK

Toole was probably the best known and most popular comic actor of the Victorian age. Like many before him, he was desirous of conquering America and opened on this night at the beginning of a long and arduous tour. Unfortunately, ten days later, while walking along the bluff at Long Branch he accidentally put his foot in a hole left by the removal of a flag-post, severely wrenching his ankle. He performed that night with a doctor in the wings applying a salve on his every exit. The next day his foot – swollen like a balloon – compelled him to relinquish any idea of further performing until its condition considerably improved. Toole had only a limited time in New York as the resident company at Wallack's was due to start their own season in October. When he recovered he had to start his tour without the New York audience having seen much of him.

1874_12_29c CINCINNATI, USA.   MR FECHTER IN FALL ON ICE

We have already noted an accident to the eminent tragedian in the companion volume and once again the poor chap was in the wars, this time outside the theatre where he slipped and fell on the ice. He injured his leg – it was rumoured to be broken but when he failed to appear on New Year's Eve his doctor issued a note stating this was due to an abscess on his leg, this considered necessary to counteract gossip that he was drunk. Whatever the injury was, it was serious enough to keep him off the stage while doctors debated whether amputation would be essential. On 28 February 1875 it was announced that amputation had been avoided, but it would be some weeks before the actor would be able to work. By June 1875, Fechter was appearing in Montreal but "playing to poor houses."

1875_08_16 STAMFORD, USA.   EDWIN BOOTH IN SERIOUS CARRIAGE ACCIDENT

After being thrown from his carriage and hurled with great force against a telegraph pole, Edwin Booth, America's leading tragedian, sustained injuries that were at first feared to be possibly fatal. Fortunately, these turned out to be two displaced ribs and the ulna of his left arm broken near the elbow. However, these were enough to put him out of action immediately, but he expected to fulfil his engagement at the Fifth Avenue Theatre, New York, scheduled to begin on 4 October. Daly the manager had contracted to pay the actor $1000 for each of 36 performances. After that season Booth was to undertake an extensive tour of the South and West giving 100 performances visiting many cities.

His recovery took place at his home, "a lovely place on the shore, looking out upon an estuary of Long Island Sound." In the event, his return was not until 25 October when he played Hamlet at the Fifth Avenue Theatre and was unable to use his left arm at all.

1876_01_21 HUNTINGDON.   TERRIBLE FATAL RAILWAY ACCIDENT

A loaded coal train arrived at Abbots' Ripton Station about six miles north of Huntingdon during a heavy snowstorm that made travelling difficult and dangerous. Signals were obscured by these wintry conditions in the dark of night. The goods train comprising 30 trucks arrived at 6.45pm and was signalled into a siding to permit the Edinburgh 10.30am express to pass on its way to King's Cross where it was due at 8.00pm. All but four trucks had passed when the express train hurtled into them.

89.   The engine was derailed on its side, several carriages were crushed and broken up.

Before anything could be done in the way of rescue, a northbound express crashed into the debris causing another shattered train, and complete blockage of the railway. Over 20 people were seriously injured and there were 13 fatalities. Among the dead was Dion William Boucicault (22) eldest son of the famous actor and playwright Dion Boucicault. Because the telegraph wires were down owing to the ferocious weather, his parents, who were acting at the Adelphi in London, did not receive the news until the following day.

1876_01_25 PRESTON.   RAILWAY ACCIDENT NEAR PRESTON

[Frederic Maccabe was the leading ventriloquist of the age. Born in Liverpool of Irish parents, he started out as an amateur actor and was one of the trio of young actors that included Henry Irving spoofing the Davenport Brothers spiritualist act (see 1865_02_24). Maccabe went on to specialise in ventriloquism not using dummy figures but, rather in the manner of Charles Mathews's At Homes, created the illusion of other characters being on stage by voice alone. He had a long career that included successful visits to Australia and the USA. His books on ventriloquist techniques are still valued. After a glittering career he retired in 1898 but illness and poverty blighted his final years and he ended up in Ormskirk workhouse hospital, dying there in 1904. At the time of this accident he was at the height of his popularity].

90.   Once again an accident was caused on the railway by a stationary coal train on the line when an express train was expected. Not as alarming as the one detailed above, but the fast train was bearing Frederic Maccabe advertised to appear at the Guildhall, Preston. Though shaken up, he was otherwise uninjured through his own presence of mind. He duly turned up at the Guildhall but was unable to appear because of the shock to his nervous system. The following night he was still unable to face the audience, and a doctor's certificate was pasted outside regarding the cancelled performance.

1876_02_18 NORWICH.   ACTORS SAVE CHILDREN FROM DROWNING

Pull's Ferry is a charming spot in the city of Norwich. Actors Brien M'Cullough and Walter Mason, were just disembarking from the ferry when shouts of alarm were raised. An eight-year-old boy was pushing a pram – bearing an infant – somewhat erratically along the path when both he and pram fell in the river. Without hesitation Mason, throwing off his coat, plunged in the rapidly flowing stream. M'Cullough took a headed dive and, being more agile than his friend, reached the children first. The pair landed the children to cheers from the onlookers, "amongst them being several who were *dressed in male attire*, but who had *not the courage* to emulate the example" set by the actors.

1876_12_22 ARBROATH. THESPIANS ALMOST DROWNED IN STORM

91. *Osmond Tearle*

Osmond Tearle, his acting manager Walter Hastings, and low comedian Will Fergus were walking the cliffs on the roughest day for some time, as they wished to see the splendour of the storm. They alighted on the flat rock described by Sir Walter Scott in *The Antiquary* when Fergus was swept off by a wave. Tearle rushed further down the rock and watching the return of the wave seized his companion by the arm. But the wave, sweeping back seawards, took with it both men, clinging together, Fergus now being insensible. Hastings, finding a firm hold on the rock, awaited the men's return and clutched them as they came in. Thus they were all saved from an awful death by drowning.

1877_01_10c PARIS, France (d'Hiver) UNBELIEVABLE DEATH OF YOUNG EQUESTRIAN

Any circus artiste knows that, if he performs an act of skill and daring, he is tempting injury and death at every performance. But he would surely think himself out of harm's way playing billiards! Robert Nyland (19) was an equestrian at the Cirque d'Hiver and while away from the show playing a game of billiards a wager was made that he could not jump over the cue, which presumably was set upright. While trying to win his bet, the cue caught in his trousers and entered his body. He was picked up barely sensible, and taken home where he languished suffering the most acute pain for a week before dying of mortification on 17 January.

1877_11_12 SHEFFIELD (Alexandra). THEATRE TREASURER IN FATAL TRAFFIC ACCIDENT

Thomas Greaves treasurer and secretary made up the evenings accounts on Monday night as customary, then set off in a cab for his home, with the lessee Mr Brittlebank. As it was a fine night and he was smoking, Greaves elected to travel outside. The cab had not gone ten yards when he fell off into the road, lying on his face. He was returned to his office, had his faced bathed, and consumed some brandy, after which he recovered and was sent home inside a cab. There, attended by Dr Gwynne, he took to his bed. He died at 6.30am on Tuesday morning due – it was assumed – to "an apoplectic seizure". He was 37 years of age and left a widow and three children

1878_12_04 DYTCHLEY. DEATH OF MR GYE OF COVENT GARDEN

We have met Mr Gye on two previous occasions – one a fire, the other an explosion. On 29 November, Frederick Gye the impresario of the Italian Opera at Covent Garden for almost 30 years, went off to enjoy a day's shooting with Viscount Dillon of Dytchley Park near Oxford. In the course of that day a gun exploded causing a severe wound to Gye's groin, and Mr Symonds an eminent surgeon of Oxford was summoned to attend. Symonds was at first doubtful of recovery, but as time passed he became more sanguine, and while not stating that his patient was out of danger, his diagnosis became more optimistic. His optimism was misplaced as Frederick Gye, who had remained at Dytchley Park, died there almost a week later on 4 December.

1879_04_30 LONDON. FATAL OMNIBUS ACCIDENT

Black-face minstrels were very popular at this period and one such troupe was the Mohawk Minstrels. They were resident at the Agricultural Hall at Islington for 27 years. On this night they were

183

doubling with Foresters' Music Hall at Mile End. The troupe travelled in their privately chartered omnibus and on the way between venues they passed under a railway arch in Bethnal Green. One of the troupe named Evans, sitting on the open top deck of the bus, hit his head on the brick arch and was hurled to the ground. He was totally insensible when picked up, and immediately taken to the London Hospital. He lingered until noon the following day when he expired due to internal injuries and concussion to the brain.

1879_06_29 BATH. FATAL BOATING ACCIDENT TO OPERA SINGERS

On their Sunday off, some members of the company appearing at the Bath theatre in *HMS Pinafore* decided to go on a boat trip up the River Avon to Batheaston where there was a picturesque weir. The singers were Florence Hyde, Annie Walsh, and Mr Ives, the other two members of the party were citizens of Bath. A jolly time was had by all, with a lunch stop at a riverside inn, after which it was decided to row nearer to the weir. This was a notorious spot for accidents at the best of times, and a particularly unwise suggestion that day because heavy rain had caused the river level to be higher than normal and water rushing over the weir was flowing faster than usual. The boat turned over, casting all the party into the water, and Miss Hyde and Mr Ives were drowned.

1880_08_20c LYONS, France. TRAVEL ACCIDENT TO CIRCUS AGENT

184 Charles E Stuart was the advance man or agent for the George Sanger Circus. Stuart, thrown from his trap on the way to Lyons, was severely cut about the head. The wounds were progressing favourably for a week or so when lockjaw set in. He was hoping to return to England, but paralysis of the nerves developed and he "was rendered quite helpless". He was languishing at a hotel in Nevers-Neivre awaiting the arrival of the circus. Eventually, although improved, but still not fully recovered, he returned to London – at the expense of his employer, who provided a first-class sleeping car for whole of his return journey.

1880_09_05 HULL. FATAL ACCIDENT TO POPULAR SINGER

Charles Williams (27), a young singer of extempore and topical songs, was involved in a traffic accident, being thrown from his trap and suffering injuries to his face and head. He was taken to his hotel where Dr Mason went to attend to him. He was greatly shaken up and unlikely to be able to work for some time. He died on the following Sunday 12 September. A committee was formed to raise funds for his wife and two young children. This was well supported as Williams was a popular young man in the profession. It was particularly unfortunate that he had gone riding in a trap with a reckless man after they had both enjoyed a convivial evening.

1881_02_23 LONDON. ROAD ACCIDENT TO MRS KENDAL

[Dame Madge Kendal (1848–1935) was reputedly the youngest of 22 children of an Anglo-Danish couple. One of her brothers was T W Robertson, the dramatist known for his tea-cup dramas. In 1869, she married W H Kendal and the two thereafter acted mostly together in Shakespeare and classic comedies. The couple, important managers as well as actors, made their American debut in 1889, spending most of the next five years there. The Kendals continued to appear in popular plays without interruption until 1908, when they both retired. She was appointed Dame in 1926. The following accident happened during her West End hey-day.]

While Mrs Kendal was on her way to the St James's Theatre in a four wheel cab, the horse bolted and the cab, having dashed against a lamp-post, was shattered. Mrs Kendal suffered injury to her forehead, and her arm pierced by some vehicle wreckage. She was bleeding profusely, and as a surgeon's house was nearby, he gave assistance in staunching the flow. She was unable to continue working for a couple of weeks, returning on 12 March to the hit play *The Money Spinner* with John Hare and William Kendal.

1881_08_06 SHEFFIELD.   ROAD ACCIDENT TO BOUCICAULT JR AND MRS BEERE

Mr Boucicault Jr and Mrs Bernard Beere, while appearing at the town's theatre, were travelling in a trap when the horse shied at a passing tramcar, became unmanageable and bolted. The horse slipped on the rails and fell, the two passengers were thrown out, Mr Boucicault's head striking the pavement. Both were taken to an adjacent surgery in a semi-conscious state, but after medical attention they were both able to appear at the theatre that night.

1883_05_27c WEST HARTLEPOOL.   MANAGER FORCED TO CLOSE TOUR

Mr Burgess, boss of a comedy and burlesque company, suffered a nasty accident while trying to climb over a wall. He slipped, and his hand caught a butcher's hook which ripped the flesh of his hand from palm to forefinger, leaving the bone exposed. He intended having it treated at Dewsbury his next venue but, alas, was compelled to abandon the tour. That wound sounds very nasty indeed.

1883_10_20c PARIS, France.   STREET ACCIDENT TO LOUIS SOURNIS

Louis Sournis the esteemed ex-singing master at the Opera Comique was knocked down by the typical clumsy driving of a boulevard cabman. The wheel of the vehicle went over his body causing internal injury as well as breaking his right arm.

1883_12_18 LONDON.   ACCIDENT TO WELL-KNOWN MANAGEMENT FIGURE

Bruce Phillips, former secretary to the Westminster Aquarium and later manager for several touring productions, lived in Walsworth Road. When a fire broke out in a neighbouring building he went to assist with the fire fighting. During this, somebody rescuing things from the building threw "a bale of goods" from the window. This knocked Phillips down, and with his leg broken in two places he was taken to hospital where he was to spend at least two months before recovery. A letter to *The Era* from Mr Smily, Treasurer of the Globe Theatre, said Phillips had been out of work for three months and was due to start a new job which would have taken him to August 1884. He was offering to start a fund for his friend, having already been given five amounts – from £2 to 10/- – from well-wishers. Further contributions followed, including two guineas from Charles Dickens & Evans, a publishing company run by Dickens Jr and his brother-in-law.

Phillips had recovered by late February 1884, and a benefit was held for him on 16 February at the Imperial Theatre. Thereafter, he started a tour as business agent for Florence Wade. To add to his woes, on 31 March 1884 his beloved four-year-old daughter Ethel died suddenly of croup.

185

"The people long eagerly for just two things: bread and circuses." Juvenal 60-130 AD

1884_10_21 LONDON.   DOUBLE ROAD ACCIDENT TO MUSIC HALL ARTISTES

This accident happened at 10pm in Poplar High Street when two independent vehicles were on the way to Queen's Palace of Varieties. As was mentioned earlier, music hall artistes were often contracted to play at more than one hall a night, thus one vehicle was a brougham taking Mr and Mrs Cairns to their next gig, the other was a mini-bus taking the Letine troupe of trick cyclists to the same venue. Both collided with a fire engine that was presumably charging off to some fire. The brougham overturned, leaving the Cairns shaken and frightened but not physically hurt. The engine then cannoned into the mini-bus, overturning both vehicles. The firemen were thrown to the ground, two receiving severe injuries. The cyclist performers, three men and three women, were all very shaken but none injured, although the bicycles were all bent. You will have read of Mr Letine's murder earlier in this book.

1884_11_18 LONDON.   VIOLINIST HAS HER HAIR CUT OFF

This is a very strange one. American violinist Nettie Carpenter, was a former child prodigy who became a well-known soloist. She had gained first prize at the Paris Conservatory and studied under Sarasate. As a young woman she seems to have deserved the epithet 'brazen' bestowed by Whistler, mainly on the grounds of jilting the same suitor twice. She was walking in Westbourne Grove when "some miscreant cut off her beautiful hair in broad daylight". Even stranger, she did not notice until she got home. I remain intrigued but none the wiser. (*but see also* 1887_11_29).

92. *Nettie Carpenter*

186

1884_12_14 SOWERBY BRIDGE.   RAILWAY ACCIDENT

Mr Melville's *Millions of Money* company left West Hartlepool on the 6.40am train to Bolton. Around noon it arrived at Sowerby Bridge where the company's carriage was left for hitching on to the Bolton train when it arrived. The engine, on arrival, hit the carriage with such force that it was completely shattered, and the entire company thrown about with the shock. The two leading members of the company, Miss de Yonson (Mrs Carlisle) and Mr Murray, were carried out unconscious. Though the summoned doctor pronounced them seriously injured they, with the rest of the company, were carried on to the train and proceeded to Bolton. However, it was not possible to open as planned owing to the lack of the leading players – Mr Murray requiring a few days to recover, and Miss de Yonson not expected to resume her professional duties for two weeks.

1884_12_20c ARROWTOWN, New Zealand.   SERIOUS ROAD ACCIDENT ENDS COMPANY

This accident gives a glimpse at the adventurous thespians who, not content to tour the theatres of the UK year after year, went to the antipodes to ply their craft. Georgie Smithson, travelling with her company on the Ontago goldfields, was nearing Arrowtown when the coach horses took fright and the driver, aware of a 100ft precipice on one side, drove his team into the bank at the other. The coach overturned, and the Smithson company was battered and broken. Miss Smithson herself suffered a broken arm, and all her players were injured to a greater or lesser extent, so inevitably had to disband.

1885_09_18 WIGAN (Ohmy's Circus). STILT WALKING CLOWN TOPPLED

This was certainly an accident, but not in the circus ring. On reaching a town it was the custom of a travelling circus to make a grand parade entrance through the streets. When Ohmy's Circus marched into Wigan, the popular clown Tony Felix strode out on his 14ft high stilts. Some small children ran between his legs tripping him up, and he fell violently to the ground, breaking his left arm and two fingers.

1885_11_06c PRESTON. BIRLEY ARMS HOTEL DESTROYED BY FIRE

This pub owned by Mr Miller was totally destroyed leaving the family with no home, furniture, clothing, money or livelihood. But worse than anything, the Millers lost their daughter Jane (11) who was burnt to death. Harry Yorke the manager of the Gaiety Theatre organised a benefit for Miller. However, Yorke's main concern was to start a subscription for Macolla, the left-handed Paganini. This young man had been living in the pub and, to save his life, dropped from the third storey window, alighting on his heels smashing both his ankles. All his clothing, music, and travelling gear was destroyed, leaving him entirely destitute.

On 30 January 1886, a letter appearing in *The Era* called attention to the unfortunate young chap. He had been in hospital since the accident – three long weary months – with only seven visits from professional friends. Macolla had been the sole support of his widowed mother for the last seven years, and the few shillings he had received while in hospital sent to her to keep the wolf from the door. Rent of four times the money sent being due, the writer was begging for more no matter how small. Macolla had not the least particle of anything except the shirt he escaped in. To add to the grim picture, Marcolla had recently tried managing on crutches but, slipping on the hospital floor, had been returned to bed as bad as ever. It is frightening to see how a fit young man could be, in the twinkling of an eye, reduced to a parlous state. The appeal brought in 10/-, 5/-, 2/6 (2), 2/- (2), 1/- (5). It makes you weep; sometimes, compiling these tales of woe, I wish the afflicted were still alive so that I could send them something more substantial!

1886_07_12 WIMBLEDON. ROAD ACCIDENT TO THESPIAN GROUP

Colonel Gordon Alexander, leading a scratch company named the Pastoral Players, was rehearsing a production of *Becket* for a special performance in Cannizaro Woods. While returning to London, the entire troupe was thrown out of their carriage when it overturned. Most escaped unhurt but Leonard Outram suffering a broken arm was taken to the nearby barracks to be attended by Dr Page. This injury had serious repercussions as Outram's regular job was at Toole's Theatre playing Abel Newton in *Hand and Heart*. By taking this extra one-off gig, he ended being out of action for some weeks. In March of 1887 he sued Alfred Johnson, who had provided the carriage, for damages caused by negligence on the part of his servant. Johnson, denying his servant was at fault, blamed the condition of the road. Verdict was for Outram for £75.

[Outram was an established player in reputable companies, including Irving's. In 1901 he was touring America with E H Sothern's company as Player King in *Hamlet*. In March, he lost his wife actress Annetta Ripley in a hospital operation. On 4 May, after the show in Pennsylvania, he went to stay with his brother-in-law for the weekend where he complained several times of the "grippe". His host, going to rouse him at 8am on Monday morning, found Outram dead in bed in peaceful repose.]

187

1886_11_07 WIGAN.   RAILWAY ACCIDENT TO THEATRE COMPANY

On the usual Sunday journey the *Alone in London* company was *en route* for Wigan, its next venue. The carriage was put in a siding to await hitching to the next Wigan bound train. The shunter omitted to put on the brake and, as the carriage had been left on an incline, obeying gravity it started rolling until it hit the buffers. Several of the ladies fainted and John Henderson was cut about the head and face. Medical aid was summoned and after a delay the troupe was sent on its way. Rose Tennyson was unable to appear, but the rest, including Mr Tennyson, carried out their "professional duties". The Lancashire & Yorkshire Railway Co met the claims of the sufferers "in a most liberal manner".

1886_11_24 LONDON.   ACTRESS INJURED IN FOG ACCIDENT

Julia Roselle was on her way to the Princess's Theatre in a pea-souper fog. At the Gloucester Road railway station the fog was so dense she was unable to see the edge of the platform, and tumbled on to the lines, breaking her leg. She was picked up by a gentleman only just in time to prevent her being cut to pieces by the next train. It could be the start of a Mills & Boon story, but wasn't.

1887_05_07 LONDON   ROAD ACCIDENT TO HENRY IRVING

Around noon, Henry Irving, the greatest star of the era, was in a Hansom cab going to the Garrick Club, presumably for his lunch as he had a matinee that day. The cab, colliding with a van in St Martin's Lane, was overturned. Irving had to crawl out on his hands and knees but, quite uninjured, carried on walking to the club. He performed with vivacity in *Faust* at the matinee.

188

1887_05_15 COLNE.   CARRIAGE ACCIDENT ON WAY TO STATION

On Sunday, Augustus Creamer was organising the move of his company from Colne to St Helen's where it was due to open on Monday. He was at the station when he received a message saying Mrs Creamer, Mrs Holt, and Bracey his baggage master had been in an accident. Arriving at the scene, he found the carriage smashed on a steep hill, Mrs Holt insensible with a cut head and broken leg, the driver with broken ribs, Bracey with a dislocated shoulder, and his wife unhurt, except for a slight forehead wound. Mrs Holt was not of the company, but a Colne friend, so she was taken to her home. The Creamers travelled the following day to St Helen's where Mrs Creamer performed in the play that night.

1887_05_27 TIVERTON.   RAILWAY ACCIDENT TO ACTOR AND DAUGHTER

Most of Clarice Trevor's Company after performing at Tiverton had travelled to the next date at Teignmouth by an earlier train. Travelling together later, were actors Mr Norman and Tom Wilson, "a comedian of the first rank", with his family of wife, son and daughter Marie (7) in a train bound for Tiverton Junction, where it would meet the main line train. A mile before the junction, with the train travelling at its full speed of 35mph, the little girl, who had been leaning on the door, fell out. Father Tom instinctively leapt out after her, actually landing on his feet, but the impact was very severe, causing concussion of the spine. On reaching the junction Mrs Wilson, in the greatest distress, informed officials who promptly sent the train in reverse to where father and daughter were picked up and placed in the guard's van. Having got the pair to the local Infirmary, the girl was found to be badly hurt about the shoulder, with her face cut and bruised, while Tom was paralysed from the waist down, and partially so in the arms. On 10 June, Mrs Wilson issued a bulletin to say little Marie was rapidly recovering, her husband remained the same. On 23 June, it was announced Tom had died. The Great Western Railway Co accepted no liability for Tom's death but awarded compensation of £100 for the injuries to the child which "may be considered a substantial *solatium* (consolation)". This would be £11,200 in today's money.

1887_06_16 NEWCASTLE.   PLEASURE ROW TURNS TO TRAGEDY

Charles Octavius Wood (22) was the scenic artist at the Tyne Theatre, taking a position his father had held before him. Charles, out boating in the afternoon with two friends of a similar age, was doing the rowing as his pals Samuel Price and John Griffiths had never been in a boat before. When they were at Elswick where the river was deep, feeling rather hot, he decided to strip off and swim for a bit asking his pals to follow him while he swam. He had only been in the water a few minutes when he called out for help, shouting for them to row quickly. Through lack of experience, Sam and John were inept and unable to get to Charles who – going under – failed to come up again. Eventually reaching the shore, they alerted competent people who went searching and dragging the river. Charles's body was found at a late hour.

1887_11_29 NEW YORK.   VIOLINIST LOSES HAIR WHILE OUT SHOPPING

Nettie Carpenter the violinist at the Metropolitan Opera House was out all day shopping with her mother. Her hair was gathered in a knot, and her hat secured by long hat pins. On returning home and removing her hat she found that her back hair came off with it. Some vandal had cut it in a crowded dry goods shop. This was remarkably identical to a misfortune in London three years previously (*see* 1884_11_18). There has to be more to these two incidents than was revealed in the press paragraphs.

[There appears to be no cogent reason why Miss Carpenter suffered this indignity twice, and one suspects a publicity stunt. However, further research indicates that having one's hair chopped off in the street was not as rare as it would seem. The explanation may be that Nettie's hair was particularly long, lustrous and attractive. In Paris, there was a trade in human hair for the manufacture of wigs, poor people often selling their hair to earn money. Fantine in *Les Miserables* sells not only her hair, but also some teeth. A goodly supply of hair came from convents where the nuns were shorn, and also from corpses. However, the most sought after was 'live hair' and one of the cheekiest methods of gaining it was to cut off somebody's hair by robbery. "An important part of the business of collecting hair is done in the streets of Paris, where the rag gatherers are said to collect every day an average of 100lb of human hair."

I have not found much printed evidence, but on 29 April 1885 in Sheffield a young woman had her hair – worn in a long plait – cut off while looking in a shop window. On 4 February 1887 a mill girl in Clackmannan was attacked by two tramps who stole her boots and chopped off her hair. So while Paris may have been the centre of the trade, illicit hanks of hair were purloined in other countries too.]

1888_07_13 NEWPORT, USA.   CIRCUS CRASH ON THE RAILWAY

Because of the vast distances in America, circuses travelled mainly by rail. Adam Forepaugh's

Circus was en route to its next stand when two cars of the train were derailed and wrecked, injuring two men and killing four horses. It happened at a switch junction and Forepaugh's loss was estimated at $10,000.

1888_09_22 WORKINGTON.

93. *The Majiltons (poster)*

A CHAPTER OF ACCIDENTS

This is an example of the courage, patience and hardiness required by a thespian in Victorian times. On Saturday night, after a successful week at Workington, the Majiltons Theatre Company packed up their equipment on to a wagon to be taken to Whitehaven, there to be loaded on a steamer to Belfast where the company was due to open on Monday. The luggage left at 10.15pm and the company followed in a large brake at 10.45pm. "The night being thick and foggy and the driver of the brake in a like condition mentally" some three miles down the road the vehicle crashed, and the passengers pitched out into a hedge. As they stood pondering their fate, a couple of butchers' carts appeared. Mr Majilton persuaded the butchers to take the women of the troupe to the nearest village of Distington, while the men made their way by foot. This achieved, another brake was hired, and the troupe sallied forth again. After a mile they were obliged to stop once more as the road was blocked with a broken-down wagon. It was their luggage wagon with a broken axle. A return was made to Distington and another goods wagon hired. Thus they were able to transfer the equipment from old to new and proceed to Whitehaven where, arriving 2½ hours after they expected, found that the steamer had not yet left. Hurrah!

1888_10_02 BRISTOL.   TRICYCLE ACCIDENT TO LIONEL RIGNOLD

Comic actor Lionel Rignold – a member of the large theatrical Rignold family of which George and William were the most well-known – was playing Alderman Doddipods in *Pleased Co* at Bristol. Obviously a farce! On Tuesday afternoon, riding along on a tricycle, he hit a large stone and was thrown to the ground, injuring his head. He was carried unconscious to the Royal Infirmary. That night his role was taken by Marshall Moore who acquitted himself admirably. Rignold was thought likely to be off work for some time.

94. *Lionel Rignold*

1889_03_18 BIRMINGHAM (Prince of Wales).   GUN ACCIDENT TO ACTOR IN LODGINGS

Glenn Wynn was an actor in the Bateman company currently playing *Master and Man*. He was found in his lodgings on Monday morning unconscious and bleeding from a gunshot wound in his forehead. Although known to carry a revolver, it was not clear whether this was an accident or attempted suicide.

Taken to hospital, on recovering consciousness he claimed no recollection of what happened, but said he was removing a cartridge from the pistol chambers when it exploded. His friends, meanwhile, chose to reveal that he was of a respectable family in Birmingham and had formed an attachment with a young lady of equal family standing. However, embarking on a stage career resulted in the young lady's father taking an objection to him, his friends shunning him, and the young lady herself spurning him.

On the death of the girl's father the attachment rekindled. Wynn was known to have visited the lady on Sunday night and was in the best of spirits. That seems to be the extent of any useful information, but perhaps it is not too melodramatic to wonder if, after rekindling the affair by post, then meeting again in person, the young lady decided parting was the better idea after all. Wynn being an actor of melodramas, then put his pistol to his temple. Pure surmise, reader!

1889_04_10 FINEDON.   MUSIC HALL TROUPE IN ROAD ACCIDENT

Le Blond Minstrels were travelling in a dogcart when, colliding with a heap of bricks, it overturned, throwing the passengers violently to the ground. Mr Dewey had his ribs fractured and knee-cap displaced, Will George's wife and child incurred severe injuries, the driver suffered a broken collar bone, and the horse was killed.

1889_09_01 CREWE.   RAILWAY ACCIDENT INVOLVING ARTISTES

At 11.45pm on entering Crewe station the Scottish mail train was turned into a loading bay instead of alongside a platform. The train crashed into the end of the bay with great force damaging the locomotive and several carriages. Some passengers, including the Brothers Horne – known for their boxing sketch – and Miss Tyndale were badly injured and detained in Crewe Hospital instead of travelling on to Aberdeen where they were all engaged at Cooke's Circus.

Although able to return home within a fortnight and then recuperate at Brighton, it was several weeks before they were fit enough to resume professional duties. Other artistes on the train were Bessie Bonehill and Harry Bass. Harry Randall was supposed to be on the train but "was fortunate enough to miss it".

1890_01_13 BISHOP AUCKLAND (Theatre).   RIDING ACCIDENT TO ACTING-MANAGER

Mr W H Morgan of Housden's *A Mad Passion* company was riding in the theatre's advertising trap when the horse bolted throwing him to the ground. Landing on his head, he was seriously injured.

1890_05_06 LONDON.   ROAD ACCIDENT TO MR FRANK OSWALD

Mr Oswald, driving his trap in Piccadilly, was thrown out on to the ground when his horse bolted. He suffered serious injuries to his head and broke his arm. Mr Oswald was due to start a tour with his comedy-drama company on 2 June which had to be abandoned.

1891_01_11 BOLTON.   SERIOUS TRAIN COLLISION WITH 32 INJURED

Owing to fog, the traffic at Bolton station had been delayed for most of the day. The Preston train due at 11.47 did not arrive until 12.23, when a large group of waiting men climbed aboard. A train bound for Manchester due at Bolton at 11.27 but an hour late, charging into the station, crashed into the stationary train. Among the passengers injured was Oscar Leroy the slack-wire walker who was detained in his hotel room for many days suffering from a very severe shock to the system and concussion of the brain. The physicians said it would be six months before he was fully recovered, but the man himself had given up all hope of ever walking the wire again.

In February he was moved to the Royal Hotel at Southport. To add to his misery, on 18 September his only son, five-month-old Oscar Jr, died. However, in October he presented a jewelled ring to his friend the juggler Jules Poule as "a mark of esteem". He must have liked giving presents as in February 1892 he gave a gold bracelet to Ada the Second Sight Wonder. He then appears to have taken up the Bath Hotel in Cheltenham that contained a bar for entertainments, and Mrs Leroy gave birth to a daughter. So he seems to have self-fulfilled his auguries.

1891_01_19 LIVERPOOL.   TRAIN ACCIDENT TO MUSIC HALL CHILD

Mr and Mrs Tom Traynor, playing the week at the Argyle Theatre, Birkenhead, were travelling by train through the Mersey Tunnel around 1.30pm when the door of their third-class carriage flew open and their four-year-old child fell out. The alarm instantly given, the train stopped as soon as possible. Found lying between the rails in the tunnel, the little one was taken into a carriage and the train carried on. The child had had a miraculous escape as on examination it was discovered – incredibly – there was but little injury. In those days children could fiddle with the door locks, and we have already had a very similar, but more serious, previous case (*see* 1887_05_27).

1891_06_20 LONDON.   FATAL BEDROOM FIRE ACCIDENT TO ACTOR

Augustus Yorke (28), an amusing young actor appearing at Terry's Theatre, was badly injured at his rooms after the show on Saturday night around 2.30am. It was surmised that while in bed, after lighting a candle, he threw down the match which remained on the floor, still lit. Reaching with his slipper to slap it out, his nightshirt caught fire from the candle and instead of throwing off his garment or rolling himself in his bedclothes, quite losing his head he fled out into the street where he was grabbed by a more sensible fellow who, throwing him down, extinguished the flames. Yorke was taken to St George's Hospital where he remained until tragically dying ten days later.

1892_01_07 BELFAST (Theatre Royal).   SHOOTING ACCIDENT TO SON OF HENRY IRVING

95.

Laurence Irving was Henry Irving's younger son who, after a university education and three years in Russia studying to be a diplomat, sallied forth as an actor. Very wisely he chose to make his debut with the Frank Benson company playing under the name of Mr Lawrence. On this evening he was due to play Lorenzo in *The Merchant of Venice*. During the afternoon while going over his lines he managed to shoot himself with a revolver. Four surgeons, immediately summoned, decided that they would not perform any surgery until they had deduced the path of the bullet. Some days later when Laurence seemed to be getting on well they decided no harm had come to any organs so surgery would not be needed or attempted. Within three weeks he was pottering around his lodgings. It was never officially determined whether it was an accident. He left Belfast at the beginning of February intending to spend some weeks in France.

1892_01_07 LONDON (Novelty).   PREMIERE DANSEUSE INJURED SLIPPING ON ICE
    Although there have been many travel accidents, I have not said much about the weather as my remit is to show up the dangers of working inside a theatre. But as a reminder that performers had to travel just as other people this is an example. After leaving the theatre at the end of her evening's work, Mdlle Marie Surtees, hurrying for the bus in the Strand, slipped upon the ice falling heavily on her right arm, breaking it in two places. She was taken to Charing Cross Hospital, patched up and sent home. This accident ensured she would not appear for the rest of the pantomime season and possibly not for some weeks thereafter.

1892_06_09 JOHANNESBURG, South Africa.   FATAL CARRIAGE RIDE OF MISS ST ANGE
    Josephine St Ange was an actress with experience of the Lyceum company under Bateman, and in Charles Wyndham's touring company. She was on this day in the company of Genevieve Ward touring South Africa. During the week she had been playing Ophelia, and around 4pm on a Thursday was returning to her hotel in a light dog-cart when the reins broke and the horse bolted down a slope into a ditch where fellow passenger Mrs Wills was thrown out. The horse careered on passing the hotel, and Miss St Ange, hurled from the dog cart, hit her head on the ground. Staff from the hotel rushed out to find her unconscious and bleeding from nose and mouth with a deep wound on her forehead. She was placed on a temporary stretcher and on the way to hospital she recovered consciousness, sat up for a brief moment, then fell back dead.

193

1892_06_18 LONDON.   STREET ACCIDENT TO BESSIE BELLWOOD
    [Bessie Bellwood (1856–1896) born Catherine Mahoney, was a popular music hall singer of

96. *Bessie Bellwood*

Coster songs, including What Cheer Ria! She assumed her stage name in 1876 when first going on the stage at the age of 20. She was an abrasive but loveable character with an ability to argue down even the toughest of hecklers. A devout Catholic, she became a popular figure in London for her many charitable acts of kindness to the poor, which included giving away her own money and possessions, taking in laundry, cleaning homes and looking after children. In 1890, she was briefly declared bankrupt as a result of lending a substantial amount of money to the Duke of Manchester which was never repaid. In later life, Bessie Bellwood suffered from alcoholism, a Bohemian lifestyle, and declining health. She died in London, aged 40.]

    Arriving home after work on Saturday night, she was descending from the carriage when the horse, taking fright, started off. Bessie was thrown down into the road with her dress caught in the door which closed on it instantly. She was dragged along the road getting her face and arms badly cut and bruised, but fortunately no bones were broken. She was welcomed back to normal business on 4 July at the Tivoli.

1892_11_13 WOLVERHAMPTON.   COMEDIAN IN RAILWAY ACCIDENT

On a typical Sunday thespian journey Emma Hutchison's *Pink Dominos* company was moving from Walsall to Gainsborough and the company's carriage, detached at some place seven miles from Wolverhampton, was put in sidings to await attachment to another train. Compulsory on trains from 1868 was an external communication cord running in guides on the edge of the roof, connecting to a bell in the guard's van and to a whistle on the locomotive.

During the shunting procedure the communication cord, through negligence, was not detached from the rest of the train and as a result the iron loops through which the cord passed were torn away. Mr Charles Stone the principal comedian of the company was sitting near an open window through which some of these iron loops came, striking him in the face and severely injuring one eye. The company had to move on leaving the poor chap in Wolverhampton Eye Hospital where it was deemed likely he would lose the sight of the eye. Miss Hutchison started a public appeal with £5, as Stone had a large family dependent on him. On 1 December, Stone wrote from the hospital thanking everybody for their financial contributions.

1893_07_10 LONDON.   ROAD ACCIDENT TO MRS BANCROFT

[Effie Bancroft (1839–1921) was born Marie Effie Wilton at Doncaster, and as a child appeared with her parents, who were both actors. She made her London début in 1856, at the Lyceum Theatre as the boy Henri in *Belphegor*. She won great popularity in several boy roles, and for some years was at the Strand Theatre, taking various general roles. In 1867, she married fellow actor Squire Bancroft, leading man at the Prince of Wales Theatre which she had been managing for two years. Now as Mr and Mrs Bancroft they instituted a new regime of realistic domestic comedies by T W Robertson that were nicknamed 'cup and saucer drama' because they reproduced typical modern settings and everyday social behaviour. They also improved their theatre by alterations and elegant decor, abolishing the pit and creating carpeted stalls, comfort making the venue fashionable.

97. *Effie Bancroft*

In 1879, the Bancrofts moved to the Haymarket Theatre (*see* 1880_01_31) where they continued their successful presentations of drawing room comedies until both retired from management in 1885, having made a considerable fortune. They were still in demand as actors, and Squire Bancroft was knighted in 1897. The accident below indicates how the fashionable West End player was treated, compared to the little known music hall performers already encountered.]

Mrs Bancroft, while employed with her husband in the play *Diplomacy* at the Garrick Theatre, was travelling in a Hansom cab when the horse suddenly fell. The lurching of the cab sent Mrs Bancroft hurling into the gutter striking her head on the kerb. The horse, having got back on its

194

feet, moved forward, the wheel of the cab running over Mrs Bancroft's leg. A number of people witnessed the accident and a group gathered urging her to be taken to St George's Hospital. However, Mr Blakeley an actor at the Criterion – and formerly of the Bancroft company – who happened to be passing by at the time organised for her to be taken to her house in Berkeley Square. There, Dr George Bird, Mrs Bancroft's regular medical attendant, was summoned, together with Sir William MacCormac who dressed her injuries which were a flesh wound on her leg, cuts and bruises on her forehead and arm. The shock to her system was considered more detrimental than her slight wounds. "Mrs Bancroft never lost consciousness and bore the pain of her injuries with characteristic courage." Mr Bancroft was walking through Bond Street to be stopped by an American lady who said "I can see you are Mr Bancroft, and I can see that you don't know what has happened." Hearing the news Bancroft hurried home.

Mrs Bancroft, unable to appear in her usual role of Lady Fairfax, went to Sheringham to recuperate. She recovered to be able to take up her next engagement – a five venue tour of *Diplomacy* with John Hare and the Garrick company opening at Liverpool on 11 September.

1893_09_16 FRESHWATER.   ROAD ACCIDENT TO MDLLE JANOTHA
[Natalia Janotha (1856–1932) a Polish pianist and composer performed her first public recital in 1868 and toured throughout Europe as a concert pianist becoming known as an interpreter of the music of Chopin, whose sister was a very close friend of her mother. In 1885, she became Imperial Court pianist in Berlin, and had the eccentricity of performing only as long as her dog was on stage within her view. Miss Janotha composed some 400 works, mostly for piano, and was also a noted mountain climber.]

195

After her successful concert on the Isle of Wight, Mdlle Janotha was driving a dog-cart with her friend Miss Ward to pay a call at Brook House, the home of Mr Seely MP. When nearing their destination the horse fell and both women were thrown out. Miss Ward escaped with a severe shaking and a cut on her face, but Mdlle Janotha remained at Brook House tended by Dr Paley who, as a friend of the Seely family, was present in the house when the accident occurred. She convalesced at Brook House and was visited by Cardinal Vaughan and had "gracious enquiries from Balmoral". She returned to her concert schedule on 28 October at Crystal Palace.

1894_03_26 LONDON (Crystal Palace).   ROAD ACCIDENT TO ONE OF THE ROMAS
The Three Romas had been performing at the Crystal Palace. Two of the trio had returned by train, the third Mr Roma was going home in a horse-drawn vehicle with others. On leaving the vicinity, with the carriage descending a steep hill, the horses became unmanageable, one bolting. The vehicle, overturning, was wrecked with one horse killed and Mr Roma seriously injured. That night the trio were to have started an engagement at the Cambridge Theatre which, of course, was then impossible.

1894_03_29 LIVERPOOL (Prince of Wales).   FATAL OUTING TO THE GRAND NATIONAL
It was the penultimate day of the longest running pantomime in the country. It was also Grand National Day – the biggest holiday attraction of the year in Liverpool. A group of players from the panto company hired a four-in-hand coach to take them for a jolly day's outing at the races. All had a

super day and were nearly back at the theatre when the coach, losing a wheel lurched sideways, turning on its side throwing all the passengers into the road. Mr Williams dislocated his shoulder and broke his collar bone, his wife was cut and bruised and likely to be crippled for life, Miss Rogers sprained her ankle, and Arthur Wilkinson was totally insensible with injuries of "an alarming nature". He was taken by ambulance to the Northern Hospital where, found to have a fractured skull, he never rallied and died around midnight. That night the manager went before the curtain to explain what had happened, and to ask the audience if they wished the show to go on. Surprisingly, it was decided to proceed, which it did with understudies as necessary. The last night went off in sadness and depression. The deceased was a well-liked genial comedian and singer, known from appearances with the Carl Rosa Opera Co. He was 34 and left a widow and one child.

1894_05_28 SPALDING.   FATAL ROAD ACCIDENT TO MRS BARRINGTON BOTT

This is an example of an everyday sort of mishap that strangely ended in death. The W H Terriss Company was travelling by road from Crowland to Spalding where it was due to play for a few nights at the Drill Hall. On nearing their destination the ladies suggested they would walk into town. In alighting, Mrs Bott caught her dress and fell to the ground. She was assisted by her husband and Mr Terriss to walk to a cottage close by, where a doctor was sent for. He arrived to find "life ebbing fast" and she died soon after his arrival.

1894_08_20 LONDON (Palace).   CHILD KILLED IN PARENT'S LODGINGS

Shortly after 11pm a fire occurred at 5 Gerrard St in the apartment of Mr & Mrs Bettinson which backed directly on to the Palace Theatre where Mr Bettinson was Assistant Stage Manager. His wife – professionally known as Madame Marie – had on this day been attending a rehearsal at the Trocadero. She returned, after having been out all afternoon and evening, to find a fire in the bedroom and her three-year-old son lying dead half out of bed. She screamed for help, and Mr Vessey, a baker living nearby, bravely entered the blazing apartment, succeeding in getting the child out – burned around face, hands and legs and dead from suffocation. The flames were soon extinguished as only bedding, curtains and furniture had been ignited before rescue arrived. At the inquest it was revealed that the child had been left in the care of the couple's servant Margaret Spelman with strict instructions to put the child to bed in the dark and not to leave a candle burning. Miss Spelman denied that she had ever been given such instructions, maintaining that the child was habitually left with a candle burning. She had on this occasion left a candle on a side table unfortunately close to a curtain which had caught fire. The jury returned a verdict of Accidental Death and offered sympathy to the parents. RIP John Hubert Charles Bettinson, aged 3.

1895_01_07 BELFAST.   COMEDIAN DIES IN FATAL ROAD ACCIDENT

Fred Bawcombe, a comedian with the Mannon Troupe of sketch performers, was riding on a freight wagon when he was thrown off into the roadway. He was taken to the Royal Hospital where he was found to have a wound at the side of his head and a broken collar bone. The wound was treated and the bone was set. Bawcombe remaining in his lodgings found the recovery was very slow, although neither of the wounds were life-threatening, with the head wound not to the cranium. However, he died on 18 January. The post mortem revealed that the collar bone was not yet fused but

196

had been set perfectly, and the head wound was to the flesh only, neither of which would have caused death. His internal organs were examined and he had an enlarged liver and copious amounts of fat with the right lung "congested and flabby". His death was attributed to *delirium tremens*.

1895_02_03 GREENOCK.   ACTOR'S FATAL DASH FOR EARLY TRAIN

Isabel Bateman's Company had been playing *Heart of Midlothian* at Greenock and with the next date being at Aberdeen, the company had to assemble at the station at 5am on Sunday to catch a train to Glasgow. Edward Price, a long-standing member of her company, in his hurry to keep the appointment fell down the stairs in his lodgings and broke his leg. While the company left for Aberdeen, poor old Price remained behind in Greenock hospital with a threat of amputation hanging over him. By Friday 8 February, the threat disappeared because he died at the age of 55 while still in hospital.

1895_03_04 MILWAUKEE, USA (Davidson)   RAILWAY ACCIDENT TO MRS MANSFIELD

[Richard Mansfield (1857–1907) was a noted actor-manager in America best known for his performances in the play Dr Jekyll and Mr Hyde. His first engagements were in the UK with the D'Oyly Carte touring company playing the principal patter roles. In 1882, he went to the USA performing in several D'Oyly Carte productions followed by plays for other managements. In 1887, his big break came with a dramatisation of the recently published novel Dr Jekyll and Mr Hyde. Expecting to repeat the success in the UK, subsidised by loans from Irving he took the play to the Lyceum where it flopped. Mansfield retreated to his successful American career. In 1889, he attempted another UK visit with Richard III hoping to wipe out his debt to Irving. It did not do so, and the prickly actor also managed to slander Clement Scott the foremost London critic. However, he had now become one of America's foremost Shakespearean and melodramatic actors, championed the plays of G B Shaw, and repaid the Irving loan five years after the borrowing. He married actress Beatrice Cameron in 1892 she becoming his leading lady, and the sufferer in the accident below. She retired in 1898.]

When touring in the USA, Mr and Mrs Mansfield lived in their own railway car, as did Irving and Terry on their American tours. Because of the vast distances, it was a practical way to travel in order to cover the principal cities in the nation. These sumptuous living carriages were hitched on to the various inter-city trains. While the carriage was in a siding at St Paul an engine forcibly ran into it throwing Mrs Mansfield and several servants to the floor. Mrs M was knocked out and got a cut over her eye. "Completely prostrated from the shock" she was unable to perform for several days.

98. Beatrice Cameron

1895_04_22 READING (Princes).   FATAL DROWNING ACCIDENT

On this Monday, Marie Dagmar's *Betsy* Company had arrived to play at Reading. After a morning rehearsal, Gadge Nolan, one of the actors, went for a sail on the Thames with fellow actor Eardley Howard, the acting manager J A Ibberson, and Dr Whitely a local friend. They had not proceeded very far when a gust of wind overturned the boat and the seafarers ended up in the water. All swam for the shore and, while three were rescued, Gadge Nolan was drowned. In the evening, in lieu of the dead player, Mr King an actor who happened to be in the town read the role of Capt McManus. A "clever local comedian" subsequently played the rest of the performances. In gratitude to this local amateur – named Ben Dawes – Miss Dagmar presented him with "a pair of handsome fruit stands and a clock to match" as a slight memento of services rendered.

1895_04_23 WOLVERHAMPTON.   DEATH OF PADDY DOYLE

My remit is to describe accidents in the theatre, but theatrical performers were as prone as anybody else to suffer accidents outside their workplace. I have included many instances of travel accidents as the unfortunates were on the way to or from work, but a few more 'extra-mural' ones are included to remind the reader that death lurks in many forms. Like Gadge Nolan (*see* above) Doyle was an Irishman, not an actor but a vocalist and comedian in the Music Hall act Dermot & Doyle. Around two weeks prior to this date, Paddy Doyle cut his hand when opening a bottle of mineral water. The wound did not heal and Doyle died in great agony on this day, leaving a widow and one child.

1895_05_18 MAIDSTONE (Corn Exchange).   ACCIDENT TO NOTED VOCALIST

George Alleyn, principal tenor with Livermore's Court Minstrels, was to give a solo recital, and in preparing for the show went from his dressing room to the lavatory next door with a match to light the gas. There was a mighty explosion in which he was severely burnt on his head, face, arms and hands. He was taken to West Kent Hospital. The same issue of *The Era* that informed of the accident carried an advert "Wanted for Livermore's Court Minstrels: Good solo tenor."

1895_07_09 LONDON (Herne Hill).   MUSIC HALL SPORTS DAY

This was the Seventh Annual Meeting in aid of the Music Hall Benevolent Fund, and 5000 people turned up to watch the great and good competing against each other in cycling and athletic contests. Among the serious events there were comic ones where the result was "Fred Griffiths, oneth; Dan Leno, tooth, C Crackford, thud." The reason this item is included is that Fred Folkestone had an accident during the day that prevented him from walking and working. This was a blow because he performed with his brother. The couple were able to resume work doubling the Queen's, Poplar and the Cambridge on 5 August. On 10 August, while in the act at the Queen's Fred slipped, damaging the cartilage of his knee, and the doctor ordered another rest of three or four weeks. Misfortune comes not as single spies.

1895_09_12c LONDON.   ACROBAT CYCLIST RUNS MAN DOWN

"Alfred Bale, acrobat, was summoned to the Bow Street Police Court yesterday for riding a bicycle on Waterloo Bridge to the common danger. Defendant knocked down a man who was crossing the bridge. He stated that he was between two cabs, and had used every precaution. Sir J Bridge observed that since the introduction of bicycles the streets were infinitely more dangerous than formerly. He fined the defendant 10/- and costs." *Nottingham Evening Post* 1895_09_17.

1895_10_14 LONDON.   CINQUEVALLI IN ROAD ACCIDENT

[Paul Cinquevalli (1859–1918) was born Paul Kestner in Poland of German parents who moved to Berlin when he was two years old. Spotted in a school gymnastics display at the age of

99. *Cinquevalli*

twelve, he subsequently embarked on a circus career aged still only 14, joining an acrobatic troupe led by an Italian, Giuseppe Chiese-Cinquevalli. Initially he performed on high wire and trapeze, but took up juggling while recovering from a fall. He first appeared in England in 1885 and was such a great success he settled permanently in London. It is not often a juggler can become a star but Cinquevalli was a top attraction until 1913, after which his German nationality made appearances in the UK impossible. He had appeared in the first Royal Variety Performance in 1912 but thereafter worked overseas until retiring in 1918.]

Paul Cinquevalli, the foremost juggler of the age, was travelling along the Strand in his trap which was run into by another vehicle with such force that he was thrown out on to the pavement. He was unconscious when picked up, with an injury to his shoulder. Due to appear at the Star Music Hall in Liverpool on Monday evening but prevented by his injury, he was obliged to delay his first appearance until the Thursday, after which he continued for the rest of the week and all the following week.

1895_12_11 LIVERPOOL.   SINKING SHIP COLLISION WITH THEATRICAL TROUPE

The White Star liner *Germanic* had left Liverpool to journey to New York; the Glasgow steamer *Cumbrae* was bound for Birkenhead with 30 passengers including a touring theatrical company on board. In dense fog near the Crosby Lightship the two vessels collided, but remained in contact while the passengers from the *Cumbrae* were transferred to the liner. On parting, it was seen that the hole in the *Germanic*, large enough to drive a horse and cart through, was fortunately above the water line. A boat with a volunteer crew was lowered – to return to the *Cumbrae* to rescue things of importance, but the steamer had sunk beneath the waves.

The touring company had been on an 18 week tour of a play – ironically called *Saved from the Sea* – which had ended on 7 December at Grangemouth. Some of the personnel were travelling to Liverpool for a fortnight's break before resuming the tour. Also among the passengers were the music hall artistes Walter Purssord, Sidney Lee and the Flying Pheros who "lost every scrap of their baggage and property."

1896_12_21 LONDON (Lyceum).   ACCIDENT TO SIR HENRY IRVING

The previous evening in a tremendous first night, Irving had revived his *Richard III* in a brand new lavish production. After the show, some 500 people thronged the stage to shower him with congratulations. It was midnight before he was able to quit the theatre and, to unwind before attempting to go to bed, he went to the Garrick Club with his friend Professor James Dewar for supper. After that conviviality, the pair went to Dewar's rooms to have a cigar and further gossip, finally walking over to Irving's bachelor apartment where they chatted and smoked until Dewar said goodnight and returned home. Going upstairs to have a bath, something he did nightly after the show no matter how late, Irving slipped, cracking his knee against a chest on the landing. The bath forgotten, he managed to make it to his bed where he

100.

collapsed in pain. He had ruptured the ligatures of his kneecap putting him out of action for some weeks.

The Christmas period without Irving at the Lyceum augured a financial disaster. The misfortune was not helped by Ellen Terry being away from the theatre all winter in Monte Carlo. When she returned at the end of January, *Cymbeline* was tried , then *Olivia* until the end of February. The season had lost £10,000 (well over £1million today) before Irving's return on 27 February. Throughout the closure Irving paid his staff and actors at the same rates as if they had been working.

1897_01_21 LONDON.   DRASTIC TRAVEL ACCIDENT TO ACTOR

American Spenser Kelly (29) was the leading baritone engaged with Clark's *The French Maid* Company at the Lyric Theatre, Ealing. After the show on this night, when boarding a train at Turnham Green station to take him to his home in Richmond, he slipped off the footboard of the carriage which was covered with ice. Thrown on to the rails and dragged along by the train, suffering major injuries, he was taken to West London Hospital where his leg had to be amputated. Influential colleagues organised a benefit and a general appeal fund made to the public. On 8 April, the sum collected amounted to £6. 11. 6d. A special benefit matinee was held for him on 10 June. In August he was reported to be in very straightened circumstances. Another benefit was given on 2 May 1898 in the Grand Hall of Hotel Cecil and, as Kelly had many friends and sympathisers, some 60 artistes, many well-known, volunteered their services in a concert that went on until midnight. On 14 June, Kelly brought a suit for damages against the L & SW Railway Company whose defence was that he had attempted to board a moving train. The jury members, unable to agree, were discharged. At a further hearing Kelly lost his claim. Happily, the accident did not prevent his career from eventually continuing – in a curtailed form – as a solo baritone in American vaudeville.

1897_02_06 STOCKPORT.   RAILWAY ACCIDENT: MUSICIAN FATALLY INJURED

Around 7pm, a passenger train from Hull was held by a red light at Brinnington Junction about a mile from Stockport. A train from Derby coming down the same line, crashed into the rear of the stationary train. The rearmost carriage was actually a heavily laden goods wagon which helped to cushion the impact, but the two rearmost passenger carriages were completely shattered. Three people on the train were injured – Mrs and Miss Mouland and the guard Aspland. The ladies were taken to Stockport Infirmary where Mrs Mouland had treatment for injured legs, while Florence Mouland had a broken ankle and head injuries. Florence (19) of the very talented musical Mouland Family, having just concluded an engagement as a solo flageoletist, was shortly to embark on the Moss & Thornton circuit with a sister in a musical speciality. Her father was the MD at the Empire, Sheffield, one sister was harpist at an Edinburgh theatre, and another was playing on the continent. Florence died from her injuries on 10 February.

The cause of the accident was revealed at the inquest when signalman William Schofield admitted to ignoring the basic system. Schofield, who had the reputation of being one of the finest signalmen employed by the company, was tried for manslaughter. He pleaded that so many train movements in a short time resulted in an excessive burden, especially as he also had 11 different telegraph and telephone machines to deal with. His defence lawyer said Schofield had admitted his mistake all along, and had evidence that when he realised his error, he phoned the next signal box.

200

The lawyer also considered that the box was undermanned and there should be an extra employee there. Finally, he said if the company had used the 'interlocking system' instead of the 'block system' the accident could not have happened. The verdict was Not Guilty and the prisoner discharged.

1897_08_20c BIRMINGHAM (Grand).   MANAGER IN FATAL CYCLING ACCIDENT

J Dennistoun the genial manager had an accident falling off his bicycle. His knee was damaged but, with nothing more than a bruise to show – which gave him little trouble – he was able to carry on with the aid of a stick. However, in January 1898, he started suffering great pain in his knee which the doctor pronounced was congealed blood that had to be removed. Mr D gave up his position temporarily for the operation, expecting it to heal in a few weeks. This was not to be, and he was still suffering at Easter. It then became clear that the limb would have to be amputated which was done at the end of April. This was thought a success, but later it was found disease had taken a firmer root and his lungs were affected. The lingering and painful illness came to an end with the poor chap's death on 7 July 1898. So falling off your bike is no laughing matter.

1897_08_29 SOUTHPORT.   NOTED MUSICAL DIRECTOR IN CAR ACCIDENT

Edmund Bosanquet, the conductor from Liverpool Empire, took his daughter to Southport where she was engaged for the week. Planning on returning to Liverpool on Monday morning he accepted the offer of a friend to do the journey in a motor car. Only a mile after leaving, the car swerved for some unknown reason and Bosanquet, thrown out on to the ground, suffered a broken leg. He was taken back to the New Southport Infirmary where it was discovered to be more serious than first assumed as he had broken the leg in two places and doctors had to remove two pieces of bone. He remained in hospital until 6 November then resumed his position in the orchestra pit with his leg still in plaster.

1897_09_05 LONDON.   ACCIDENT AT PADDINGTON STATION

The special train from Bristol bearing George Edwardes No 1 *Circus Girl* Company arrived at Paddington station, the company disposing themselves and baggage into waiting cabs. The cab containing Mrs Blythe and Coralie Blythe suddenly fell over on its side with a tremendous crash. The roof giving way through the excessive weight of baggage placed upon it, unbalanced the vehicle. Millie Hylton, who was sharing the cab but not yet entered it, had a narrow escape, as a heavy trunk just missed hitting her on the head. The two women inside escaped with nothing but a few cuts on their hands.

1897_11_01 TWICKENHAM.   ROAD ACCIDENT TO GERALDINE ULMAR

[Geraldine Ulmar (1862–1932) was an American singer and actress, best known for her performances in Gilbert & Sullivan operas. She performed extensively in both the USA and the UK. Her last stage role was in 1904 when she retired to turn her talents to teaching.]

Miss Ulmar was driving her dog cart with a friend and coachman down Church Street in Twickenham where she lived when her vehicle was hit by a bus of the New London and Suburban Omnibus Company, and the three occupants thrown out to the ground. Miss Ulmar suffered a compound fracture near the ankle of the left leg and an operation became necessary which was done on 6 November by Dr Keatley. She remained in hospital until 20 November and then recovered at home.

On Monday 23 May 1898 her claim for damages was heard in court. Dr Keatley was asked his fee, which he said was 50 guineas for the operation – a difficult one as both bones were broken – plus 8 guineas for subsequent visits to her home. He said he usually charged theatrical performers less than that but, as Miss Ulmar earned star money, in her case there was little reduction. The counsel for the omnibus company asked if he would charge the same fee if there had not been the chance of getting the amount from the bus company. The good doctor said he always asked the same fees, but regrettably often had to lower them for less well-off patients. He would never lower them for an omnibus company.

101. *Geraldine Ulmar*

After the accident Miss Ulmar had been unable to work, and indeed could only walk with the aid of two sticks right up to two weeks previous to the court case. Her income was from £40 to £100 a week. Witnesses said the omnibus had pulled out to pass a bicycle leaning against a wall, and wheel tracks on the ground indicated it was 3ft away from the wall when the accident happened. It was travelling at 5mph. Miss Ulmar had pulled her dogcart in as close on her side as possible and was almost stationary when struck. The jury declared in her favour and she was awarded damages of £750. She returned to the boards on 21 November 1898.

202

1897_12_22 LONDON.   **FATAL ACCIDENT ON OMNIBUS IN OXFORD STREET**

Ernest Wood, a well-known provincial actor who had toured for a long time with J A Atkin's Company playing the comedy part in *Grip of Iron*, was travelling on the upper deck of an omnibus when he felt faint. He rose from his seat with the intention of leaving the bus and taking a cab, but staggering fell from the bus into the road, breaking his back in the fall. He was taken to Middlesex Hospital where he died exactly a week later.

1898_01_03 DUNBAR.   **RAILWAY ACCIDENT INVOLVING TRICK CYCLISTS**

This was another railway accident where carriages were rammed together. In one carriage – telescoped by the one in front of it – was the Minting Trio of bicyclists travelling to Kirkcaldy for an engagement, they being Mr & Mrs Fred Minting with their son aged three, and Fred's brother A H Minting. The only other occupant was a Mr Porteus a teacher from Thurso. A H, dozing, but wakened by the shock of the crash, was remarkably unhurt whereas his brother and Porteus were trapped by the legs, his sister-in-law was trapped by the ankle, and the toddler was safe having fallen between the seats. A H struggled to free his kin, with no effect as he had no tools. Eventually help arrived and all were released, Mrs Minting being the last to be extricated "bearing her sufferings with great bravery". Abject from shock and cold, they were taken to the Royal Hotel where two doctors attended to the wounded.

1898_07_06 LONDON.   **ROAD ACCIDENT TO MRS THRUM**

Mrs Thrum, a professional vocalist, was standing in Wandsworth Road to board a tramcar from which passengers were descending when an empty coal wagon belonging to Cameron & Co ran into the back of her, knocked her down, a wheel passing over her leg. Her right knee, hip and shoulder were badly hurt and she suffered internal injuries. In May 1899, she took Cameron & Co to court for damages, the charge against the coal company being the driver had recklessly driven his wagon within 3ft of the tramcar while it was at a stop exchanging passengers. The verdict was given to Mrs Thrum and she was awarded £175 damages.

1898_07_15 MANCHESTER.   ACCIDENT TO BERNHARDT'S 'PALACE ON WHEELS'
    Madame Sarah Bernhardt was a perennially fascinating figure to the public. All her doings were of interest to the newspapers, and she constantly fed them with stories. If 'Twitter' had been invented in her day she would have had millions of followers. She travelled in what was dubbed a "special palace train" and it was in this she made the journey from Liverpool to Manchester. Having arrived at the destination Madame and her company alighted, which was fortunate as during shunting operations a goods train smashed into the "palace on wheels". The damage resulted in the complete destruction of Madame's sleeping saloon, two first-class carriages and one composite carriage.

1898_08_09 LONDON.   ROAD ACCIDENT TO HARRY LUNDY
    Harry Lundy was the popular manager of the Oxford Music Hall. On this night, while going down Tottenham Court Road his horse swerved and ran into a post. Lundy, thrown out of his carriage and striking his head on the ground, was taken to University Hospital critically ill with concussion of the brain. When he was recognised, his friends were summoned to take him home. Some degree of the man's popularity can be gained from the brief paragraphs recording his progress of recovery. At first he was not allowed any visitors, when that period was past, he said he felt sufficiently recovered to go down to the Oxford but this was vetoed by his doctors. By the end of August he was "recuperating at Datchet" and by 7 September was well enough to attend the AGM of the Music Hall Benevolent Fund of which he was the retiring president, where he offered himself for re-election. He returned to his regular duties at the Oxford on 8 October after an eight weeks' absence.

1898_09_11 LONDON.   ROAD ACCIDENT TO DAN LENO

102.

[Dan Leno (1860–1904), born George Wild Galvin in London, was the pre-eminent comedian of the late Victorian years. His parents were lowly music hall singers and after his alcoholic father's early death, his mother married an actor/comedian who performed as William Leno. As a youth George adopted the name Dan Leno and built up a reputation for comic songs and character comedy. A fixture in Drury Lane pantomimes for some sixteen years, Leno was the top panto dame of the era, and flooded with offers to appear in many farcical musical comedies. Together with his continuing music hall performances he was fully booked for three years ahead. By 1901 "The funniest man in the world" had become an alcoholic with a ruined constitution. In 1903, he was committed to an asylum for several months. On his release he attempted to pick up his career, but was too incompetent. He died at the age of 43. His recordings are still available on You Tube. Perhaps the accident described below helped to unhinge him?]

On finishing his work at the Canterbury Music Hall, Dan Leno was travelling home in his brougham. Suddenly the horse bolted and through the skill of the driver several obstacles were avoided. But bad luck triumphed when the carriage hit a post, brought down the horse and overturned the brougham. The coachman, thrown on to the horse, was not badly injured, whereas the horse suffered cuts and lacerations. Leno escaped through one of the doors, considerably shaken but otherwise uninjured.

1898_10_11c LONDON.   EADE MONTEFIORE INJURED IN ROAD ACCIDENT

Mr Eade Montefiore the noted actor-manager and author was currently playing the dashing hero in Dion Boucicault's money-making hit *The Streets of London* which had at that point exceeded 700 performances. When Montefiore was injured in a traffic accident, the news was not released for three weeks, and he was languishing at home not able to even dress himself. Montefiore had many irons in the theatrical fire often simultaneously and both Laurence Irving and Edward Gordon Craig worked for him.

1899_01_20 STROOD.   ANOTHER RAILWAY ACCIDENT

The train bearing E Graham-Falcon's *Dick Whittington* Company had left Sittingbourne for Maidstone. The carriages carrying the company, scenery and baggage were detached at Strood to await coupling to the Maidstone bound train. A misguided engine crashed into the standing carriages, throwing the performers from their seats. All but the three detained by injuries were able to proceed within two hours, performing as planned that evening in Maidstone. The management engaged some understudies and rearranged the casting to enable the tour to continue. On 2 February, *The Stage* announced that Mrs Coleridge – still confined at the Bull Inn at Rochester – had deteriorated, suffering from concussion of the spinal column as well as the brain. Miss Vyner, another victim, was said to be improving and hoped to return home in a couple of weeks, but the rest of the tour had been cancelled because of the accident.

1899_07_01 CROYDON.   ROAD ACCIDENT TO JENNY VALMORE

Jenny Valmore, a popular serio-comic of the day, was on her way in her brougham to the Palace of Varieties at Croydon when it collided with a trap containing an entire family who were thrown into the road, as was Miss Valmore. Her horse bolted, the vehicle was wrecked, the recaptured horse injured so badly had to be shot. Miss Valmore was taken to Croydon Hospital suffering from a fractured jaw. She was unable to return to work until the end of October having endured a long tedious convalescence partly at Folkestone.

1899_11_29 DUBBO, Australia.   FATAL GUN ACCIDENT TO STAR MAGICIAN

[The Great Dante (1869–1899) was born Oscar Eliason, a Mormon from Salt Lake City. He took up magic at an early age and during the mid 1890s he toured with his wife – professionally known as Madame Edmunda – throughout Texas, Mexico, Cuba and Canada. By 1898 Eliason had adopted the name of Dante the Great and embarked on a successful career in the antipodes. Not to be confused with the far better known Harry August Jansen (1883–1955) the Danish magician who worked under the name Dante the Magician.]

While appearing at Dubbo in New South Wales, Eliason was invited to join a party going rabbit shooting. During the day he was accidentally shot in the groin. Three days later after asking for a glass of champagne he died. He was only 30 years old.

1899_12_07 LONDON.   WELL-KNOWN COMPOSER RUN OVER BY BUS

Denham Harrison, run over by an omnibus and taken to University College Hospital, was diagnosed with a compound fracture in both legs. Still an inmate at the end of January 1900 and with a prediction that it would be months before he could walk again, Mr Cayley Calvert master-minded a fund to support Harrison's deprived family. After having had the plaster casts removed and beginning to become active, on 5 March Harrison broke his leg again, necessitating a return to the hospital where he had just obtained his release. He was expected to leave hospital again the first week in April. Harrison had a rough time as he only became convalescent in August 1900 when a manager offered his theatre for a benefit performance which Harrison declined on the grounds that he had "already received substantial help from professional friends."

1900_03_05c PARIS, France.   MDLLE YVETTE GUILBERT'S NARROW ESCAPE

One of Frances's greatest stars, Yvette Guilbert, after an operation at the beginning of winter, was recuperating at home. During the day, while reclining on a couch dozing, the hangings round the grate caught fire. Fortunately she awoke and cried out for assistance whereupon her attendants rushing in decided – as she should not be shaken – to carry her out on the couch. This proved to be too wide for the door! Bundled up in blankets Mdlle Guilbert was delicately transferred to another room. Once she was safe, the fire was quickly dealt with. Her medical attendants trusted her "iron nerves and strong physique" would save her from any "retardation of her convalescence".

205

103. Yvette Guilbert

1900_04_19c FLORIDA (USA)   NEAR DROWNING OF CISSIE LOFTUS

[Cissie Loftus (1876–1943) born Marie Cecilia Loftus Brown, was a versatile Scottish actress, singer, and music hall performer. In 1893, at the age of 17 she made her debut as a music hall artiste at the Oxford. Her act was mainly impressions of popular performers of the day such as Yvette Guilbert. She went into musical comedy, and later straight theatre, even attempting Shakespeare. In 1902, Sir Henry Irving engaged her to play the roles for which Ellen Terry had become too old. In 1905, she played Norah in Ibsen's *The Doll's House*, and Peter in the second production of *Peter Pan*. In 1912, she was one of the stars who appeared in the first Royal Command Performance. She wrote music and lyrics, and in later life appeared in a number of films.]

Cissie Loftus had been engaged at Keith's Theatre in Boston but ended her season prematurely on 17 April in a low state of health suffering from "nervous prostration". She was recommended to take a holiday break at Old Point Comfort a fashionable seaside resort. She

104. Cissie Loftus

resided at the Hotel Chamberlain and took a late night walk on the pier. The next anybody knew was that a sailor on a training ship fished her out of the water. He said he had seen her "fall into the sea." Press rumours arose that Miss Loftus had attempted suicide, but these were immediately and forcibly denied by her companion Marie Bishop who said Miss Loftus had fainted as they were both sitting at the end of the pier. For the last fortnight she had endured fainting fits daily. She was well enough to open In New York's Fifth Avenue Theatre on 7 May, but booked her passage home in June.

1900_06_05 LONGON. A FATAL TRIP TO THE LAVATORY

Lewis E B Stephens (36) was an established actor and playwright with experience gained in many touring companies. He and a party of chums were, on this night, celebrating the capture of Pretoria. Returning home around midnight in the best of health and spirits – possibly an excess of the latter – Stephens tottered down to his lavatory which, as customary until modern times, was situated at the bottom of the garden. He is presumed to have taken a spirit lamp with him to light his way. Mr Williamson a commercial traveller who lived next door, hearing shouts from his neighbour's garden, scaled the dividing wall to see flames issuing from the lavatory building. He found Stephens enveloped in fire, all his clothing ablaze. Dousing the flames, as other help arrived, a doctor was summoned and did what he could before despatching the poor chap to the Great Northern Hospital, where he died shortly after arrival.

1900_10_07 TWICKENHAM. RAILWAY ACCIDENT TO OPERA COMPANY

Morell & Mouillot's *Geisha* Company left by express train from Bristol making for Kingston. The special coaches were detached at Twickenham ready for coupling to a local train to Kingston. A signalman, thinking the coaches had been shunted into a siding, allowed a train on to the same line and the two collided. Twenty members of the company were in the derailed coaches, a similar number having travelled on an earlier train. The singers were suffering from shock and minor injuries when they opened at Kingston the following night. As the curtain rose the audience cheered the singers lustily for several minutes to show sympathy with the company's plight.

Queen Victoria died on 22 January 1901

ILLUSTRATIONS:
Adelphi Project: 6
Book of Words, Programme and Songs: 90
Bygone Liverpool (1913): 5
Cassell's Universal Portrait Gallery(1895): 96
Cincinnati Enquirer: 76
Dan Leno Hys Book London (1899): 101
Dick's Penny Plays: 53
Digital Commonwealth: 41
Find a Grave: 28, 95
Folger Shakespeare Library) (CC BY-SA 4.0): 7, 8, 9, 29, 44, 45, 80, 86, 94,99
Frederick Maitre et son temps (1876): 83
Harper's Weekly 59
Harvard Theatre Collection, Houghton Library, Harvard University: 35
Histrionic Montreal: 89
Illustrated Sporting News and Theatrical and Musical Review: 19, 27, 91
Kenny's Illustrated Cincinnati (1875): 58
L'Illustrated Journal Universel: 17
La Semaine Illustrée: 78
Le Journal Illustré: 67
Le Monde Illustré: 72
Le Petit Journal Supplement Illustré: 74
Library of Congress, Poster Collection: 22
Library of Congress, Prints and Photographs Division: 42, 48
Life and Art of Richard Mansfield (1907): 97
Memories of Fifty Years (1889): 85
New York Clipper 1907: 98
North East Lore: 65
NYPL digital: 30, 68, 102
Old & New London (1818): 36, 50
Old Curiosity Shop (1841): 64
Our Theatres Today – and Yesterday (1911): 46
Perils of the Deep (1885): 82
Post Card (1907): 79
Poster (1876): 92
Project Gutenberg: 31
Tallis's Illustrated London (1851): 3, 4, 51,
The Bancrofts: Recollections of Sixty Years (1909): 60
The Magic Lantern its Construction and Use (1890): 1, 2
Theatrical Times (1846): 37
Wellcome Collection (CC BY 4.0): 39
Wikimedia: 11, 16, 18, 20, 21, 23, 24, 25, 26, 34, 38, 43, 47, 52, 55, 57, 62, 63, 69, 71, 73, 81, 84, 88,
  www.gallica.bnf.fr/ark: 87
Newspaper images © The British Library Board. All rights reserved. With thanks to The British
Newspaper Archive (www.britishnewspaperarchive.co.uk): 10, 13, 14, 33, 49, 54, 56,
61, 66, 70, 75, 77

Jeopardy within the Victorian Theatre

The intention of this book was twofold, firstly to focus on the many dangers that lurked backstage ready to entrap stagecrew members and actors and performers in the offstage regions of the stage house; and secondly to record the many varied dramas that take place in the auditorium.

But when all is said and done the point of an entertainment venue be it opera, music hall, drama, circus or pantomime is what happens on the performance space. The auditorium is simply the place where viewers join together to watch the show and everything backstage is there to assist the people on the stage to do their job.

Perils of the Victorian Stage

"The play's the thing" and it is astonishing how many things can go wrong in the performance of a drama, or melodrama, and those things in Victorian times often led to financial disaster, injury and even death. Scenery could be unsafe, trapdoors left open; and rostrums prone to collapse.

The Victorian actor had to be adept at fencing as so many plays of the time called for duels between hero and villain – Macbeth v Macduff, Hamlet v Laertes – the number of accidents and even deaths is not to be wondered at. Strangely, the most popular stage weapon was a gun and even 'blank' pistols caused many injuries and some fatalities.

Gymnastics were hugely popular especially when performed by young children, and high wire walkers like Blondin the 'Hero of Niagara' inspired lesser artistes to attempt stunts beyond their capabilities. Mid-century, Léotard invented the flying trapeze and from that moment the race was on for artistes to outdo whatever had gone before. The first triple somersault was achieved in 1896, but a great many injuries and deaths had happened along the way.

The performing space, be it a stage, music hall platform, circus ring, or outdoor gala, could be, and often was, a dangerous place. Surprisingly, female dancers were major sufferers as their flimsy costumes were prone to catching fire. A special feature covers a hundred and sixty such cases with some forty fatalities.

A companion volume to this present book is now available. In similar format, the new book encompasses a miscellany of accidents ONSTAGE IN ACTUAL PERFORMANCE.

A companion volume
Perils of the Victorian Stage
ON SALE NOW

OTHER BOOKS OF THEATRICAL INTEREST BY ALAN AND BRENDA STOCKWELL

What's the Play and Where's the Stage?

The lives of eminent London actors of the Regency period are more than amply recorded. This book ploughs a more unusual, rarer, furrow. It reveals the theatrical lives of a family of provincial players who tramped the highways and byways bringing the latest London hits and classic plays to unsophisticated audiences in tiny country theatres and large manufacturing towns. The author offers not a specialist tome for theatre historians - although they will find previously unknown material and new revelations here - but a beguiling story of a family of three thespian siblings, their spouses and their children. This is a Regency world far removed from the novels of Jane Austen. There are highs and lows, riches and poverty, twists and turns, and extraordinary events as in the script of any modern television saga. The marked difference being that - for the Jonas and Penley Company of Comedians - this was real life.

ISBN 978-0-9565013-6-3 *Hardback* 420 pages **rrp £16.95** (do not pay more!)

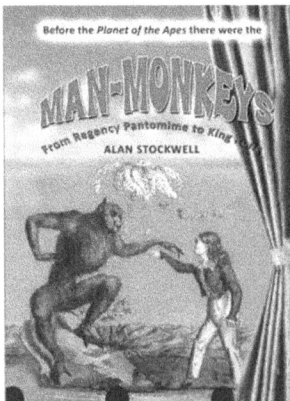

MAN-MONKEYS: From Regency Pantomime to King Kong

This is the first and only book about the man-monkey phenomenon and its major stars. From the first stage play to feature a chimpanzee as a character back in 1801 to the present-day popular film franchises of 'King Kong' and 'The Planet of the Apes', many actors have played apes and gorillas – some rising to stardom earning top money, others coming to a sadder and more tragic end. Men-in-fur like the ill-fated Parsloe who fell from fame in London to suffer an early and lonely death in America, the irascible almost legless trouble-maker Hervio Nano, Teasdale who found God in prison after stabbing his wife, and the simpleton East End potboy who was transformed into Monsieur Gouffe attracting the *bon ton* of London and making a fortune. Within these pages you will find some of the oddest, most unfortunate, ill-requited, and doomed performers who ever chose to tread the boards – the artistes known as 'man-monkeys'.

ISBN 978-0-9565013-7-0 *Paperback* 234 pages **rrp £8.99** (do not pay more!)

VESPER HAWK

for further information visit www.vesperhawk.com   amazon

MATCHBOX PUPPETS

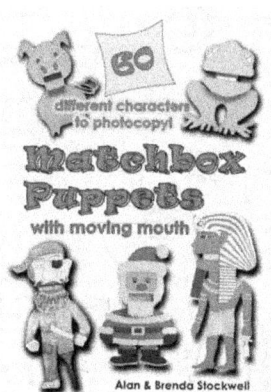

This delightful collection of easy-to-make puppets will be a boon to all parents, teachers and entertainers of children. The puppets are based on an ordinary household-size matchbox which enables them to have opening mouths. The pages are designed to photocopy on to A4 card, cut out and colour as fancy takes. With a choice of some sixty different characters there is something for all ages and abilities in these simple but clever constructions. The collection varies widely from a simple flower to the Minotaur, a whale to Henry VIII, octopus to Roman emperor, and a selection of characters which can be topical at different periods of the year - turnip lantern, Easter bunny, scarecrow, Father Christmas etc. The puppets have been designed by Alan and Brenda Stockwell who for over forty years toured primary schools throughout the UK and abroad with their educational puppet show conducting many puppet-making workshops for teachers. Now retired, they are placing their expertise in the hands of future generations. In 2000 Alan Stockwell was awarded an MBE for services to education, a rare honour for a professional puppeteer.

ISBN 978-0-9565013-3-2 A4 *paperback* 126 pages **rrp £9.95** (do not pay more!)

MR DICKENS AND MASTER BETTY

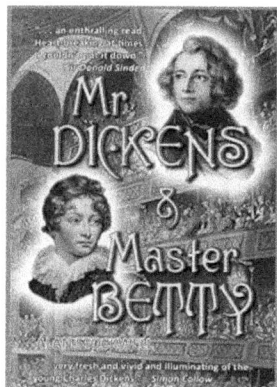

Charles Dickens, the nascent novelist, is employed to write the life story of the former infant prodigy Master Betty known as Young Roscius. Dickens, a self-proclaimed "delver into the human soul", clashes with his employer's overweening arrogance and revenges himself by unearthing the hidden truths lurking in the older man's psyche. The story tells of two teenage boys, both with feckless spendthrift fathers. One scrapes a miserable existence in a boot-*blacking factory for six shillings a week; the other earns fifty guineas a night* idolised by the highest in the land. *"The sad decline - heart-breaking at times - of the infant prodigy compared with the upstart young genius. It makes an enthralling read. I couldn't put it down - it is a history of the time."* (Sir Donald Sinden - eminent actor and historian). This unusually-written short novel reeks of the atmosphere of the early 19th century; through its pages weave many historical personages in this true story imaginatively told. *"Very fresh and vivid an illuminating of the young Charles Dickens."* (Simonn Callow - noted actor and writer).

ISBN 978-0-9565013-2-5 *paperback* 190 pages **rrp £8.95** (do not pay more!)

VESPER HAWK

For further information visit www.vesperhawk.com

amazon